Revolutionary Womanhood

Stanford Studies in Middle Eastern and Islamic Societies and Cultures

Revolutionary Womanhood

FEMINISMS, MODERNITY, AND THE STATE
IN NASSER'S EGYPT

Laura Bier

Stanford University Press
Stanford, California

Stanford University Press
Stanford, California

Printed in the United States of America on acid-free, archival-quality paper

Library of Congress Cataloging-in-Publication Data

Bier, Laura, author.
    Revolutionary womanhood : feminisms, modernity, and the state in Nasser's Egypt / Laura Bier.
        pages cm.—(Stanford studies in Middle Eastern and Islamic societies and cultures)
    Includes bibliographical references and index.
    ISBN 978-0-8047-7438-3 (cloth : alk. paper)
    ISBN 978-0-8047-7439-0 (pbk : alk. paper)
    1. Women—Government policy—Egypt—History—20th century. 2. Feminism—Egypt—History—20th century. I. Title. II. Series: Stanford studies in Middle Eastern and Islamic societies and cultures.
HQ1236.5.E3B54 2011
305.48'89276200904—dc22
                                                        2010051610

To Ganoby

CONTENTS

ACKNOWLEDGMENTS

THE STEREOTYPICAL PICTURE of the academic at work is that of the solitary writer in an oak-paneled study, brow furrowed, toiling in obscurity and isolation. While I can certainly testify to the furrowed-brow part, this book is yet more proof that no work of scholarship can be produced without the aid and generosity of what seems like a cast of thousands.

The research and writing of this book were made possible by the generous support of the Fulbright US Student Abroad Program and the Fulbright-Hays Research Abroad Program; the Institute for Advanced Studies at New York University; a Dean's Fellowship from New York University; and the National History Center's 2007 Decolonization Seminar.

In Egypt, many thanks go to the staffs of Dar el-Kutub, the archives at the Ministry of Education; the National Center for Criminal and Sociological Research; and the libraries at 'Ain Shams and Cairo Universities and at the American University in Cairo. Special appreciation goes to 'Asim Disuki, my Fulbright faculty advisor.

This project owes much to the existence of a vibrant, supportive community of scholars and students at New York University (and surrounding environs). I want particularly to thank Zach Lockman, whose wisdom and support have been unwavering. Molly Nolan and Lila Abu-Lughod have also been an incredible source of inspiration and guidance—as scholars, as women, and as politically committed individuals. The members of the Middle East Studies writing group and the History of Women and Gender writing group commented on very early versions of chapters and provided many valuable suggestions. Michael Gilsenan, Khalid Fahmy, and Linda Gordon deserve particular commendation for opening their homes so that we could meet and exchange ideas. Seteney Shami began as my boss at the Social Science Research Council and ended up as a mentor and a friend. Her energy and her intellect are a perpetual reminder of why I wanted to be an academic in the first place.

This project also owes much to the support of my colleagues at Georgia Tech, especially Amanda Damarin, Marin Klawiter, Jenny Smith, Wenda Bauchspies, Bill Winders, Amy D'unger, Rajaa Aquil, Narin Hassan, and Nihad Farooq. John Krige and Carole Moore took me under their respective wings from the day I started at Tech and have been exemplary mentors and friends. Ron Bayor, the Chair of the School of History, Technology, and Society, has graciously supported all sorts of requests, which made completing this project that much easier. Finally, special appreciation goes to Larry Foster and Steve Usselman, for going above and beyond the call of duty in an unexpected emergency.

Many individuals have read, heard, and commented on various parts of this work. Thanks to Hibba Abugedieri, Sabri Ates, Koray Caliskan, Samera Esmeir, Khaled Fahmy, Nihad Farooq, Michael Gasper, Michael Gilsenan, Linda Gordon, Andrew Haley, Narin Hassan, Wilson Jacob, Hanan Kholoussy, John Krige, Christopher Lee, Shawn Lopez, Silvia Marsans-Sakly, Ellen McLarney, Shana Minkin, Lisa Pollard, Megan Reid, Mario Ruiz, Josh Schreier, Sherene Seikaly, Elizabeth Smith, Danielle Sypher-Haley, Jessica Winegar, and Marilyn Young for their insights and generous willingness to give of their time and critical faculties.

At Stanford University Press, Kate Wahl has my gratitude for shepherding this project through the publication process with professionalism and an infallible sense of what authors need to survive that process with sanity intact. I would also like to thank Joa Suorez for her assistance. Three anonymous reviewers for the Press offered their thoughts and critical engagement, providing a supportive and insightful road map for revisions. This book is much the better for their keen insights; it goes without saying that any errors and omissions are my own.

Both inside and outside the academy I have been tremendously fortunate to have been blessed by the company and friendship of an extraordinary group of people. Members of my "virtual family," Reem Morsi, Ellen McLarney, Megan Reid, Lisa Pollard, Hibba Abugedieri, Nancy Stockdale, Mario Ruiz, Jessica Winegar, Elizabeth Smith, and Miriam Pierce, have been an unending source of inspiration, amusement, and assistance. I am especially grateful to my former Brooklyn *shilla*, Samera Esmeir, Michael Gasper, and Wilson Jacob, for their irreverence, their brilliance, and their extraordinary empathy in times of triumph and tribulation. Danielle Sypher-Haley and Andrew Haley deserve a ten-page acknowledgment of their own for sticking with me for over twenty years, through Faulkner, food poisoning, and other crises, with humor, wisdom, and strength.

I am eternally grateful to my parents, Susan and Robert Bier, for their unceasing support and encouragement, and to my late grandfather, Thomas Rowland, a treasure trove of odd historical facts and expansive stories about life in early twentieth-century Mississippi, who was the first to give me an inkling that history wasn't just a bunch of boring facts.

This book is dedicated to Mohamed Elganoby, my partner in crime, *fadfada*, and life in general, whose unfailing patience, humor, and love make all the hardest things bearable and all the best things even better. It is no mean exaggeration to say this book could not have been written without him. Last, but of course not least, my acknowledgments would not be complete without mention of the fabulous and indomitable Zahra, whose unexpected (but much welcome) arrival at the end of this project was the very best incentive imaginable to finishing it.

A NOTE ON TRANSLITERATIONS

ARABIC WORDS AND NAMES have been transliterated according to a simplified system based on the guidelines provided by the *International Journal of Middle East Studies*. For the sake of expediency, all diacritical marks have been omitted except for the *'ayn* (') and *hamza* ('). Arabic words in common usage in English, such as *Nasser* and *ulama*, remain in this Anglicized form. Arabic names of those who have published primarily in English have not been transliterated (so Aziza Hussayn is referred to throughout as Aziza Hussein); for authors who have published in both English and Arabic, alternate spellings of their names may appear. All transliterations, unless otherwise noted, are my own.

Revolutionary Womanhood

INTRODUCTION

SPEAKING SEVERAL YEARS AGO at a conference about the decline of secularism in Egypt, a prominent member of Egypt's supreme constitutional court delivered a talk entitled "The Egyptian Judiciary Between Secularism and Islamization." He touched on topics ranging from court challenges aimed at making Egypt's largely secular body of law more in line with Islamic *shari'a* to the politicization of the lawyers' syndicate, and then he turned to a less predictable subject: women's fashion. Reminiscing fondly about his days as a young lawyer in the years following Egypt's 1952 revolution, he said, "Egypt was a different place. Women were very elegantly dressed, more fashionable, more Westernized. On the streets of Cairo you saw them all the time wearing short dresses, short skirts." He went on to mention the various gains Egyptian women had made over the course of the last half century—in the labor market, in education, in how social practices had changed to favor marriages between men and women on the basis of affection and compatibility rather than familial arrangements—gains that stood to be rolled back by the sweeping Islamization of Egyptian society and the increasing strength of Islamist political forces. "Now," he said, referring to the proliferation of *hijab* (the religiously prescribed head covering often translated into English as "veil") among young, educated urban women, "the streets of Cairo look very different."

The evocation of the chicly dressed, Westernized woman in the miniskirt might seem somehow out of place in a talk about the Egyptian judiciary and the legal challenges it faces in an age of globalization and Islamic resurgence. However, as Egypt's secular past has increasingly become a site of political

1

contestation over the country's future, the gendered aspects of that past remain a crucial focal point of present debate. Whether among establishment intellectuals and cultural brokers longing for a more secular past in which modernity was a collective national project and women were liberated from the strictures of tradition and backwardness, or from Islamists who view the consolidation of the secular nation-state as a wrong turn on the way to the construction of a more authentically Islamic society, the figure of the Egyptian woman remains a potent symbol for engaging wider political and social changes that occurred over the last half of the twentieth century. The wider questions that animate this study are thus as much a product of the present moment as they are historical and theoretical preoccupations.

How do the gendered political and social orders put in place with the establishment of postcolonial nation-states change as nation-states themselves respond to changing political and social forces? How has the framing of "the woman question" by various social and political actors limited, or enabled, the sorts of claims women themselves could make for inclusion? What are the linkages between secular nationalist projects—like that pursued by the Gamal Abdel Nasser regime in Egypt in the 1950s and 1960s—and the seemingly diametrically opposed gender politics of Islamism?

Focusing on various social, political, and cultural projects aimed at transforming women, as historical individuals, into "the Egyptian woman," as national subject, this book explores the interrelated attempts of political elites to fashion a new nation-state and a "new" yet authentically Egyptian womanhood during a particularly formative and turbulent era of modern Egyptian history. The period following 1923 witnessed Egypt's nominal (and later actual) independence from its British colonial overlords, the birth of mass politics (and mass culture), a revolution that overturned the existing political and social order, the rise of Egyptian president Gamal Abdel Nasser as a global symbol of the struggle against colonial domination and oppression, the genesis of "the Arab dream" of Pan-Arabism and socialism, and finally the devastating shattering of that dream by Israeli forces in 1967. My central aim is to chronicle how postindependence political and social projects, which were increasingly inclusive of women as political subjects, also produced new sorts of gendered and classed hierarchies exclusive to the process of forging a particularly Egyptian vision of modernity.

In order to do that, this study begins with the interwar period and then moves rapidly to its primary topic of concern: the emergence in the wake of the 1952 revolution of new discourses and practices of citizenship, which Mervat

Hatem has termed elsewhere "state feminism."[1] State feminism entailed the recognition of women as enfranchised citizens and the explicit commitment by the Nasser regime to liberate women in order to guarantee their inclusion and participation in the postrevolutionary nation on an equal footing with men. Through laws, social programs, and the creation of new institutions that redrew the parameters of the public, state feminism aimed to make women into modern political subjects by dismantling traditional patriarchal structures in the family, creating new gender subjectivities, and mobilizing them in the service of national development.

Such measures were part and parcel of wider state attempts at reform and modernization. Over the course of the nineteen years of Nasser's rule, the revolutionary regime embarked on an ambitious program of political and social reform that included rural land redistribution, the nationalization of foreign companies, and eventually the creation of a distinctly Arab Socialist state. These measures were orchestrated by a newly hegemonic state elite of middle-class technocrats, planners, and professionals who drew inspiration from a proliferation of other non-Western socialist models of modernization. Egyptian socialist planning aimed at eradicating the "backwardness" of the nation and creating a modern citizenry capable of carrying out a program of national advancement.

"The woman question" (debates about gender roles in the family and society), long a preoccupation of nationalist reformers, was taken up by state elites in this new, future-oriented, decolonizing world where the liberation of women, like modernization itself, appeared not only as a goal but as a historical inevitability. The promises of the revolution were embodied in glossy photos appearing in newspapers, magazines, textbooks, and state-authored pamphlets of "the Egyptian woman" working in factories and offices, going to school, waiting to obtain birth control from state family planning clinics, and presiding over her kitchen, which featured the latest in Egyptian-manufactured domestic appliances. Nor was the role that women were to play purely symbolic. For the first time, the state exhorted women to assume their role in building a modern Egyptian nation as fully enfranchised citizens and national subjects. In 1956 women were granted the right to vote and hold public office; subsequent measures abolished formal gender discrimination in hiring, established social protections for working mothers, and guaranteed women's equal access to higher education. Later as the regime gradually adopted the ideology of Arab Socialism, focus shifted from issues of formal rights to the social and material contributions Egyptian women were expected to make to modernization and state-building. Women thus emerged as both symbols and beneficiaries of a new and vibrant revolutionary culture.

WHY GENDER?

The gendered aspects of Nasserist state- and nation-building, which this book takes as a central concern, have been largely overlooked by scholars. Although the literature exploring various aspects of the Nasser period is vast, more than fifty years after the revolution not a single monograph has taken the gender politics of Nasserist rule as its central focus. Most historical accounts of the Nasser period have been confined to studies of political economy or of the formal politics of the Nasser era: foreign affairs, the adoption of a one-party system, the rule of the military, and the relationship of the regime to various oppositional political movements and corporatist groupings.[2] When studies have dealt with women, they have mainly focused quantitatively on such issues as entry into the labor force and the participation of women in the public sector, but have largely failed to consider the regime's attempts to restructure gender relations as significant to its vision of development.

In fact, most scholars have assumed that with the consolidation of military rule and the imposition of a one-party system, politics ceased to occur at all but the highest levels of government within the framework of the state, understood as a set of legal institutions set apart from Egyptian society. What such studies leave out are the countless struggles to define the content and meaning of the Nasserist project that occurred in other arenas. It is not simply that these arenas—those of culture, of social relations, of the family, and of everyday practices—provided the terrain upon which ordinary Egyptian citizens negotiated the politics of the revolution. They were, as well, important areas of concern to the historical actors—intellectuals, policy makers, technocrats, and culture producers—who by virtue of their emerging status as state elites were most responsible for defining and implementing a vision of what post-revolutionary Egypt was meant to look like.[3]

By foregrounding the politics of gender, *Revolutionary Womanhood* aims to refocus attention on the relatively neglected social and cultural aspects of Nasser's revolutionary project, locating them as central to the formation of the seemingly more important arenas of state and public. The "politics of gender" as I use it here has two mutually interactive aspects: the uses to which gender is put in the process of organizing, legitimating, and attacking political (and other forms of) power; and the multifarious struggles by which gender is continually constructed. Gender is a social construction; it refers to the social meanings constructed upon anatomical differences. Gender ideologies work to legitimate social inequalities between men and women; but gender also serves as a reference in the conceptualization and legitimation of other kinds of power. Thus the politics of gender do not exist in a vacuum: they are constitutive of (and constituted by) other political claims, narratives, and frameworks.[4]

STATE-BUILDING AND THE POLITICS OF MODERNITY

In its attempts to write gender back into accounts of Nasserist rule, this study locates itself within an expanding body of literature within Middle Eastern women's and gender studies that problematizes the multifaceted ways that gender identity formation shaped (and was shaped by) modern state- and nation-building.[5] *Revolutionary Womanhood* shares with this scholarship the epistemological viewpoint that women of the region should be studied, not ahistorically in terms of a monolithic vision of Islam and Islamic culture, but through highlighting the construction and reproduction of gender inequalities inherent in the incorporation of national and ethnic collectivities into modern nation-states.[6]

To approach a study of gender in modern Egyptian history in this way is ultimately to call into question how the assumptions of modernization theory have informed both academic and popular discourses on Middle Eastern women. Modernization narratives take the axiomatic position that—in contrast to "traditional Islamic" societies, which suffer from religiously derived patterns of systemic and pervasive gender inequality—newly Westernized or modernized societies, whether indigenously inspired or imposed upon from the outside by colonization, produce new sources of openness, emancipation, and possibilities for women.[7]

The tenets of modernization theory have been particularly prevalent in accounts of Egyptian women in the post-1952 period, when the state granted women equal citizenship rights with men, including the right to work, the right to education, and the right to vote—in other words, the right to participate in the public space of the nation and its politics. Emancipated within this modern public sphere, where the rights of all individuals regardless of gender are recognized, Egyptian women in this period have been portrayed as continuing to be oppressed by the premodern Islamic and tribal values and structures that govern the private space of the family and that recognize men and women, not as equal individuals but as essentially different, unequal be-ings. Confined to the home and traditional gender roles, women in the Nasser period have been assumed to be quite marginal to the male world of public politics.[8]

This is not the only story that scholars and others have told about women during the Nasser period, however. The other is a more triumphant story, one in which debates about the status of women in Egyptian society are seen to disappear as Egypt became more modern under the Nasser regime. In such nationalist histories (nationalist in the sense that the progress of women par-allels that of the nation itself), the Egyptian state is portrayed as an agent of women's emancipation; by awarding legal rights to women, the Nasser regime is seen as having settled the vexing question of women's public participation consistently with the dictates of a modern world.[9] Remaining gender inequali-ties, in both of these arguments, can then only be the product of traditional male privilege in the private sphere, which has failed to give way to the eman-cipatory forces of modernization and development.[10] More fundamentally, however, what these diametrically opposed pictures of women during the Nasser period share is an unproblematized understanding of modernity as a universal teleology against which the progress of any given society can be objectively measured.[11]

Alternatively, this study suggests we must look more skeptically at the var-ied effects that state modernization projects have had on women's empower-ment, as well as interrogate more critically the claims that are made on their behalf.[12] Like Lila Abu-Lughod's volume that explores projects of "remaking women" in the Middle East over the last century, I ask "how modernity—as a condition—might not be what it purports to be or tells itself, in the language of enlightenment and progress, it is."[13]

Such an epistemological critique of modernity is central to framing this study of gender and Nasserist state-building. In arguing that the Nasser re-gime's attempts to "liberate" women brought novel forms of state intervention into women's lives as well as new notions of equal rights—which were con-tingent upon gender-specific obligations that women were expected to meet as proper national subjects and citizens—*Revolutionary Womanhood* explores what Abu-Lughod terms "the politics of modernity," namely, how new ideas and practices, identified as "modern" and progressive and implanted in Euro-pean colonies or simply taken up by emerging local elites, ushered in not only new forms of emancipation but also new forms of social control and coercive norms.[14] In revolutionary Egypt one of the key sites where the politics of gender met the politics of modernity was state feminism.

WHY FEMINISM?

Expanding on the work of Mervat Hatem, I understand state feminism not just as a policy or series of policies, but as a constellation of normalizing discourses, practices, legal measures, and state-building programs aimed at making women into modern political subjects. Such a definition unites various initiatives and projects that seem quite divergent in their aims. Some, like the legal protections and social policies established to encourage female participation in the labor force, were explicitly couched as necessary for women's empowerment. Others, such as the establishment of a family planning program, subordinated discourses of female empowerment to the developmentalist discourses that characterized the regime's state-building measures. Still other issues, such as the dress and comportment of female civil servants, remained largely outside the purview of official state policy but were nevertheless a critical site for defining and negotiating the contours of a Nasserist public sphere. What they had in common was a normative vision of female "liberation" as necessary to the task of building a modern, independent nation capable of overcoming the debilitating legacies of colonial and monarchical rule.

In light of studies that have traced the history of feminism in Egypt, applying the term "feminist" to Nasserist state- and nation-building would seem to have a certain irony. According to many of the scholars who have ably charted the history of Egyptian women's movements in the first half of the twentieth century, the advent of the revolution signaled the beginning of the end of independent feminist politics in Egypt, at least until the 1970s when the greater openness of the Sadat era marked a reemergence of "competing discourses" on women, gender, and feminism.[15] For many politically active women, the revolution represented a new hope that long-standing political and social grievances could be rectified. Following the Second World War, the political crises and social displacements that characterized the period brought the entrance of new actors and social movements to the political arena. Among the Islamists, trade unionists, populist reformers, student organizers, communists, and others who crowded the postwar Egyptian political scene was a new generation of women activists who built on a rich tradition of feminist activism from the first part of the century to make new claims for rights, inclusion, and citizenship. The abolition of the monarchy, the resolutely anti-British and anti-imperialist stance of the Free Officers, as well as the revolutionary regime's promise to end the three ills—poverty, ignorance, and disease—which had plagued the Egyptian nation throughout its colonial and immediately postcolonial past, caused many to support the new order as a means to abolishing the power of a corrupt ancient regime, achieving social justice for the poor and the marginalized, and ending the continued vestiges of British colonial control and interference. In its first decade, the revolutionary regime realized many of the demands of feminist activists, including the right to vote and the right to run for and hold public office, in 1956, and the passage of extensive labor protections for female workers. The expansion of free public education gave tens of thousand of young Egyptian women access to secondary and higher education, and the expansion of the public sector brought increasing employment for female high school and university graduates.

The state's championing of gender issues, however, coincided with the suppression of dissenting voices and alternative visions. Egypt's multiparty system was abolished in 1954 in favor of a succession of mass, single-party organizations (the Liberation Rally, the National Union, and in the 1960s, the Arab Socialist Union) aimed at mobilizing support for the regime. The Muslim Brotherhood was outlawed in 1954 and much of its leadership jailed or executed over the course of the next decade, as were many Marxist activists. Prominent feminists, such as Duriyya Shafiq and Inji Aflatun, were incarcerated. Women's formerly independent social and charitable organizations, which had provided much of the basis for early activism, were placed under control of the Ministry of Social Affairs in 1964.

If we understand feminism to refer to a social movement authored by women for women, as most of these accounts have, then it is difficult to argue against the position that the Nasser era marks a profound rupture in Egyptian feminist politics. Certainly that's how some women who were politically active in the post–Second World War period experienced it.[16] This study, however, argues for a more expansive definition of feminism. *Revolutionary Womanhood* views feminism not only as the speech of women but as "a system of ideas . . . a particular constellation of political practices . . . tied to a particular history—of capitalism, of personhood, political and legal arrangements" that were international in origin but local in iteration.[17] It acknowledges that Egyptian feminism, like other postcolonial feminisms, rested on highly complex historical and epistemological preconditions that included disparate elements which were not themselves "feminist" (in the sense of being self-authored prescriptions for, as Margot Badran has put it, "evolv[ing] a more equitable gender system involving new roles for women and new relations between women and men").[18] Framing feminism as a historical narrative about how Egyptian women developed their own (local) national feminism has had the benefit of stressing women's agency and has successfully challenged politicized assertions that Egyptian feminism (or particular articulations of it) are somehow culturally "inauthentic" to Muslim societies or merely derivative of Western feminist projects.

And yet, any story of the emergence of the woman question in Egypt (and the Middle East more generally) and its varied and complex legacies cannot afford to overlook the entanglements between local, national, and transnational forces, in which colonialism, nationalism, visions of modernity, the emergence of new regimes of power and regulatory institutions, and class consolidation intersected in complex ways to constitute "the Egyptian woman" as an imagined political subject. The "colonial feminism" (as Leila Ahmed has termed it) of Lord Cromer—the British consul general in Egypt in the early years of the twentieth century, whose claims that British tutelage would rescue Egyptian women from oppressive Islamic practices such as veiling—legitimized British imperial rule, the endeavors of local women activists like Huda Sha'rawi (whose pioneering activities in social service provision were predicated on the assertion that the empowerment of Egyptian women was an integral part of the Egyptian national project following independence in 1923), and the later attempts of Nasser era technocrats to create modern families by instituting a national family planning policy; all of these projects would appear, at first glance, to have little in common.[19] They were shaped by political and social forces that occurred at distinct historical moments; they envisioned different outcomes and possible political futures for Egypt; and they differed in the forms of power and authority they legitimized. These differences shouldn't be minimized. Despite their differences, however, such projects shared a normative conception of Egyptian womanhood (however defined) as the key to social and political transformations that overflowed the boundaries of the woman question narrowly posed. Egyptian feminism, as Tani Barlow has argued for the case of China, "was already other things as well."[20]

Using such a broad understanding of feminism and applying it to Egyptian postrevolutionary state- and nation-building projects has a number of advantages. It allows for a more nuanced understanding of the motives, reactions, and responses of the women who were among the architects and advocates of the policies, discourses, and practices, as well as the objects, of state feminism. It helps to call into question the universalizing claims feminism makes for itself by insisting on the historical and social specificities of Egyptian projects that foreground "woman" as a foundational category. Finally it helps to situate state feminism within the context of other projects of "remaking women" in Egypt, the Middle East, and other parts of the postcolonial world.

This historically situated approach to categories, which informs the entirety of this work, also necessitates a brief disclaimer, as it marks this study's difference from much of the work already done on the 1952 revolution and its aftermath. Two of the questions that have preoccupied Nasser period historians are the extent to which the revolution was actually "revolutionary," and whether Arab Socialism was in fact socialist in form, content, or intention. These are not unimportant questions. The intention of this study, however, is not to assess whether or to what degree the Nasser regime was truly, objectively socialist as defined against some ideal type, nor to simply weigh in on the extent to which 1952 was actually a "revolution." Rather, it tries to understand how concepts like "nationalism," "revolution," and "Arab Socialism" were defined and enacted by state elites during this period, and how visions of womanhood became central to such definitions. What sort of political and ideological work did such labels perform? What was the nature of the changes (or continuities) they legitimated?

Like many other projects of social and political transformation that had preceded it, state feminism was a project that embodied the aspirations, desires, and normative assumptions of a professional urban middle class (*effendiyya*) and often targeted urban working-class and rural women as objects of intervention. Over the course of the 1950s, members of the *effendiyya* came to provide the bulk of the middle and upper ranks within the public sector, which by the early 1960s included not only agencies dealing with social service provision but also the press, the cinema, and publishing. They were journalists, writers, culture producers, social scientists, engineers, medical personnel, and policy makers who had benefited from the prerevolutionary expansion of education and the postrevolutionary expansion of the civil service. They belonged to an emergent and increasingly powerful state elite who, as Roel Meijer has argued, derived their authority and influence from their claims to be agents of modernization.[21]

Given the regime's authoritarian nature, it is perhaps tempting to view the women who became part of this state elite—either as state functionaries who uncritically embraced the regime's secular modernizing agenda, or as feminist heroines who used their position to challenge the more patriarchal aspects of Nasserist state-building—as either resisting or complying with interventions in largely self-evident, uncomplicated ways. But an examination of the ways in which Egyptian women and men of all classes negotiated, reacted to, and made sense of state feminism in its various manifestations suggests the need to see motives and outcomes as more complicated. Were women who responded to the state's calls to have fewer children resisting traditional patriarchal control over the family? Were those who criticized a campaign to reform family law, which would have expanded women's right to divorce and retain custody of their children, somehow more invested in traditional, religiously sanctioned marital roles (and thus less "modern") than those who championed change? Were commentators who articulated concerns about women's dress and deportment in newly co-ed workplaces simply reproducing Islamic notions about the corrupting nature of unrestrained female sexuality?

Not only does posing questions of agency in this way risk oversimplifying the complexities of historical experience; it forecloses a more historically, politically, and socially situated account of feminism's history in the Middle East by taking as axiomatic the assumption that "culture," in the context of state- and nation-building projects, stands as a retrogressive force that has failed to give way to the forces of emancipation and progress. Historicizing both Egyptian nationalism and Egyptian feminism as cultural or discursive projects (and not just as political movements) that are intimately tied to the politics of modernity not only helps to get beyond the binaries—between complicity and resistance, patriarchy and feminism, the traditional and the modern—that such a notion of culture presumes, but also helps to raise questions about some of the foundational tenets of feminism itself.

Notions of liberation, inclusion, participation, emancipation, and citizenship have provided both the terrain of feminist struggle and the terms of feminist critique since the nineteenth century. A now well-established body of work, much of it grown out of the experiences and histories of women of color, has argued for the need to historicize and engage critically with feminism's foundational categories by asking, "Whose liberation?" "Whose inclusion?" and "Whose feminism?" In spite of such efforts, the project of displacing feminism as a universal category remains incomplete.[22] One need look no further than Laura Bush's speech justifying the United States' bombing and invasion of Afghanistan in 2001 on the grounds that it would liberate Afghan women from the horrors and oppressions of Taliban rule to see that such a project is not only a necessary intellectual endeavor but also a political imperative.

A project like state feminism, which lays claim to citizenship, inclusion, and the liberation of women, represents, I argue, a small but fruitful site through which to historicize notions of freedom, liberation, and emancipation, as well as an illustration of some of the conceptual challenges presented in doing so. State feminism was a project that made universal claims for itself. It spoke in the singular name of "*al-mar'a al-misriyya*" (the Egyptian woman), but its assertions of universality were bolstered by contemporaneous state feminist projects in other countries: China, Cuba, the Soviet Union, and in Eastern Europe. In this, it was consistent with the developmentalist discourses that characterized Nasserist state-building (and many other contemporaneous statist projects in other parts of the formerly colonized world). The liberation of women, like modernization itself, appeared in state feminist discourses not only as a goal but as a historical inevitability. And yet, that sense of inevitability, imbued with all of the promise of the new, went hand in hand with a consciousness of difference. Progress (*taqaddum*), development (*tatawwur*), and renaissance (*nahda*) were the watchwords of the day, but what the state elites who were charged with diagnosing and curing Egypt's social and political ills most often saw when they looked at the countryside and in the old quarters of Egypt's cities was reaction (*raj'iyya*), backwardness (*takhalluf*), and the persistence of outmoded customs (*taqalid*). The challenge here is to uncover the ideological work of categories that presume a teleology of history rooted in universal Enlightenment thought and that consigned many local forms of knowledge, belief, notions of personhood, and patterns of social relations to an outmoded past while also acknowledging that their promise lay in their nation-based specificity. It was through claiming both the terrain of the modern and that of Egyptian particularity that Egyptians who invested their hopes and dreams in the revolutionary project aspired to be part of universal progress.

If we take the imperative of historical and conceptual specificity seriously, then state feminism (and Nasserism itself) appears, not as a project of failed modernization whose progressive promise was curtailed by tradition, reaction, and backwardness but as a project fraught with ambiguities and complications that were internal to the larger project of creating a secular, postcolonial nation-state and that were shaped by Egypt's encounter with colonial modernity.[23]

COLONIAL LEGACIES AND POSTCOLONIAL TRANSLATIONS: SITUATING STATE FEMINISM

Scholars of postcolonial nationalism have offered ways to "provincialize" feminism (to borrow a phrase by Dipesh Chakrabarty) as a universal project by looking at the genesis of the woman question in the context of anticolonial nationalist projects—and how they were shaped by what Partha Chatterjee has termed "the rule of colonial difference" (difference and inferiority attributed to the colonized by Europeans).[24] Writers on colonial and postcolonial nationalism in India have suggested that the nationalist resolution to the woman question resolved a fundamental tension within nationalist thought among colonized peoples: the desire to modernize the nation and its subjects (including women) and thus to demonstrate worthiness for independence, and the desire to preserve an "inner sphere" of cultural sovereignty (located discursively within the domestic realm) that remained ostensibly untouched by foreign habits, mores, and practices.[25] Identifying women as bearers of the values of the timeless inner sanctum of national culture (which was immune from the potentially corrupting elements of modernity) served to reconcile the seemingly contradictory dictates of anticolonial nationalism and was foundational to postcolonial secular modernist projects.

What was true of other postcolonial nationalist projects was true of the Egyptian context as well. Since the turn of the twentieth century, debates about women and gender have occupied a central place in Egyptian national discourse as a focus of both political activism and social anxieties. Situated at the intersection of British colonial and imperial discourses on the "backwardness" of native women and societies, and anticolonial nationalist discourses, the woman question emerged as a site for the formation of anticolonial struggles and a vehicle through which the forms and institutions of the nation-state were "imagined" and contested.[26] "The Egyptian woman" as a category came to mark the uneasy, shifting boundary between being modern and being authentic. Which aspects associated with modernity and progress were acceptable and worthy of emulation, and which were not; what constituted authenticity (and worthiness of preservation), and what was simply backward, were questions that set the terms of debate on the woman question and that were central to the process of translation, which postcolonial scholars have argued marked the colonized's encounters with modernity.

If the notion of translation is useful for understanding how the dynamics of colonial encounters produced new forms of cultural and political hybridization, it also points to the importance of attending not only to the overlaps in posing "the woman question" between and across different colonial and nationalist projects but also to its historical specificities. The bifurcation of the "inner sphere" of cultural sovereignty and the "outer sphere" of material progress was never as fully enacted in Egypt as Partha Chatterjee has argued it was in India. Egyptian women during the Nasser period stood not only as a representation of "authenticity" but also (and more frequently) as symbols of the Nasser regime's success in transforming the outer sphere. More critically, however, "the home" and the gendered cultural practices and relationships associated with it were not perceived as separate from the imperatives of material progress and state-building but rather as fundamental to it.[27] Projects aimed at development, social engineering, and inclusion sought to transform women as a locus both of culture and of advancement. This helps to explain the seemingly contradictory nature of state feminist discourses in which the concept of rights granted to the universal (purportedly ungendered) citizen coexisted with gender-specific obligations that women (and men) were expected to meet. The construction of women's "complementary" work within the family, and the discursive separation of ungendered labor in the public sphere from the gender-specific labor performed by successful wives and mothers, are suggestive of the ways in which difference was being configured in new ways specific to Egypt's project of socialist development. In such formulations, cultural transformation and national uplift went hand in hand.

Thinking critically about translations also serves as a reminder that nationalist projects aimed at transforming women as a means of social uplift were also reformulated as nation-state political projects and visions of political community changed over time. Much of the work on the history of the woman question in the Middle East has focused on tracing the emergence of nationalist movements or on colonial roots of the gendered institutions, discourses, and practices of postcolonial nation-states, a preoccupation it shares with works on gender in other formerly colonial contexts.[28] Another, more recent, trend in Middle Eastern studies has been the proliferation of works dealing with gender and Islam in the contemporary world.[29] For the most part, however, the question of what lies between the emergence of the woman question in various Middle Eastern contexts and the (seemingly) radical transformations wrought on gender politics as the result of the emergence of Islamism as a political and social force remains largely unasked. Inevitably (in the Egyptian case at least) there is an implicit or explicit assumption of continuity with the earlier colonial and liberal-nationalist periods, and one of disjuncture with the era following the early 1970s, in which the hegemony of secular national states began to be challenged from within by Islamist social and political projects (as well as their own political failures), and from without by the forces of globalization and neoliberalism.

In seeking to explore what happened to the woman question in post-1952 Egypt, *Revolutionary Womanhood* argues for attending both to the historical burdens that feminists, policy makers, intellectuals, and others grappled with as they struggled to define a new notion of nationalist womanhood, as well as to the particular historical conditions that shaped those engagements. If Nasserist state feminism was not "revolutionary," neither did it simply reproduce gender inequalities and hierarchies that had been established during the earlier period of nation-state building. Rather, the constellation of norms, discourses, practices, and epistemologies associated with earlier colonial and nationalist projects that were aimed at remaking women were taken up by a new state elite and transformed in the context of postcolonial state- and nation-building. The nexus formed between national liberation, gender, and modernity, so foundational to anticolonial Egyptian nationalism in the first decades of the twentieth century, continued to set the terms within which groups of varying ideological orientation, goals, and outlooks conceptualized (and contested) gender issues of all sorts.

There were, however, significant differences in the various discourses, policies, and practices that characterized state feminism as a project of national uplift; differences, I argue, that derived in part from critical changes to debates around gender, institutionalized models of gendered citizenship, and social reform, which occurred in the interwar years following the establishment of the Egyptian nation-state. These included a growing divide between secular and religious visions of modernity; the constitution of gender as a social scientific category, which marked the institutionalization of nationalist discourses on womanhood and the family within projects aimed at rural reconstruction; and the appearance of a new generation of historical actors who emerged to challenge and rewrite the gendered terms of the liberal-nationalist order. In the tumultuous years following the Second World War, these embryonic changes became more apparent as the woman question was taken up by social and political movements ranging from the Islamist Muslim Brotherhood, to liberal reformers, to the radically secular labor movement. The period also witnessed the birth of new forms of feminism and women's activism, which rewrote older colonial and nationalist debates on gender to make new claims for rights and inclusion. These changes helped to set the stage for postrevolutionary transformations.

What was different in the post-1952 period, however, was that the revolutionary regime claimed responsibility for solving the woman question in a way that was consistent with the dictates of a secular nation-state project and the notions of secular modernity that underpinned them. The public battles over gender, national culture, and women's participation were largely over by the time the revolutionary regime had consolidated its rule during the first few years it was in power. Debates over issues such as veiling, whether women should be allowed access to higher education, and the extent to which women should be allowed to participate in the workforce, which had featured prominently in the interwar period, largely disappeared from public discourse. The debate over women's suffrage, which had raged in the press and parliament in the late 1940s and early 1950s, was resolved when women were granted the franchise by the 1956 constitution. The questions now posed around gender shifted focus from the inner realm of cultural sovereignty to the "outer realm" of material development, making Egyptian womanhood central to progress in both. Public discussions of women in the workforce now revolved not around whether women should work but around how the state could mobilize women to participate in the labor force and in the material tasks of state- and nation-building. Representations of "woman as nation," so prevalent twenty years before, were replaced by representations of women as symbols of the state and the successes of state-driven modernization.

The shift in the terms of debate and discussion around gender issues was, no doubt, in part a result of the regime's authoritarian nature. As I noted before, many of the voices that had crowded the postwar Egyptian political scene were suppressed. But more fundamentally the shift reflected the extent to which secular notions of modernity and the state's claim to them had become hegemonic. The Nasser regime created new sites for the transformation of women as historical individuals into "the revolutionary woman." The constitution of gender as an object of social scientific investigation that occurred during the interwar period found its full expression in the social engineering projects of the Nasserist state. Underpinning these changes were fundamental changes in the state itself, which not only assumed new regulatory functions, bringing it into the everyday lives of Egyptian women on an unprecedented scale, but also adopted (and institutionalized) a resolutely secular vision of modernity, which consigned alternative visions (chief among them variations of Islamic modernism) to the terrain of the traditional, the backward, and the reactionary. The example of contemporaneous state feminist projects emerging in other parts of the global South—places like China, Cuba, India, Iraq, Vietnam, and Senegal—provided both new sources of inspiration to state elites eager to assert Egypt's position at the vanguard of global anticolonial struggle, and sites through which to debate the various merits (and pitfalls) of modernization on Egyptian women.

For policy makers and everyday Egyptian citizens alike, revolutionary gender politics prompted new questions: How could women reconcile their duties as workers with their duties as mothers and wives? How should they behave, and what should they wear as they left the home to take up their obligations to participate in the task of building the nation? What rights should they have to obtain a divorce? How many children should they have? Such subjects were taken up in film, literature, and the fashion and advice columns that were a standard feature of the women's press, as well as in social scientific studies, policy briefs, textbooks, and conference proceedings.

I argue that the contradictions, ambiguities, and tensions that underlie such questions (and the attempts to answer them) were internal to the project of creating a secular, postcolonial nation-state, not external to it. Women became actors in a new national drama even as they became subject to new forms of control and discipline. The (purportedly) gender-neutral rights women held as citizens coexisted with new, gender-specific responsibilities they were to fulfill within their own individual families and within the reconstructed Nasserist family. Moreover, anxieties about the ability of women to act as modern citizens made them targets of state intervention and tutelage. Women themselves, far from being either passive objects of social control or apologists for the Nasser regime, played an active role in shaping and contesting the parameters of state feminism throughout the period.

SOURCES FOR THE STUDY

Understanding state feminism as more than a constellation of state policies allowed me to chart the construction of Nasserist gender politics across a wide spectrum of texts and in multiple sites, including political speeches, policy studies, the women's press, film, and literature. Such an approach not only allowed me to get beyond the rigid dichotomy between state and society characteristic of much of the Nasser period literature but was also necessitated by the archival challenges of working on post-1952 Egypt. For a period when state institutions, projects, infrastructure, and personnel were growing and proliferating at an unprecedented rate in Egyptian history, there are fewer official state documents remaining and publicly accessible to scholars than there are for even the late nineteenth century. Court records, police reports, documents outlining the implementation and effects of policy measures, papers that shed light on the day-to-day running of institutions—all used to good effect by scholars of earlier periods in Egyptian history—are unavailable for the post-1952 period. This is, in part, a reflection of the security concerns of the Egyptian government, which continues to restrict access to post-1952 documents. It also reflects the lack of protocols set up by the Nasser regime and its predecessors for depositing documents in the national archives. How many documents exist and are just unavailable for public scrutiny and how many have been lost or destroyed is an open question. What the post-1952 period lacks in official and quasi-official state documents, however, it makes up for in published sources: government reports, conference proceedings, memoirs, literature, films, and the press. These types of sources represent a rich and largely untapped resource for scholars interested in working on the Nasser period.

The Egyptian press, in particular the women's press, has provided much of the material on which this study is based. As early as 1954, the Nasser regime had begun to implement a systematic policy of control over the media.[30] The journals of several opposition parties and various political organizations such as the Muslim Brotherhood were closed, a trend that continued until 1960 when the press was nationalized. Control over the press was turned over to the National Union and later the Arab Socialist Union (the mass political organizations created by the regime as an alternative to a multiparty system), which was to supervise the publication of all newspapers and journals through five major publishing houses. The movie industry, which was the center of filmmaking for the Arabic-speaking world, was also nationalized in the early 1960s.

The gradual tightening of state control over the press, coupled with state subsidizing of media and cultural output, resulted in more words (and because of the impact of education, a larger readership), but fewer voices. This was true not only for media generally but for the Egyptian women's press in particular. The women's press has been among the most utilized sources for Egyptian gender history in the modern period. Studies have focused almost exclusively on the Egyptian women's press in the first half of the twentieth century.[31] However, there were important differences between the women's press before and after the 1952 period. One of the most striking differences was in the actual number of women's magazines published after the revolution.[32] In the 1920s there had been no fewer than ten journals aimed at a primarily female readership. By 1958 *Hawwa'* was the only remaining periodical aimed primarily at a female readership.[33] *Hawwa'*'s major competitor, *Bint al-Nil* (Daughter of the Nile), had been closed down in 1957 when its founder and editor, Duriyya Shafiq, was placed under house arrest for her criticism of the regime's increasing authoritarianism.

While much of the content of the women's press at this time was thus consistent with the general vision and policies of the regime—state control over the press demanded nothing less—it also reflected, in part, the generationally specific intellectual and political orientations of its authors. Thus it was an important vehicle for the construction of, and contests over, the gendered meanings of Nasserist ideology.

Amina Sa'id, the woman who was appointed as *Hawwa'*'s editor in chief when the magazine was founded in 1957, is emblematic of the backgrounds and orientations of journalists and other culture producers of the Nasser period. The daughter of a physician who was active in nationalist politics, Sa'id was an early beneficiary of the 1930s educational expansion under liberal-nationalist rule. She became a journalist (a common career path for newly higher-educated women with professional aspirations) and in 1959 was appointed as the vice president of the journalism syndicate. Out of 1,000 members of the syndicate, 250 were women. They were primarily educated, middle-class women who had come of political age in the 1930s and 1940s, and were the first to benefit from the successes of the early Egyptian feminist movement in opening higher education and the professions to women. For many, however, their own political orientations constituted a conscious break with the liberal-nationalist feminism of the previous generation.[34] They saw themselves as part of "the new generation" (*al-jil al-jadid*) whose political and social outlooks were shaped by their rejection of the elitism of early feminists and the climate of radical political protest against British imperialism, the corruption of the monarchy, and the vast social ills that had beset Egypt since it gained independence in 1923. The new political and social movements that emerged during this period also challenged notions of identity based on Egyptian territorial nationalism, in favor of alternative visions of national belonging that incorporated supranational affiliations and orientations.[35] Through these articles, Egyptian writers, many of them women, fashioned notions of community, identity, and secular modernity in ways that both reproduced and challenged official versions of state feminism.

Amina Sa'id, for example, was an outspoken advocate of the revolution and the vision of secular modernity that it embodied. The pages of *Hawwa'* (particularly its editorial content) reflect this. There is a danger, however, of reading *Hawwa'* (and the Egyptian press generally) as merely propaganda or an unmediated reflection of regime policies. Sa'id, while lauding state feminist policies, also used her position to critique what she saw as its failures. While much of the content of the Egyptian press at this time was thus consistent with the general vision and policies of the regime, the press was also an important vehicle for the construction of, and contests over, the meanings of Nasserism and Arab Socialism. While locating voices of outright political dissent in the press during the period is difficult, debates over the meanings and consequences of the social changes brought about by "the new society," and the policies designed to encourage the formation of that new society, were commonplace.

In sum, what the Egyptian press and other published sources offer is a picture of the views and orientations of the educated elite who were Nasserism's proponents and architects. They are less useful as a source for the voices of those who were most often the objects of state policy—the peasantry and the urban poor—although those voices occasionally appear in highly mediated forms. How to locate the voices of non-elites during this period is a question this project has largely not attempted to answer. Another question this project in large part has not addressed is the extent to which the press and other types of cultural production can be used as a source of social history to understand how state feminism was experienced on an everyday level by ordinary Egyptians. Both of these issues are well deserving of studies of their own, but I leave them to future research.

OUTLINE OF THE BOOK

Over the course of five chapters, *Revolutionary Womanhood* reveals how various political regimes and movements took up the woman question as part of their attempts to envision and build a modern Egyptian nation-state. It further shows how normative discourses on Egyptian womanhood translated into concrete policies, practices, and prescriptions aimed at transforming actual women into proper national subjects. By treating the construction of gender and the construction of the nation-state as intersecting processes, this study suggests that the ambiguities, tensions, and contradictions in both are not easily attributable to the persistence of traditional patriarchy or "Islam" as overarching explanations, but rather reflect the particular historical conditions within which the Egyptian nation-state was formed and transformed over the course of the twentieth century.

Chapter 1 traces the roots of state feminism by laying out the historical development of the woman question and examining how the gender politics of liberal-nationalist elites became institutionalized in the newly independent Egyptian nation-state. It then goes on to explore how notions of Egyptian womanhood and the gendered underpinnings of the state itself began to change in the first decades of self-rule. The interwar years following the establishment of the Egyptian nation-state brought critical changes to debates around gender and institutionalized models of gendered citizenship. This chapter sets the stage for the following chapters of the book by tracing the gradual emergence and consolidation of state feminism as a project, situating it both within the transformations that occurred during the interwar and postwar period, and within attempts by an emerging technocratic state elite to formulate a distinctly postcolonial, revolutionary culture and program for national development in the years directly following the revolution.

Chapters 2, 3, and 4 serve as case studies of various locations and iterations of state feminism. Chapter 2 examines how state feminist discourses reconfigured notions of labor and space by focusing on the figure of "the working woman" in labor policies, popular culture, and debates about women's work. Chapter 3 considers the intersections between gender, law, and notions of marriage by exploring the Nasser regime's restructuring of the confessional court system and a campaign waged by activist women and their male supporters to reform laws that governed marriage, divorce, and child custody. Chapter 4 looks at how state feminism was linked to social reproduction in considering the Nasser regime's efforts to address the problem of "overpopulation," leading to the establishment of a national family planning program. Finally, Chapter 5 grounds Egyptian state feminism within a broader transnational context of anticolonial politics by examining how depictions of non-Egyptian women in the Egyptian women's press were a vehicle for the construction of gendered national identities and visions of a "new society," as well as a medium through which Egyptian women wrote about and negotiated state feminism.

The term "fashioning," which appears throughout this book, captures both the notion of working within already existing conventions and the sense of creative adaptation inherent in such projects. The policy makers, reformers, culture producers, feminists, and others whose stories this book tells did not fashion their notions of Egyptian womanhood out of whole cloth, nor did they simply reproduce older patterns; rather, discourses on gender, modernity, and the nation that had played a constitutive role in the formation of anticolonial politics during the period of British rule were taken up in a new, future-oriented, decolonizing world where the liberation of women, like modernization itself, appeared not only as a goal but as a historical inevitability. The term also serves as a reminder that while hegemonic postcolonial state projects like the one described in *Revolutionary Womanhood* "ushered in new forms of gendered subjugation (in the double sense of subject-positions for women and forms of domination)," they could also provide the means for individual women (and men) to engage in the process of fashioning new selves, identities, and futures.[36]

1 EGYPTIAN WOMEN IN QUESTION
The Historical Roots of State Feminism

"To whom does this free will, which the Egyptian people managed
to extricate from the heart of the terrible battle, really belong?"[1]

WHEN IT WAS PUBLISHED IN 1960, Latifa al-Zayyat's novel *The Open Door* was heralded as both a path-breaking work in Arab literature and a bold manifesto of women's liberation. The story's protagonist is Layla, a young girl from an upper middle-class Cairene family coming of age during a particularly turbulent and formative period of Egyptian history. The critical personal events of Layla's life take place against the backdrop of a decade that witnessed an unprecedented uprising of mass popular opposition to the Egyptian monarchy, British control, and the liberal-nationalist political system; the Free Officers revolution of 1952; Gamal Abdel Nasser's nationalization of the Suez Canal; and the Israeli-British-French attack that followed it.

When the novel opens, in the mid-1940s, Layla is a schoolgirl. Her understanding of what it means to be a woman comes with the onset of menstruation and her father's traumatized realization that Layla has grown up. She discovers that she is now subject to an elaborate set of rules, which affect almost every aspect of her life: what she may or may not say, where she is allowed to go and with whom, posture, dress, polite behavior, and whom she is (and is not) allowed to love. Her experience of entering womanhood is tantamount to "enter[ing] a prison where the confines of one's life were clearly and decisively fixed. At its door stood her father, her brother and her mother."[2] Layla's attempts to rebel against the constraints of bourgeois society are frequently thwarted by an older generation whose corruption is figured not only by their narrow, individualistic social concerns and their treatment of their daughters as commodities to be auctioned off in "the marriage market," but also by their lack of political commitment.

But it is not only the authority wielded first by her parents that circumscribes Layla's attempts to transcend her narrow, particularistic world. Layla, like other young women of her generation, is trapped by the conflict between desire and expectation, between the constraints of a society that is already coming to be outmoded and a future full of promise, but not yet realized:

> Our mothers knew their situation, whereas we are lost. We do not know if we are in a harem or not, or whether love is forbidden or allowed. Our parents say it's forbidden, yet the government-run radio sings day and night about love. Books tell women they are free, and yet if a woman really believes that, a catastrophe will happen and her reputation will be blackened.[3]

It is through political activism and her commitment to the higher cause of Egyptian nationalism that Layla ultimately finds the courage to break free of the stifling social conventions of her bourgeois family. Abandoning the life laid out for her by social and familial expectations, she goes to Port Said after Abdel Nasser's nationalization of the Suez Canal to participate in the resistance movement against the invading British, French, and Israeli forces. Her choice to stand in defense of her nation also allows her to realize her love for Husayn, a fellow political activist and comrade-in-arms. It is Husayn who urges her: "Let go, my love, run forward, connect your self to others, to the millions of others, to that good land, our land, to the good people, ours. . . . It is a love that makes one grow: love of the nation, love for its people. So let go, my love, run forward, fling the door open wide, and leave it open."[4] The novel's resolution and its chronicle of Layla's transformation from a passive victim to a strong and independent woman is a poignant and passionate statement of the intimate and inseparable relation between personal liberation and the political freedom of self-determination, as well as an allegory of the historical progress of the nation itself.

Al-Zayyat's novel is the product of a historical moment when many doors appeared to be opening for Egyptian women. Two years after *The Open Door* was published, a committee made up of representatives from Egypt's "progressive forces" issued the "Charter for National Action" (Al-Mithaq al-Watani), a document that laid out the blueprints for Egypt's development from a backward, impoverished society still suffering from the crippling legacies of colonial rule to a strong, modern, independent nation-state capable of providing equality and social justice to its citizens. "The Egyptian woman" was, along with workers and peasants, explicitly addressed by the charter as both a beneficiary of the Nasserist state- and nation-building project, and an agent of social and political transformation. The section of the charter devoted to the creation of an Arab Socialist society stated, "Woman must be regarded as equal to men and must therefore shed the remaining shackles that impede her free movement so that she might take a constructive and profound part in shaping life."[5]

With the publication of the charter and the adoption of Arab Socialism as the official regime ideology, state discourses declared "the woman question" as such definitively answered by the realization of national liberation. In 1956, the new constitution had made women fully enfranchised citizens, granting them the right to vote and to run for public office. Later measures were enacted to guarantee women's access to education and mobilization into the workforce. All citizens, regardless of gender, were granted the right to vote and the right to public education and were charged with the duty of public labor on the nation's behalf. It was through their inclusion in the Egyptian nation as citizens that groups formerly excluded from the body politic, women among them, were to be liberated from past oppression.

The woman question, however, was not a blank slate on which the regime could draw its own normative vision of gender relations in the new revolutionary society. In many respects the terms in which gender issues were conceptualized and confronted had already been set in the earlier period. Visions of the "new" revolutionary woman were the product of more than half a century's worth of debates about gender, feminism, and modernity that produced a secular narrative of progress institutionalized in the postcolonial nation-state.

The purpose of this chapter is to look for the roots of "state feminism"—the Nasser regime's answer to the woman question—in the discourses, debates, state-building processes, and social changes of the first half of the twentieth century. It argues that ultimately the state which emerged as a result of the 1952 revolution embodied both the promises and the limitations of the preceding half century of modernizing discourses on feminism, the nation, and inclusion. The first sections connect the emergence of anticolonial, nationalist visions of womanhood both with British colonial discourses on Egyptian women and with local debates about political authority, modernity, and the domestic practices of Egyptians, which converged after Egypt was granted quasi-independence in 1923 to produce the reformed bourgeois family as a model for the modern secular national state. Egyptian women, as "mothers of the nation," were imagined both as a potent symbol for the modernity of the independent nation and as boundary markers of national culture and group identity, while actual Egyptian women were excluded from formal political participation.

The chapter goes on to examine how the political crises and social displacements of the 1930s and 1940s intersected to challenge the gender regime of liberal-nationalist rule, producing novel articulations of feminism and modernity as well as transformations in the discursive, epistemological, and material structures of the state as a modern regime of power. These interwar transformations helped pave the way for the rise of mass political movements after the Second World War, movements that mobilized increasing numbers of politically disenfranchised Egyptians to challenge the elite paternalism of liberal-national rule even as they reproduced some of its gendered tenets. Women who were active in these movements asserted their own visions of political solidarity and liberation, which differed both from previous gendered models of citizenship and from those posited by their male compatriots.

THE GENEALOGIES OF THE WOMAN QUESTION

At the end of the nineteenth century, Egyptian reformers such as Qasim Amin, whose 1899 book *The Liberation of Women* touched off a firestorm of controversy, began to call for a transformation in the status of women in Egyptian society at a time when many Egyptians, chafing under a seventeen-year British occupation, had begun to pose fundamental questions about the nature of Egyptian society, politics, and the conditions of possibility for an independent, postcolonial future. In *The Liberation of Women* and his follow-up book, *The New Woman*, Amin advocated a number of changes necessary to advance the position of Egyptian women, including abolishing the *hijab*, ending practices of gender segregation, establishing schools for girls, and reforming divorce laws to curb practices like polygamy.[6]

Amin's call to reform Egyptian womanhood as a means to the betterment and uplift of Egyptian society reflected a much longer-standing preoccupation by Egyptian elites with questions of modernity. In the context of a changing world order in which political, social, and economic structures were being transformed by the spread of global capitalism and European colonial expansion, what were the sources of Egypt's seeming failure to advance along the trajectory of historical development? How could Egypt's "backward" populace be transformed into productive subjects? Such questions were posed as early as the first decades of the nineteenth century but gained new urgency and political valence with the assumption of British colonial control in 1882.[7]

Emerging in the late nineteenth century at the intersection of discourses on domesticity, culture, and modernization, Egyptian womanhood became the terrain on which British colonial officials and an emerging nationalist bourgeoisie contested Egyptian moral and political authority for self-rule.[8] Colonial critiques of native practices centered on the figure of "the Muslim woman," whose ignorance and oppressed condition was asserted simultaneously as cause and result of the deplorable domestic practices to be found in Egyptian homes and families. Polygamy, early and arranged marriages, gender segregation embodied in the institution of the harem, and the practice of veiling—the latter singled out as the most visible marker of the difference and inferiority of Islamic societies—became symbols of the oppression of women and the backwardness of Egyptian society.

Yet the promise of "civilization" that was used to justify colonial authority ultimately served the construction of a nationalist, anticolonial politic of reform. Colonial assertions of the ignorant condition of Egyptian women and the degraded state of the Egyptian family intersected with the aspirations of nationalist reformers and intellectuals to produce a didactic discourse on scientific childrearing and domestic hygiene that targeted women (and Egyptian mothers particularly) both as ignorant and backward and as a locus of reform and cultural uplift.[9] The establishment of girls' schools, whose curricula centered largely on *tadbir al-manzil* (household management); the training and certification of nurse-midwives; and the proliferation of pedagogical articles in a burgeoning women's press, discussing how to maintain the requisite standards of hygiene to ensure a happy home and a healthy family, were all measures aimed at "remaking women" as a means of modernizing Egyptian society.[10]

This process by which the status of women, the domestic practices of colonized Egyptians, and the modernity and political legitimacy of the Egyptian nation were linked was neither univocal nor uncontested; the connections forged between family and nation, and in particular between liberal-nationalism and bourgeois domesticity, were the product of numerous discursive and material struggles between reformers, nationalist activists, ruling elites, and colonial officials.[11] Certainly, Amin's strident condemnation of veiling led to vocal opposition, often couched in the language of preserving Islamic cultural authenticity in the face of Western encroachment. At the same time, calls for reforming local domestic practices (and women with them) were not solely the purview of secular, Westernized reformers but were also a preoccupation of reformers working within the Islamic modernist tradition.

Neither solely a product of imposed colonial modernization, nor the un-problematic adoption of Western gender norms and ideals by Westernized reformers (or their rejection by religious traditionalists), the woman question made gender central to attempts to define the parameters of a new national identity that was both "modern" and authentically Egyptian. These debates were not solely (or even primarily) about women's political agency or their status as rights-bearing citizens. They were about claims to political author-ity asserted by various groups within the emerging nation-state. Normative claims about Egyptian families and the women in them were simultaneously: a means by which colonized men affirmed their fitness for self-rule against a colonial power, a rising native bourgeoisie asserted their authority to lead against both traditional elites and subaltern men, and a means to envision the shape of a future independent nation. Over the next several decades, as competing and inchoate notions of women, family, and nation continued to crystallize, the vision of Amin and reformers like him would become foun-dational to the emergence and consolidation of what scholars elsewhere have referred to as *effendiyya nationalism* and the secular nation-state forms that underpinned it.[12]

As the calls for female education and national reform spread during the first two decades of the twentieth century, women took an increas-ingly public role in the project of national renaissance. Women's journals, which flourished during this period, elaborated a concept of "maternal citizenship," which glorified women's roles, on the one hand as moth-ers and custodians of a reformed domestic sphere based upon bourgeois models of companionate marriage, scientific childrearing, and rational household management, and on the other as national subjects with a duty to participate outside the home in the everyday struggle against colonial domination and local "backwardness." Indeed the two roles were seen as being part and parcel of one another. Women of elite backgrounds and middle-class women, who had been early beneficiaries of the calls to edu-cational reform, founded charitable organizations in which they contrib-uted to the vocal public debates around women's status by writing for and founding magazines, attending salons, and giving talks. They were joined by middle-class women who worked as teachers in girls' schools. These activities, and the female networks and engagements that they enabled, established a base for the organized women's movement that emerged after the 1919 revolution.

THE GENDER REGIME OF LIBERAL-NATIONALIST RULE

Anticolonial political and social unrest, which had been brewing for the previous decade, culminated in a mass uprising of Egyptians against British colonial control led by the Wafd (Delegation) Party under the leadership of Egyptian lawyer Saʿd Zaghlul.[13] The 1919 revolution witnessed mass strikes, demonstrations, violence, and economic boycott throughout Egypt in which forty British and hundreds of Egyptians were killed. Women's activism in the 1919 revolution was public and militant and transcended class barriers. Lower-class women, some of whom became national martyrs when they were shot and killed by police, participated in street protests with men. Elite women, including Huda Shaʿrawi, whose husband, Ali, was one of the leaders of the Wafd, organized demonstrations and formed the Wafdist Women's Central Committee, signaling their intention to take an explicitly political role in anticolonial activism.

The 1919 revolution was a turning point of modern Egyptian history, not only because it culminated in Egyptian quasi-independence from British colonial rule in 1922. As a result of the unrest in 1919, the British ended Egypt's status as a protectorate and Egypt became independent, although Britain preserved its control over key Egyptian institutions and infrastructure, including the military, the police, the Suez Canal, and parts of the judiciary. It also marked the moment in which a century's worth of debate, discussion, and reform over modernity, womanhood, and the family brought "the private politics of the domestic realm into the spotlight of the political arena."[14]

The order and structure of the modern bourgeois household, defined by the presence of enlightened mothers and responsible fathers, became enshrined within the political iconography of the nation and national struggle. The home of Zaghlul, the Wafd Party's founder, was christened the *bayt al-umma*, or "house of the nation," and his wife, Safiyya Zaghlul, was designated *Umm al-Misriyyin*, "mother of the Egyptians." Political cartoons featuring mother Egypt nurturing *al-shaʿb al-misri* (the Egyptian people) to independence, as well as images of male nationalist leaders in nurturing, mothering roles, demonstrate the extent to which family, home, and gender had become a part of Egyptian nationalism.[15] Domestic images helped to cement the relationship between the privileged elites who ran the country and the masses by incorporating both into the metaphorical family.[16] Such representations, appearing in political speeches, cartoons, literature, and the popular press, were not merely rhetorical strategy deployed as a political tool by the Wafdist leadership and its supporters in order to mobilize the Egyptian population in nationalist struggle; they engendered liberal-nationalist rule.

The purpose of this section is to show how notions of nationalist womanhood, embedded in visions of the modern domestic realm and elaborated in the decades leading up to Egyptian quasi-independence, became institutionalized in the "gender regime" of the liberal-nationalist political order following Egyptian independence. According to Robert Connell, the gender regimes embodied by the nation-state contain a structure of cathexis, a gendered structure of power, and a gendered division of labor. In the case of the emerging independent Egyptian nation-state, what linked symbolic depictions of the nation, elite liberal-nationalist constructions of authority, and the structure of the state itself was paternalism.

In her study of gender, citizenship, and the civic order in mandate Syria and Lebanon, Elizabeth Thompson has defined paternalism as a system of power defined by the ability to control the distribution of benefits, not by the recognition of rights to benefits. It signifies a system of negotiated relations and hierarchies in which elite men continually reconstruct their authority over women as well as subaltern men. The benefit of using a concept of paternalism in the Egyptian case is that it allows consideration of the ways in which the system of liberal-nationalist rule accorded elite women authority over subaltern women and, in some cases, subaltern men. As she writes:

> A mediating elite emerges between the state and mass of citizens to broker these benefits by winning privileged access to them from the state, and by using that access to control the unprivileged majority . . . it defines authority as that of the father; that is as essentially male and passed down from one male to the next. Male authority thus flows continuously from the formal realm of politics through to the informal politics of the household. . . . In a paternalistic system of rule, the ruler distributes benefits according to his will, not by the right of the ruled, and power is devolved in a mediating hierarchy of males enjoying a priori authority over females and the power to discipline weaker men.[17]

Thus, paternalism is distinguished from patriarchy by its fluidity. While patriarchy connotes the structural subordination of women to men, paternalism signifies a system of negotiated relations and hierarchies in which elite men continually reconstruct their authority over women as well as subaltern men.

The paternalistic gender regime that characterized liberal-nationalist rule was made tangible by the familial symbols and gendered imagery of *effendi* nationalism. In the Egyptian "family romance" of nationalist history, the nation was conceived in anticolonial struggle and birthed out of the triumph of the 1919 revolution by the male leaders of the nationalist Wafd Party. Lynn Hunt, drawing on the work of Sigmund Freud and Frederic Jameson, defines "family romance" as "collective, unconscious images of the familial order that underlie revolutionary politics."[18] While Hunt's contention that images of the family and familial order are constitutive of (and constituted by) political orders is compelling, I would argue that there was nothing unconscious about these images in the Egyptian case. The politics of the family and the politics of the Egyptian nation were seen very consciously to be constitutive of each other, not only because the very notion of nation and narratives of nationhood are explicitly built upon "imagined" ties of kinship between the nation's members, but because the domestic practices of Egyptian families were so central to colonial claims that Egyptians could not govern themselves. As the founding fathers of the liberal-nationalist order, Wafdist politicians very self-consciously authorized their claims to rule on the basis that they were members of *al-sha'b* (the people), legitimate sons of mother Egypt, and paternal guardians of the national family and its interests.

The gendered construction of political authority had significant ramifications for Egyptian citizenship and the building of the postcolonial state. The 1923 constitution enshrined the fraternal character of the nation by recognizing only adult male citizens as members. While it recognized all Egyptians as "equal before the law . . . enjoy[ing] civil and political rights . . . without distinctions of race, language or religion," the electoral law promulgated three months later granted universal suffrage to male Egyptians only.[19] Article 32 also declared that this fraternity of citizens was the source of all legal and political power in the new parliamentary system, presided over by a constitutional monarchy. While the horizontal bonds between male citizens were thus enshrined in provisions on voting rights as well as those that obligated all Egyptian males twenty-one or older to participate in defense of the nation, other measures highlighted the existence of vertical bonds among male members of the nation, which underpinned class and ethnic hierarchies institutionalized in the power structure of the new nation-state.[20]

Consistent with maternalist constructions of citizenship, the only right women were accorded was the right to primary school education. The refusal of the nationalist government to award the vote to women led to a split within the membership of the Wafdist Women's Committee, and in 1923 Huda Sha'rawi joined several other former committee members to found their own organization, the Egyptian Feminist Union (EFU). The EFU is traditionally credited as Egypt's first independent feminist organization.

The centrality of the woman question to nationalist politics and the active and highly publicized participation of elite and subaltern women in the events of 1919 has led scholars to attribute the gendered exclusions of the electoral law to the patriarchal conservatism of male nationalist leaders who, once women's active participation in nationalist struggle was no longer needed, expected them to return to their "natural" place in the home.[21] Not only does this overlook the exclusions of subaltern men from political agency, but it also overlooks the ways in which secular nationalism, and the forms and institutions that underpin it, themselves embodied patriarchal norms.[22] The set of modern constitutional ideals inherited during colonial rule were gendered in such a way as to depend on a modern, reformed female presence in the home. The exclusion of women from political participation was thus a logical extension of those gendered ideals.[23]

What has been too infrequently acknowledged in accounts of elite women's activism during this period is their active complicity with the paternalism of liberal-nationalist rule. Given the emphasis placed by nationalist discourses on the condition of Egyptian families, particularly mothers and children, the lack of provisions made for the care and welfare of families by the state is striking. The Ministry of Social Affairs, the establishment of which signaled the beginnings of a state commitment to social welfare, was not founded until 1939; prior to that time, the provision of social services was monopolized by women's organizations. As male nationalist elites turned their attention to what would become a continuous struggle with the palace and with the British residency for power and control and the more "masculine" tasks of state-building, the task of "nurturing the nation" was claimed by elite Egyptian women, who though excluded from political enfranchisement, carved out a space of authority and autonomy through their involvement with social service provision.[24]

In transferring the caretaking duties performed in the home to that of the nation, elite women asserted their right to inclusion in the national project. The program of the Egyptian Feminist Union, for example, is emblematic of the ways in which the joining of maternalist conceptions of citizenship with national service made possible new demands for political and economic rights.

In a 1924 pamphlet, Huda Sha'rawi argued that women were half the nation and the caretakers of future generations, and thus they must be prepared to take up their political and social obligations to the nation aş enfranchised citizens.[25] She emphasized the need both for women's access to education and for the provision of social services and tutelage that would reform women's condition and allow them to act fully as proper political subjects.

Elite women accepted the paternalism of liberal-nationalism, in part because it gave them authority over subaltern women.[26] Huda Sha'rawi's model of citizenship was explicitly class biased. Educated upper- and upper middle-class women were to be given the right to perform public work so that they could instruct working-class and rural women how to become proper citizens. The EFU's early demands for suffrage, largely abandoned by 1926, had argued that the franchise should be restricted to educated, literate women (a tiny fraction of Egyptian women). Subaltern women thus occupied a contradictory position in feminist discourses. On one hand, subaltern women were objects of elite charity and tutelage; on the other, they were also imagined as potential political agents. Their condition was of concern precisely because of their potential to be reformed. This was not the case in other contemporaneous movements, such as the labor movement.[27] Labor publications featured articles on the difficulties faced by middle-class working women but wholly ignored female factory workers as a potential constituency to be mobilized, until the 1940s. Peasant women served as a romanticized symbol of the nation, but they (like peasant men) were never envisioned as a potential constituency to be mobilized.

For the next two decades, the EFU, along with a host of other women's organizations such as the Society of Young Egyptian Women, concentrated on the provision of social services to poorer women. These activities primarily involved teaching basic literacy and domestic tasks, such as sewing and the principles of hygiene and child care. In short, as Mervat Hatem has pointed out, their goal was to enable working-class and rural women to be better wives and mothers.[28] In providing instruction to the working class, elite and middle-class reformers actively collaborated in the division of labor created by the gender regime of liberal-nationalist rule. By 1926, the feminist movement had largely abandoned any claim to political participation by way of the ballot in favor of reforming the nation through social service.

It is important here not to overstate the coherence of views on the woman question found in the women's press of the period. While some journals, including *Al-Masriyya*, *Al-Fatat*, and *Al-Amal*, explicitly tied their calls for women to serve the nation to demands for other sorts of rights, such as the rights to work and to have access to higher education, others, such as *al-Nahda al-Nisa'iyya*, rejected such formulations. What they shared was a model of gendered citizenship that endured throughout the interwar years. The ideal nationalist woman combined the fulfillment of domestic duty within her individual family with an extension of domestic tasks outside the home in the service of the nation.

A NEW GENERATION

During the 1930s, Egyptians who came of political age after the 1919 revolution began to make their presence felt on the Egyptian political scene. This "new generation" (*al-jil al-jadid*) as they came to be referred to by the press, increasingly challenged monarchal rule, the continuing economic, social, and political domination of British interests, and the existing liberal-nationalist order embodied by the Wafd Party. The failure of the Wafd Party to successfully negotiate a treaty with Great Britain after Egypt was formerly granted independence in 1922, and its often antagonistic relationship with the palace and British officials, resulted in its eviction from power and the installation of Sidqi Pasha, the head of the Liberal Nationalist Party, as head of the government in 1930. The abrogation of the 1923 constitution by Sidqi, the consequent government crackdown on press and political freedoms, and the authoritarian and elitist character of the government generated an outpouring of opposition. This opposition came largely from students, an increasingly organized labor movement, new political parties such as the fascist-inspired Young Egypt, and Islamist social organizations such as the Muslim Brotherhood. Even as they organized and agitated in favor of the Wafd, these groups were mounting alternatives to the older liberal-nationalist order.

The social, political, and economic transformations of the 1930s and 1940s not only led to the spread of the professional middle class and its increasingly important contribution to cultural and political life, but also to its increasing sense of alienation and disaffection from the established structures of liberal-nationalist rule. The early 1930s saw the economic fortunes of the middle classes challenged by the collapse of the global cotton market and economic recession. The crash in the price of cotton, Egypt's primary export commodity, was accompanied by increases in the cost of living, declines in the real value of wages, and rising unemployment. Especially affected were young, educated professional men, whose numbers had increased with the expansion of education that occurred in the period following independence.[29] By 1937, there were 7,500 baccalaureate (high school graduate) holders and 3,500 university graduates who were unemployed.[30] Others were underemployed or paid salaries that failed to keep pace with the rising costs of living.

In particular, two developments from this period stand out as significant. The first is that challenges to and critique of the liberal-nationalist order increasingly took the form of claims on the nation-state. The paternalism of liberal-nationalism was implicitly and explicitly challenged by demands from new political movements, reformers, and individual commentators that the state take a greater role as the arbiter of public order, the guarantor of individual rights, and crucially, as the agent of social reform. The second is the increasing divergence between secular and religious narratives of modernity. By the mid-1930s, the practices, institutions, and epistemological frameworks of secular nationalism had become hegemonic to the extent that they were able to claim the status of "modern" to the exclusion of alternative modes of thought, practice, and being.

GENDER AND SOCIAL REFORM IN THE 1930S AND 1940S

"[The rural population] is dead as regards healthy nationalistic life," Mirrit Butrus Ghali wrote in *The Policy of Tomorrow*, a book published in 1938 that aimed at "draw[ing] up a program which will realize the aspirations of the nation in creating a renaissance (*nahda*) and progress" through rural reform measures.[31] Ghali was a former member of parliament and came from a Coptic family with a long liberal pedigree. But his assessment of the dire condition of the Egyptian countryside was shared by many of his contemporaries, where the situation in Egyptian villages was characterized by contemporary commentators as wracked by violence and endemic economic hardship, a breeding ground for the "three ills"—poverty, ignorance, and disease—that plagued the majority of Egypt's population.[32] *The Policy of Tomorrow* advocated government involvement in the most minute details of villagers' daily lives, from the transformation of village housing, to individual instruction in hygienic practices, to the promotion of maternal and child health through the establishment of village clinics and dispensaries staffed by personnel trained in modern medical practices. Ghali's text, while influential, was hardly unique.[33] Its prescriptions reflected the emergence of new discourses of social welfare and reform in the 1930s and 1940s.

The social, political, and economic unrest of the 1930s gave rise to a new concern about social welfare in the interwar period, in which groups and individuals of widely divergent political affiliations and ideological outlooks debated "the peasant question" and a host of other social problems as a necessary component of national integration and uplift. This period marked not only the operationalization of earlier discourses on social reform but also their increasing institutionalization. Starting in the mid-1930s, the state began to claim new responsibility for improving social conditions among its largely "backward" and impoverished population, and new authority over the daily lives and practices of individual Egyptians. The Ministry of Public Health was founded in 1936; the same year saw the establishment of the Higher Council for Social Reform, an official body made up of prominent social reformers charged with drawing up plans for the foundation of a larger government entity that would address all social and labor issues in Egypt. Their work resulted in the creation of the Ministry of Social Affairs in 1939.[34] Ahmed Hussein, influential social scientist and advocate of interwar social reform, who would eventually be appointed minister of social affairs in 1950, wrote about the factors behind the creation of that ministry:

> It was no longer wise to leave the various social problems to be dealt with by haphazard efforts curtailed by opposing currents and conflicting opinions. It was the supreme duty of the State to observe and record social conditions and their development, to diagnose social diseases and defects and to study the methods of treatment; to plan . . . a comprehensive and permanent policy of social rehabilitation with a view to uplifting the poor classes, raising the standard of living of the individual as well as the family, and finally ensuring the greatest measure of social justice to the people. It is on these grounds that the Ministry of Social Affairs was created and its tasks planned out.[35]

Hussein's description of the new ministry's mandate suggests some of what was new about discourse of social reform in the interwar period, as well as their continuities. Prescriptions for social rehabilitation were increasingly couched in terms of a new reliance on expertise and scientific planning. The "comprehensive" approach recommended by Hussein and other interwar reformers entailed the development of new capacities in diagnosing, classifying, and categorizing social problems, with the goal of developing remedies to social ills; unlike the piecemeal approaches of the earlier period, these remedies were integrated, coordinated, unified, and carried out by professional experts trained in the relatively new disciplines of sociology, anthropology, demography, and social work. No longer primarily the province of charitable organizations, social reform measures were taken up and carried out increasingly by state institutions.

As Omnia El Shakry has pointed out, such developments were important not only because they laid the discursive and institutional foundations of later social engineering projects carried out by the Nasser regime, but because they marked the increasing shift from "the home" as a metaphor for the nation to "the family" as an object of regulation and governance.[36] Like the reformers under older notions of social welfare, interwar reformists drew on the language of modernity, national progress, and a normative vision of the bourgeois modern family to fashion Egyptian womanhood as both a source of backwardness and the key to cultural uplift. Social development projects advocated and implemented in the 1930s and 1940s were, in no small part, aimed at rehabilitating Egyptian families by reforming lower-class—particularly peasant—women. These projects displayed a concern not only with improving health services to pregnant women but also with instructing rural women in the principles, practices, and dispositions of domestic order and sanitation—how to keep a clean home, how to prepare healthy, nutritious food, how to inculcate an ethic of personal hygiene in their children, and so on.[37] What was different about interwar reform is that it marked the operationalization of older discourses on women, the family, and social welfare to an extent that was unprecedented in the earlier period. While an in-depth account of how this shift was enacted is beyond the scope of this study, a sense of its gendered ramifications is made clear by brief examination of interwar debates over population and contraception, which were inextricably linked to rural reform in the late 1930s.[38]

In the 1930s, reformers of various political persuasions and ideological commitments began to link the social ills that beset Egypt—widespread poverty, illness, poor sanitation, and criminality—to the elevated fertility rates of peasant and working-class families. Wendall Cleland's influential 1936 book, *The Population Problem in Egypt*, projected that Egypt's high rate of fertility would double its population in fifty-two years.[39] Pointing out that Egypt's natural resources and agricultural land were already insufficient to support its growing population, he went on to argue that, left unchecked, peasant over-reproduction would result in a generation of "half-living listless people" beset by endemic diseases and malnutrition that sapped their vitality.[40]

Confronted with the images of the benighted peasant family and a grim, apocalyptic future, reformers formulated a number of solutions to the population problem. Some, like Cleland, recommended the establishment of a national birth control program, which would produce "an average family of from three to five children with intelligent, literate parents, living healthy lives in solid, clean houses, very simply furnished, which will belong to well ordered, sanitary communities."[41] Others rejected birth control in favor of rural reform measures, which would improve the standard of living in the Egyptian countryside (this was, in fact, the most widely advocated solution to the population problem throughout the interwar period).

Such issues were debated in salons, public lectures, and conferences, where contraception was a fashionable, if controversial, subject of discussion for Egyptian intellectuals, reformers, and medical professionals. These debates have been well chronicled elsewhere.[42]

Briefly, whether the argument was that birth control was the only means to effectively curb population growth or that raising the standard of living and hygiene in the countryside would automatically result in decreased fertility, reformers agreed that the solution lay in improving Egyptian motherhood. As one contributor to the interwar population debate put it, the goal was not only to reduce the numbers of children being born but to ensure the production of "healthier and more useful mothers," who would then give birth to "healthier, more vigorous and better trained children."[43] The focus in interwar Egypt on motherhood as the means of promoting the health and fitness of the lower classes was, of course, not new; in the 1930s and 1940s, calls for the state to spread maternal and child health units throughout the Egyptian countryside, to establish schools and training programs that could instruct peasant women in hygienic domesticity or to distribute birth control on a wide scale could be viewed, in this respect, as just the latest attempts by reformers at modernizing women so they would be able to act as fit national subjects.

Despite the emphasis on motherhood, however, discussions about birth control and population in the 1930s and 1940s largely effaced the centrality of women to reproduction.[44] Women's voices, as well as the social roles that women play in child rearing, were largely excluded from public discourses on birth control and population until well after the 1952 revolution. As birth control continued to be debated throughout the 1940s and early 1950s, women figured primarily as objects of population debates rather than subjects, a move that was largely replicated in other prescriptions for social reform.[45]

The erasure of women as social actors and the instrumentalization of gender as a sphere of state interest and control were part of a process in which the claims of elite women over social reform were gradually supplanted by those of largely male reformers. Elite women and their organizations, as we have seen, couched their social welfare activities in the language of maternal citizenship, in which their efforts at "nurturing the nation" would result not only in healthy families but also in liberated, empowered women capable of taking their places as active political subjects. Thus, elite women like Huda Sha'rawi emphasized the benefits and opportunities that social reform measures would bring to women and to society. Interwar discourses of social development, by contrast, barely referenced the empowerment of women as a desired outcome of, or necessary precursor to, the wider project of social and national integration that was the ultimate goal of reform projects like those carried out by the Ministry of Social Affairs. Articulated in the masculinized vernacular of planning, integration, and engineering rather than that of nurturing, prescriptions for social reform and their enactment in the 1930s and 1940s marked the beginning of the transference of feminized social "caretaking" to the masculine realm of state-building, planning, and governance.

FEMINISMS AND DIVERGENT MODERNITIES

In the 1930s, Egyptian women increasingly challenged the boundaries of maternal citizenship to make new claims to inclusion and participation. Women activists, writers, and culture producers began to argue for wider political, social, and economic rights on the basis of national service, not motherhood. This was not a departure from earlier discourses of maternal citizenship but rather a radical elaboration of them, and was in part a result of the increasing participation and influence of middle-class women in public activism. The roles that women had formerly performed in the home and within their individual families could be transferred to the public realm in service of the wider national family. Indeed, contributors to the women's press viewed "social housekeeping" as necessary for national progress.[46] Calls for the right to suffrage, for increased access to higher education, and for "respectable" work opportunities, where women might be protected from exploitation in the workplace, were linked at various times (and in complicated ways) to the preservation and health of the family, the well-being of the nation, and fulfillment of the personal desires and aspirations of individual women.

This period is often viewed as the beginning of a particularly vibrant era in the history of Egyptian feminism, as the demands of women activists expanded to include political and social rights, and the domination of elite women over the women's movement came to be increasingly challenged by women from more humble backgrounds. Moreover, the 1930s and 1940s are also, justifiably, seen as a period when feminist activism helped realize important legal and social gains for Egyptian women, including the promulgation of the first labor legislation providing protections for female workers, matriculation of the first class of female students into Fu'ad University (which would later become Cairo University) in 1929, and the increasing entrance of women into professional occupations such as journalism, teaching, and health care. It was also, however, the period that witnessed the increasing reification of a liberal, secular modernist vision of liberation and the woman question, which undermined efforts at a unified women's movement.

During the first decades of the twentieth century, the emphasis on the woman question as a key to national transformation created a space within which women reformers, whether operating from within an Islamic modernist tradition or drawing on the language of secular Westernization, found possibilities for collaboration, exchange, and cooperation. Historians of the Egyptian women's movement have argued over the local genealogies of Egyptian feminism. Whereas some have highlighted the colonial origins of discourses on the woman question, dividing feminism into indigenous and "Western-oriented," others have stressed the local origins of women's activism. Still others have maintained that feminist impulses are universal, transcending the cultural binary between East and West, which the argument over feminism's origins presumes. However, Egyptian notions of feminisms, as they manifested themselves in the various reform projects that characterized the "women's awakening," were not simply derivative of Western prescriptions, nor were they an unmediated local response. Huda Sha'rawi, a member of an elite Turco-Circassian family and who is today lionized by nationalist narratives as the "founding mother" of Egyptian feminism, was educated by a French tutor and couched her reformist activities in the language of Westernizing reform. Yet she found common cause with Malak Hifni Nasif, known by her pen name, Bahithat al-Badiya, whose views on women's status were articulated from within an Islamic modernist tradition.[47]

Such formal and informal collaborations should not be viewed as the emergence of some sort of unmediated feminist consciousness. But they do force us not only to recognize that there were issues that drew women to make alliances on the basis of a common concern with bettering their own condition, but also to recognize the ways in which "indigenous" calls for reform shared assumptions with Western-inspired projects of modernization. From the turn of the century up to the mid-1930s, those projects, and the understandings of modernity that they were based upon, were still compatible.

By the mid-1930s, however, that space was increasingly being transformed from a space where cooperation was possible to one where differences led to conflict. The question of why that should be the case deserves a study of its own. Some answers are suggested by looking at contemporaneous developments in gender politics in other parts of the Middle East. In an article about the state abolition of the chador in Iran in the 1930s, Afsaneh Najmabadi has written how mandatory unveiling marked the moment in which feminism came to be identified with the secular modernizing projects of the state, effacing the complicated histories, overlaps, and collaborations that allowed for multiple understandings of feminism and modernity to coexist. The effect of state-mandated unveiling was to cast religious articulations of modernity as the repudiated "other" of secularism. Some women and girls who had formerly taken an active role in debating, articulating, and participating in the project of creating a modern Iranian womanhood through their involvement in education and social service provision, either chose (or were forced) to stay home rather than appear in public unveiled. In the rhetoric of Iranian nationalism, these women served as a potent symbol of the backwardness of "traditional" or religious Iranian womanhood, while the "new" unveiled woman stood as a representation of the progress promised by secular modernity.[48] In Egypt (unlike in Iran) there was no apocalyptic moment that an observer of interwar Egyptian history can point to, no particular incident that stands as the moment of disjuncture between religious and secular modernism. Yet, the new political meanings that the project of "liberating women" acquired during the interwar period suggest a similar process.

On the surface, the gender politics of secular nationalism and those of Islamic modernist movements (such as the Muslim Brotherhood, the largest and most influential of the Islamist organizations to emerge in the interwar period) would seem to be in diametric opposition. Taking the community that the prophet Muhammad had established at Mecca as its exemplar, the Brotherhood posited a return to an "authentic" Islam purged of corrupt Western influences as a solution to the political and social crises engendered by Egypt's liberal experiment. Brotherhood founder Hasan al-Banna advocated a return to veiling and exhorted women to take up their "sacred" roles as mothers, wives, and custodians of the domestic realm as a means to the transformation of the *umma* (the community of Muslim believers) and, eventually, to the establishment of an Islamic state.[49] Secular nationalism, which had provided the basis of liberal-nationalist rule in the interwar period, viewed the transformation of gender relations as a means to ending the vestiges of backwardness (*takhalluf*) that prevented Egypt from taking her rightful place among the "advanced" (*mutaqaddim*) nations of the world. Articulating a unilinear vision of progress and development, secular nationalist thought posited the liberation of women as an outward trajectory from the harem and unveiling to public participation.

In fact, Islamist and secular nationalist visions of women's roles shared more features than might seem readily apparent at first glance. Within both secular nationalist and Islamist ideologies, gender was a particularly charged site for negotiating the meanings of being "modern" and being "authentic." The gender politics of secular nationalism and Islamism reflected the growing cultural hegemony and political challenges of the *effendiyya*, the professional, urban middle classes who shaped and were shaped by modernist cultural forms, ideologies, and political engagements. Walter Armbrust, in his study of mass culture and modernism during the interwar period, has written: "Between what was seen by some as corrupt aping of Europe and by others as native adaptation of European custom lay the potential for families and individuals to negotiate their identities as 'modern Egyptians.' Negotiations of identity within such limits, more than any material criteria defined the Egyptian middle class."[50] Modernity was being claimed in new and different ways by a new generation as an organic part of local historical experience. In their rejection of the culture and politics of an elite viewed as corrupted by its ties to European colonialism, secular and Islamist intellectuals negotiated politics and identities that were critical of Western hegemony and colonialism while embracing many of its institutional and epistemological forms. Whether articulated in the idiom of Islamic reform, as in the case of the Muslim Brotherhood, or in the language of universalism and social planning, as in the case of secular socialist and leftist intellectuals, the languages of modernity with their attendant binaries (change/continuity, universalism/particularism, importation/authenticity) provided shared terms of political and social engagement and the limits of a common political field. Thus Islamists, even as they condemned the unregulated mixing of the sexes evident on the beaches of

Alexandria and in the nightclubs of Cairo, were advocates of women's education as a means to inculcating the knowledge and values necessary to social and political transformation. Secular nationalist discourses on women, even as they decried the veil as a symbol of backwardness, continued to define and debate women's duties to the nation with reference to their roles as mothers, wives, and custodians of the domestic realm and the importance of the home as a site for the inculcation of national culture.

What was different, however, was that by the mid-1930s, the practices, institutions, and epistemological frameworks of secular nationalism were able to claim the status of "modern" to the exclusion of alternative modes of thought, practice, and being. Put in another way, the overlaps, collaboration, and cooperation that had been possible between secular and religious modernizing projects in the first two decades of the twentieth century were foreclosed. Religious modernity, and the practices and beliefs associated with it, came to stand, on one hand, as modernity's repudiated "other," a vestige of the backwardness that had to be overcome by secular modernization; or on the other (according to Islamists), as the means by which Muslims might return to a more authentic way of life, which had been eroded by the imposition of modern norms and values. Thus, as some women found support for their cause in the secular state, and the cultural, political, and institutional expressions of secular nationalism became increasingly hegemonic, certain expressions of religiosity came to be viewed as "backward" and antithetical to the cause of women's liberation and empowerment, foreclosing some of the possibilities for collaborations, imaginings, and negotiations that had once been possible.

A brief analysis of the changes in Labiba Ahmad's journal *The Women's Awakening* (Al-Nahda Al-Nisa'iyya) over the course of the 1920s and 1930s provides an example of the binaries that came to be attached to the woman question in the interwar period. Labiba Ahmad, the daughter of a doctor and wife of prominent jurist Uthman Bey Murtada Pasha, began her political activities in 1919 as a participant in the "ladies' demonstration" against British rule. After 1919 she declined to join the Wafdist Women's Committee and founded a philanthropic organization, "The Society of the Women's Awakening," whose goal, according to Beth Baron, was to inculcate Islamist values, nationalist ideals, and proper notions of social and gender relations in young, primarily poor Egyptian women.[51] In 1921 she published the first edition of *The Women's Awakening*, which aimed to convey her message to a wider audience of women.

In the mid-1920s *The Women's Awakening* featured both Islamic *hijri* dates and Gregorian calendar dates on the cover next to an illustration of the famous statue "Egypt Awakes" (Nahdat Misr). The statue, a key symbol of Egyptian nationalist aspirations, featured a peasant woman lifting her veil, her other hand resting on the head of a sphinx.[52] Inside the magazine's cover, readers could find the daily timetable for prayer and, during Ramadan, articles about fasting next to articles about home economics and the latest developments in education and child rearing, which were virtually indistinguishable from those appearing in women's journals with a more secular orientation.

By the late 1930s, however, Islamic and secular symbols had begun to take on political meanings that largely precluded their easy coexistence. The illustration of "Nahdat Misr" was removed in 1934 from Ahmad's journal and replaced with arabesque and Islamic figures. Where magazines had once embraced diverse images of the Egyptian nation dressed in a variety of garbs (from Western evening wear, to fully covered in the style associated with elite Turkish women), by 1934 the new Egyptian woman, the "beauty of today," was pictured on the cover of the popular magazine *Al-Ithnayn* glamorously unveiled, her hair chicly bobbed, and explicitly contrasted with "the beauty of the past," her face covered. Such illustrations were emblematic of how "the liberation of women" was increasingly appropriated as the sole province of secular modernity, to be embraced as progressive and liberating or dismissed as a culturally inauthentic, imperialist imposition. By the time developments in post–Second World War politics created new opportunities and new spaces for women's activism, the possibilities for collaboration between women were already largely foreclosed.

REWRITING THE TERMS OF LIBERATION

The economic and social displacements of the period immediately following the Second World War, the devastating defeat of Arab troops and the creation of the state of Israel in 1948, and the corruption and political machinations that typified struggles between unstable coalition governments, the British, and the throne brought the political and social tensions that had been brewing since the previous decade to the boiling point. The post–Second World War period witnessed the rise of mass politics, in which an array of organizations of various ideological leanings—socialist, communist, Islamist, trade unionist, radicalized wings of the Wafd such as the Wafdist Vanguard, and women's unions—competed for space and influence in the political arena.

All of these groups, despite differing agendas, constituted a challenge to the existing political and social order. Their demands for national liberation, social justice, and expanded rights within the body politic represented a conscious break with the paternalistic rule of the liberal-nationalist elite. The calls for political and social reform to combat Egypt's "three ills," which had grown louder during the interwar period, increasingly gave way to diverse calls for social and political transformation that took the state as a common referent. Whether the calls were from Islamist activists who advocated the creation of an Islamic state, or from secular activists who envisioned a state that would be the primary agent of social reform (or for some social planning), the creator of a more egalitarian society, and the guarantor of citizenship rights, the shift from reform to more radical political programs occasioned new understandings of the meanings of liberation and the forging of new sorts of political and social claims on the nation.

Within this context a new generation of women activists lent their efforts to a diversified national political scene that included Islamists, the working class, students, and leftists. Women such as Amina Sa'id, Latifa al-Zayyat, Duriyya Shafiq, Suhayr Qalamawi, Zaynab al-Ghazali, Inji Aflatun, and Fatma Ni'mat Rashid, whose names would become familiar through their political participation in the postwar period, or after the revolution as leaders in their field and active participants in the revolutionary project, were from a very different milieu than their elite predecessors who founded and provided the bulk of the leadership of Huda Sha'rawi's Egyptian Feminist Union. Most, although not all, were from middle-class, *effendiyya* backgrounds and families that were sympathetic to, if not actively involved in, nationalist politics, and most had ethnic Egyptian, as opposed to Turco-Circassian, roots.[53] Many of them were among the early beneficiaries of the opening of educational and work opportunities for women that came during the liberal-nationalist period.[54] Fu'ad University (which would later become Cairo University) matriculated its first class of female students in 1929. Eight years later, there were 1,979 women holding university degrees, and by 1947 there were 4,000.[55] At primary and secondary levels of education, whereas there had been 31,000 female students in 1913 (10 percent of the student body), by 1930 the number of girls attending schools at all levels had increased to 218,164 or 24 percent of the student population.

Women's postwar activism provided a forum for new articulations of the woman question and the relationship between class, nation, and feminism. One of the most influential movements during the postwar period was the Muslim

Brotherhood. Started in 1928 as a social organization, it soon grew into a mass political movement. The Brotherhood's platform advocated the end of British and Western influence in Egypt and the institution of a state based on Islamic law. A fundamental part of their program was the return to what they argued were more authentic roles for women, which valorized women's contributions as mothers and wives whose religiously ordained place was in the home.

The valorization of domestic roles for women not only was central to the Muslim Brotherhood's political program but also served to delegitimize movements that competed with it for mass support. One of the ways the Brotherhood attempted to discredit leftist activists was by impugning the sexual morality of a group's female members.

Latifa al-Zayyat, a leader of the student movement and a leftist activist, recalled in an interview: "I fought against the Muslim fundamentalist groups which tried to defame my reputation—they called me a prostitute and other such things. . . . This turned me into a puritan. Really, because they said that communists were immoral . . . communists became puritans to maintain their relationship with the public."[56] Suraya Adham, a member of the Communist Party, was beaten by Islamists in 1948 for her political activity.[57]

However, the Brotherhood's use of gender stereotyping to advance political aims did not signify that they were opposed to women assuming a public, activist role if that in turn promoted women's roles as wives and mothers as well as the formation of an Islamic state. Zaynab al-Ghazali is widely touted as the grandmother of Islamist women's activism. In 1935, at the age of eighteen, she joined the Egyptian Feminist Union but left a year later when she became convinced that the EFU's program was "not the right way for Muslim women."[58] The same year, she founded the Muslim Women's Association (MWA). Its aim was to spread the tenets of Islam among women by holding study groups, providing social services, and more generally, advocating for the implementation of Islamic law and an end to British influence. Al-Ghazali dismissed efforts to "liberate" women as dangerous deviations from Islamic tenets, yet her understanding of the social and political crises of the time, as well as her positing a return to Islam as an authentic solution to those crises, is striking for the ways it draws on a gendered language of modernism. In an interview in the 1980s she spoke of her intentions in founding the MWA:

> Our goal was to acquaint the Muslim woman with her religion so she would
> be convinced by means of study that the women's liberation movement is a

deviant innovation that occurred due to the Muslim's backwardness; they must remove this backwardness from their shoulders and rise up as their religion commands, as it should be in Islamic lands. . . . Women must be well educated, cultured, knowing the precepts of the Koran and Sunnah, knowing world politics, why we are backward, why we don't have technology. The Muslim woman must know all of these things and then raise her son in the conviction that he must possess the scientific tools of the age and, at the same time, he must understand Islam. . . . Islam does not forbid women from working, entering into politics, and expressing her opinion or from being anything as long as that does not interfere with her first duty as a mother.[59]

Al-Ghazali's emphasis on the necessity of educating women as a means to eradicate the "backwardness" of the Muslim *umma*, her stress on the importance of creating mothers capable of inculcating proper political and social values in the next generation of Muslims, and her list of things a Muslim woman must know is evocative of the "selective repudiation" practiced by Islamist activists.[60] Rejecting "women's liberation" as a deviation from Islam, al-Ghazali's claim of authenticity occluded the significant convergences between Islamist programs and other gendered modernist prescriptions, mitigating any claim that her advocacy was somehow antithetical to women's Islamically mandated roles.

If al-Ghazali's message was a consistent repudiation of unconventional roles for women, her own life—scholars have observed—stood in sharp contrast to the message she delivered. And yet, the Brotherhood's leadership collaborated with and accepted al-Ghazali's activism, suggesting that the Brotherhood's actual assessment of what women could be allowed to do was not that different from that of the secularists and proof of al-Ghazali's own success in legitimating her unconventional choices. Nonetheless, the gender politics of the Muslim Brotherhood, which entailed coding al-Ghazali's activities as consistent with Islamist ideologies and those of leftist women activists as a form of social deviation, was emblematic of how gender worked to construct postwar political movements as mutually oppositional and helped to define the limits of collaboration and cooperation between groups.

The second major mass political movement in the postwar era was leftist and secular. Leftist organizations, which rose to prominence during this period, including communist, socialist, and labor groups, maintained a broad, ideological commitment to women's rights as part of their programs aimed at securing wider social, political, and economic rights for the lower and middle classes. These groups often included women in leadership positions; the student movement in particular saw active women's participation and leadership. For the most part, the platforms of such organizations deemphasized specific feminist agendas and relegated the woman question to the margins of politics. Nonetheless, the general atmosphere of radical political activism encouraged the formation of ad-hoc groups and committees—such as the League of Women Students and Graduates for the University and Egyptian Institutes, the Committee of Young Women, and the Women's Committee for Popular Resistance—which organized specifically around women's issues and mobilization, providing a forum for new articulations of the relationship between class, nation, and feminism, as well as the creation of networks of women.[61]

Latifa al-Zayyat contrasted the liberation of women and the liberation of society in an interview:

> It is a luxury to think of the liberation of women . . . when you see your brothers, fathers, and children strangled, scorned and exploited by foreigners and local men and women. . . . It is only when civilization reaches a certain level that the problems of women, children and minorities become urgent. Women make the most noble contribution to the liberation of society when they embrace causes outside of themselves and outside their families. . . . Women's fight for liberation implies a fight for the liberation of society.[62]

The phrase *tahrir al-mar'a* (the liberation of women) itself carried particular historical meanings for leftist women activists, evoking the bourgeois maternalism of Huda Sha'rawi's EFU, whose calls for gender solidarity they viewed as having masked the inequalities between elite and poor women. For leftists, securing equal rights without transforming the political and economic system could benefit only the educated elite and would not benefit women of the lower classes. Also, acquiring political rights did not imply that the socioeconomic structure would be changed. To become part of the governing class was simply a co-optation of the women's movement and a fragmentation of the opposition to the ruling class. As an alternative to the existing women's parties, Marxist women formed the League of Women Students and Graduates from University and Egyptian institutes. In its pamphlet "Our Goals," women were instructed to "Struggle for the widest freedoms, struggle for liberation from oppression, hunger and aggression; struggle by ourselves, for ourselves; struggle to create a free, noble life for Egyptian women under the sovereignty of a free and noble country; struggle to realize democratic freedom which cannot arrive under the shadow of the imperialist and imperialism nor under the shadow of enslavement and exploitation."[63]

Finally, drawing on a legacy of liberal-nationalist women's activism, several women established organizations focused on the struggle for political rights. Duriyya Shafiq and Fatma Ni'mat Rashid both founded organizations that coupled demands for women's political rights with calls for wider social reforms. Rashid founded the National Women's Party in 1944.[64] Duriyya Shafiq's organization, the Bint al-Nil Union, was established in 1948. Bint al-Nil Union would eventually become the larger and more influential organization.

Governed by an executive committee of professional middle-class women—university graduates, lawyers, supervisors, and Ministry of Education inspectors, as well as a few influential society members with strong political connections—Bint al-Nil sought the establishment of constitutional and parliamentary rights for Egyptian women and the diffusion of cultural, health, and social services among poor Egyptian families, and called attention to the conditions that threatened poor families, especially health matters such as maternal and child care. Over the course of the late 1940s, the organization became increasingly focused on the issue of women's suffrage, staging highly public political actions, including storming parliament in 1951 and a hunger strike that garnered Shafiq international attention.[65]

In many ways their privileging of gender as the primary basis of political solidarity as well as their adoption of some of the maternalist rhetoric of the older generation made Rashid's National Women's Party and Shafiq's Bint al-Nil Union logical extensions of the Egyptian Feminist Union. Their adoption of a universalist rights-based discourse, however, represented a clear departure from the class-based calls for suffrage made by the EFU. For Shafiq and Rashid, ties of solidarity on the basis of gender represented an antidote to the party factionalism (*hizbiyya*) and class-based exclusions that typified the politics of the immediate postwar period. In an article in *Fatat al-Ghad* (The Young Woman of Tomorrow) Rashid posited feminist politics as a moral alternative to the divisiveness of multiparty political engagements and the chaos that they engendered. The National Women's Party, she wrote, was "built on feminist principles (*al-mabadi' al-nisa'iyya*) independent of various political currents. The evidence of this is that the majority of our members have various and contradictory political inclinations. But they are in agreement the primary demand of women must be the granting of political rights."[66] Thus, the political demands of women were articulated as transcending other sorts of divisions between women. This solidarity of purpose, the ability to work for a common political goal to the benefit of both a disenfranchised segment of society and the nation as a whole, was frequently asserted by Rashid and other contributors to *The Young Woman of Tomorrow* as evidence that women were, in fact, more deserving of political rights than their male counterparts.[67]

These calls for political rights were couched in the language of national liberation, which Rashid and, to a greater extent, Shafiq viewed as contingent on the inclusion of women in the project of liberating Egypt from foreign political influence and from the conditions of ignorance and poverty that typified the existence of lower-class urban and rural women. In 1954, two years after the revolution, when party politics continued to be contentious and the direction of the revolution was still far from certain, she wrote: "I am more determined than ever to continue the struggle to obtain the rights of the Egyptian woman for the sake of Egypt and the sake of the movement to rebuild Egypt. A liberated Egypt is only as productive as her liberated daughters."[68] Shafiq's call for gender liberation within the context of national liberation, while more class-inclusive than those of the EFU, gave middle-class women a privileged role to play as architects of national unity. Bint al-Nil stressed the responsibilities educated women had to spread the ideas of enlightenment and gender emancipation, formerly espoused by elite women, to women of all classes, thus erasing class differences and creating a new basis of solidarity.

THE JULY REVOLUTION

On July 23, 1952, left-leaning junior military officers calling themselves the "Free Officers Movement" staged a coup after a period of sustained political and social unrest. The Free Officers, led by a young colonel named Gamal Abdel Nasser, seized control of the government and forced the king to abdicate, ending a dynasty that had lasted for 150 years. The date was hailed by many as the start of a new era. The 1952 "revolution," which brought Abdel Nasser to power, marked the beginning of Egypt's transition from a monarchy purportedly based on liberal-democratic principles to a republic, which by the 1960s had adopted Arab Socialism.

The men who composed the core of the Free Officers Movement were united by neither party affiliation nor ideology, nor class background. Some (like Anwar Sadat and Abdel Nasser) came from modest middle-class backgrounds.[69] Others, like Khalid Moheiddin, came from landowning families.

Many were members of the first classes to graduate from the Royal Military Academy after it became open to those of non-elite Egyptian backgrounds. Politically, their individual affiliations ran the gamut from Islamist to communist. What they held in common was a broad commitment to national liberation and social reform, which crossed party lines—political views shared by the new generation, which had become utterly disillusioned by the country's political old guard.

The political and social measures undertaken by the regime over its twenty-two-year history are well chronicled.[70] Among them were the dismantling of the prerevolutionary multiparty system and the curbing of independent political associations in favor of the creation of a succession of single-party organizations aimed at mass political mobilization under state auspices, as well as the short-lived political union with Syria under the banner of pan-Arabism.[71] Other significant measures included the nationalization of the Suez Canal, which ended the legal vestiges of British colonial control in Egypt and made Nasser an international hero among colonized and formerly colonized peoples, a role further enhanced by his participation in the Bandung Conference and Egypt's role in the Non-Aligned Movement.

Over the course of the late 1950s and early 1960s, Nasser adopted a more unified program of national development than the piecemeal reforms (such as the 1952 land reform limiting agricultural holdings) carried out in the years immediately after the revolution. Under the rubric of national planning and, eventually, Arab Socialism (defined as socialism adapted to the particular needs of an Arab society), Nasser nationalized public utilities and foreign-owned companies, implemented a state plan for economic development, and attempted to mobilize previously marginalized groups such as workers, peasants, and women through the creation of bureaucratic, corporatist institutions such as the Arab Socialist Union. Arguably, the most successful reform of the Nasser period was the spread of education, particularly primary school education. Over a twenty-five-year period (1951–76), the number of students in primary school more than quadrupled, from 1 to 4.2 million.[72] Access to secondary and university education also increased, bringing thousands of middle- and lower-class youth into the higher levels of the public education system. The growth of female education during this period is particularly striking: in 1952 there were 541,712 girls attending primary school, and by 1969 there were approximately 1.4 million. At the intermediate level, the number of girls attending increased 300 percent over a fifteen-year period.[73] Such measures altered the class structure in Egypt in fundamental ways, dissipating the old elite and bringing broader segments of the population into the middle classes, who became the primary producers of culture and knowledge and the architects of the revolutionary project.

Certainly, none of these measures were a foregone conclusion or without contradictions. During the early years of the "revolution," the Free Officers' vision was, in many respects, decidedly unrevolutionary, comprising the ouster of a corrupt ruling class, the suspension of parliament, and a temporary period of martial rule ending in the transition to a liberal democratic order, rather than a complete overthrow of the existing system. The rhetoric of the revolution was largely backward-looking, focusing on the crimes of the ancien régime rather than on promises of a vast utopian future.[74] As many scholars of the revolution have pointed out, even after the regime's vision gradually shifted, over the first four years of rule, to encompass an understanding of revolution as the transformation of the social, political, and economic bases of Egyptian life in the name of "the masses," many of its more dramatic reforms appear radical only in the context of Egypt's own past. Land redistribution (undertaken in 1952 and 1961) appears relatively conservative when placed alongside contemporaneous land reform measures.[75] Economically, Arab Socialism functioned much more like state capitalism than it did like "classical" socialism. Social revolution was intended to expand the industrial sector and swell the ranks of the Egyptian middle class rather than achieve a thoroughgoing restructuring of the class system. But rather than ending the analysis with the revolutionary and ideological limitations of the Nasser regime's rule, as is typical in accounts of the Nasser period, these contradictions should serve as a jumping-off point for asking broader questions about the nature of revolutionary change.

"Arab Socialism" was not just a convenient label for piecemeal reforms, nor was it simply a cynical rhetorical strategy used by a centralizing state to justify its own authoritarianism and increasing intrusion into the lives of its citizens. As Roel Meijer has pointed out, Arab Socialism marked the consolidation of a vision of "authoritarian modernism" that had its roots in the writings of secular liberal and left-wing intellectuals and political activists of the previous two decades, as well as in broader postwar shifts in the global political order.

Similar to other Egyptian modernist projects that preceded it, Nasserist visions of modernity were built around "a master narrative of historical emancipation from political, economic and cultural backwardness to enlightenment and personal and collective development."[76] What was novel in the post-1952 period was the extent to which this vision became embedded in the structures and ideologies of the Egyptian nation-state. Rather than taking the "democratic road" to modernity, the state appropriated the vocabulary of national liberation used by the radical nationalist movement in the years leading up to the revolution and incorporated it into a new discourse of state-led development and social engineering. Discourses of planning, premised on the notion that progress—defined objectively with reference to a teleological narrative of historical advance—could be measured by scientific criteria and achieved through the rational reconstruction of social relations, became the centerpiece of the regime's ideology and its claims to legitimacy. Egyptian society was backward, but it was redeemable through the application of technocratic expertise throughout all aspects of Egyptian life. The Nasser regime's adoption and institutionalization of an ideology of planning thus not only gave the postcolonial nation-state new powers but also accorded a central role to a new class of experts, engineers, and intellectuals, as both agents of modernization and its exemplars.

Moreover, the embrace of an avowedly "socialist" vision of modernity reflected a transformation in geographic identity among state elites, which was shared by many in the decolonizing and postcolonial world in the wake of the 1955 Bandung Conference. The Bandung Conference, in which Nasser played a major role (along with Sukarno of Indonesia, Nehru, and Tito), was an attempt by leaders, intellectuals, and activists (most of whom hailed from Africa and Asia) to forge a common ideology among anticolonial nations that could supersede the emerging cold war system dominated by the Soviet Union and the United States.

Bandung was a watershed moment in modern history, transforming not only postwar geopolitics but also global political imaginaries in ways that have yet to be fully appreciated by scholars (see Chapter 5).[77] New transnational visions of political solidarity, underpinned as they were by new visions of development and modernization, took root in individual contexts, leading to debates and continued speculation over the viability of transposing certain ideas, like socialism, beyond their place of origin. Arab Socialism was one local manifestation of this wider political trend.

For Egyptian intellectuals and technocrats, Bandung marked the moment when "the East" began to embody the promises of rationality, development, and technocracy that Egypt must aspire to. Whereas older generations of anticolonial Egyptian leaders and intellectuals had viewed "Eastern Civilization" as a repository of spiritual purity, the revolutionary generation looked to countries such as China and India as fulfillment of a higher stage in history, one in which the experiments in modernization and development pursued by formerly colonized countries—framed in the language of socialist state planning—would supplant declining Western models of politics and social organization.[78] What socialism would look like in the Egyptian context was a matter of some contestation and debate, but the fact that socialist modernity was the rubric within which ideas such as progress, planning, and backwardness were addressed by supporters of the regime in the late 1950s and 1960s tells us something important about the transnational context in which Egyptian state elites operated and formed their worldview. For many in Africa and Asia, struggling with the crippling legacies of colonial rule and attempting to forge a new world in the wake of decolonization, socialism (however defined) and modernity went hand in hand.

THE EMERGENCE OF STATE FEMINISM

Like the ideological program of Nasserism itself, the gender politics of the regime did not spring fully formed from the head of the revolution. Rather, it took shape gradually over the first decade of Nasserist rule, finding its most iconographic expression in the "Charter for National Action," promulgated in 1961, which laid out a blueprint for Egypt's socialist development. In fact, in the first several years of the revolution, the regime seemed largely unconcerned with gender issues. Unlike the National Charter, Nasser's book *The Philosophy of the Revolution*, written in 1954, makes no mention of women as a particular constituency to be mobilized.[79] Prior to 1956, there were a few piecemeal measures (such as women being granted permission to serve in militias in the national guard in 1953), but claims that the revolution would liberate Egyptian women—so prominent in later rhetoric—were virtually absent during this period. In the early years of the revolution, the wide-scale political mobilization of women, as Cynthia Nelson has suggested, may have seemed too controversial a step for a regime that was still struggling to consolidate its power. Muhammad Neguib reportedly told Duriyya Shafiq in 1952 that granting women political rights risked generating too much opposition from conservative elements of the regime.[80]

The absence of the wives of prominent Free Officers from public occasions is an interesting mirror of this state of affairs. Unlike the female members of the royal family, who were well known (and sometimes notorious) public figures in their own right, the wives of the Free Officers were rarely seen in public.[81] Naguib's wife never appeared at a public function during his short tenure as Egypt's ruler. Nasser's wife, Tahia Kazim, didn't make an official public appearance until 1955, when she stood at the Cairo airport next to her husband and welcomed Tito, the leader of Yugoslavia, and his wife, on their first state visit to Egypt.

As the regime consolidated its rule, however, it increasingly went from alternately ignoring and suppressing women's independent political initiatives, to co-opting them into its own program—a strategy it employed with other groups such as workers and peasants. The year 1956 brought a new constitution and new electoral law, which granted women the right to vote and the right to run for public office. In 1957, Rawia 'Attia (famous for campaigning in military fatigues) and Amina Shukri successfully ran for seats in the newly created National Assembly. Most politically active women were overwhelmingly supportive of the revolution initially, although the regime's increasingly authoritarian actions were to divide activists—Duriyya Shafiq, for example, was denounced as a bourgeois reactionary by other activists for her criticism of the regime in 1956 and 1957.

According to most scholars, the 1952 revolution marked the beginning of the end of independent feminism in Egypt. Former activists were arrested or silenced. Zaynab al-Ghazali and Inji Aflatun both went to prison, Ghazali in 1962 on charges that she had participated in an alleged Muslim Brotherhood plot to assassinate Nasser, and Aflatun in 1959 for her association with the Communist Party.[82] Saiza Nabarawi, a founding member of the Egyptian Feminist Union, turned her attention to international movements, and Duriyya Shafiq, as noted above, was placed under house arrest in 1957 for criticizing the increasingly authoritarian direction of the revolution. Latifa al-Zayyat continued her activities but as a writer and not as a political organizer.

If independent feminist organizing was curtailed, however, the politics of gender did not disappear with the advent of the revolution; rather, over the course of a decade, the state adopted a secular narrative in which the discourse of modernizing feminism was paramount. With the promulgation of a new constitution in 1956 and the later ratification of the charter by unanimous vote of the 1,750 members of the National Congress of Popular Forces, the questions of women's equal participation in the public space of the nation and their liberation from the "reactionary" traditions and mores that governed Egyptian society were deemed by the Nasser regime to be solved, specifically by the granting of enfranchised citizenship to all Egyptians irrespective of gender.[83] The 1950s and 1960s saw many of the demands of postwar feminists answered, including the right to vote, the right to run for public office, protective legislation for women workers, the expansion of free public education, and the creation of a vast network of social protections and welfare measures aimed at national integration and the realization of social justice for the peasantry and the working classes.

Moreover, while some voices were silenced, a younger generation of women professionals and intellectuals arose who gained prominence within the newly established economic, political, and social institutions of the modernizing state. Women like Amina al-Sa'id, who became the editor in chief of Egypt's only women's magazine, *Hawwa'* (established in 1957), and Suhayr Qalamawi, who headed up the state publishing association after the Nasser regime's nationalization of the press in 1961, had been active in the EFU's youth organization, *al-shaqiqat*. Others, like Aziza Hussein, the wife of reformer Ahmed Hussein, who became a prominent public figure as a pioneering advocate for birth control when the regime established a national family planning program in the 1960s, and social researcher Zahia Marzuq, who became an undersecretary at the Ministry of Social Affairs under Nasser, had been actively involved in interwar social development projects.

These women, and others like them who made careers either within, or under the auspices of, the public sector in the 1950s and 1960s, were neither unwitting dupes of the regime—puppet-like propagandists of Arab Socialism—nor renegades working within the system in order to fundamentally challenge its legitimacy. Like other intellectuals, technocrats, and culture producers during the Nasser period, they derived their authority from their claims to serve the cause of national liberation, social justice, and revolutionary transformation. If they subscribed to the underlying assumptions embodied in the Nasser regime's modernizing project, however, they did not simply passively endorse state policy. Instead, they used their positions to take an active role in shaping and contesting the gendered parameters of that project throughout the Nasser period.

CONCLUSION

Revolutions, by their very nature, claim the status of the new and all of the hope and aspirations that come with the emergence of "newness" into the world. At the same time, scholars have often observed that in terms of gender, revolutions simply bring old wine in new bottles. But Nasserist gender ideologies were neither the inauguration of newness nor simply the passive perpetuation of what was old. The linkages between the liberation of women and the liberation of the nation, so prominent in Nasserist discourses, were certainly nothing new. The rhetoric of secular nationalist modernity, which had become increasingly hegemonic since the 1930s, was taken up within the context of state- and nation-building but in the process was transformed. "The Egyptian woman" went from being a potent symbol of the modernity and authenticity of the nation, to being an equally potent symbol of the modernity of the state and the regime that was its custodian. If the popular slogan "*La sharqiyya wa la gharbiyya*" (Neither Eastern nor Western) reflected the regime's commitment to a policy of nonalignment in an emerging bipolar, cold war global system, it also signified attempts to forge a "third way" between the cultures of capitalism and communism that reflected the needs and specificities of Egypt in its state- and nation-building projects. Within the context of Nasserist state-building, Egyptian women stood as signifiers for both the universalized promise of socialist development, scientific planning, and modernity and the authentic roots of an emerging revolutionary national culture.

Moreover, the gender regime of liberal-nationalism, based on the paternalism of elites, was replaced by the paternalism of the new socialist state.[84] The vertical ties of patronage between elites and subalterns were to be replaced with horizontal, fraternal ties between citizens with the state as the primary arbiter and protector of national unity and the common good. And yet, there was an acknowledgment in the National Charter that the task of social revolution and national unity was far from achieved. Not only did the vestiges of social conservatism and reaction continue to jeopardize the revolutionary project, but Arab Socialism as an ideology viewed differences among different social groups and classes as inevitable. Unlike other variants of socialism, it did not acknowledge the legitimacy of class struggle as an integral part of the revolutionary process. One of Arab Socialism's most critical tasks, according to Nasser, was to create institutions that would manage the conflicts between various groups by providing social justice, promoting national unity, and integrating previously marginalized groups into the political and social order without undermining the bases of class itself. The language and imagery of paternalism, so prevalent in the liberal-national period, now provided a way to conceptualize social and political relations in the new socialist state. In a speech to the members of the Preparatory Committee for the National Conference of the Popular Forces, the body charged with ratifying the National Charter, Nasser said:

> The differences that the People [al-sha'b] have with each other are like the differences in a family between a husband and his wife and between a father and his children. . . . In the family, the master of the house [rab al-bayt] says "you may go to the cinema twice" and the children want to go five times. The master and mistress of the house discuss the matter. Will they come to blows? They will never come to blows in order to solve the problem of whether they go to the cinema. . . . Every person will have his opinion and everyone will consider his specific interests . . . and there will be opposition, and incompatibility and differences and contradiction. But this is the difference and opposition and contradiction that one finds in a single family and it doesn't affect in any way the progress of the people in its social revolution and its socialist revolution.[85]

In this new socialist national family it was the state that was to play the role of *rab al-bayt* and the people that of subordinate wife or dependent children. The basis of national unity lay not in the common investiture of Egyptian citizens with political agency nor with the abolition of class and social differences. The basis of national unity was the common relationship of Egyptian citizens as beneficiaries of state largesse. Although the state's level of penetration into everyday life never reached that of other state socialist projects (including China, the Soviet Union, and the countries of Eastern Europe), which it looked to as models, aspects of Arab Socialism appear consistent with what Katherine Verdery, writing on Rumania, has called paternal socialism. According to Verdery, instead of political rights, paternal socialism "posited a moral tie linking subjects with the state through their rights to share in the redistributed social product. . . . [T]hey were presumed to be grateful recipients—like small children in a family—of benefits their rulers decided upon for them."[86]

The gendered language of socialist paternalism had ramifications for Egyptian women and for Egyptian citizens as a whole. The shift in emphasis from reform to social engineering, which found its fullest expression in state socialism, gave the project of fashioning a new revolutionary womanhood a modern, universalist, scientific basis even as it legitimated unprecedented intervention into the daily lives of Egyptians. A rights-based discourse that linked "the liberation of women" to the social, political, and economic liberation of the nation intersected with a discourse on social welfare that marked gender relations as a realm of state governance, making both central to the operations of the postcolonial secular nation-state. Women's activism, which had throughout its history embodied multiple political claims and visions of rights and demands for inclusion, was reduced to claims that could be made only on the state as the sole agent of emancipation.

The resulting program of "state feminism" embodied all of the contradictions, paradoxes, and foreclosed possibilities of Nasserist rule as well as its opportunities and promises. For unlike in Verdery's model of paternal socialism, women, like others, were also, for the first time, recognized as national subjects and citizens with an active and necessary role to play in national development. It was at the intersection where citizens were constituted both as objects of pedagogy and performing subjects, as beneficiaries of the state yet actors in a new national drama, and it was in the doors the Nasserist project opened and in those that it closed, that the tensions, contradictions, and ambivalences of state feminism can best be explored.

2 BETWEEN HOME AND WORKPLACE

Fashioning the "Working Woman"

IN 1962 the popular weekly magazine *Ruz al-Yusuf* proudly reported that an East German magazine had run a photo spread on the opening of the Nasser textile factory in Qina, which featured a profile of the factory's five female employees.[1] The factory girls of Qina were a popular subject of articles in the Egyptian and international press, where they were represented as a symbol of the successes of Egyptian socialist planning.[2] But the path to progress had not run entirely smoothly in the Upper Egyptian city of Qina. Initial attempts to recruit women into the ranks of factory workers had prompted demonstrations by male workers who marched in front of the factory chanting, "The girls of the factory bring shame to us."[3] Resistance eventually subsided as the number of female workers grew from five to two hundred. Other changes swiftly followed, including the opening of a school where female workers could receive an education in reading, writing, and the domestic arts, and the arrival of the first ladies' hairdresser in Qina. In perhaps the most incongruous representation of change, one article featured a picture of a young woman in athletic gear straddling a gymnastic pommel horse, headed with the caption "Exercise is no longer considered shameful in Qina since the young woman entered the factory."[4]

Accounts of Qina's female factory workers framed their story as the collective story of all Egyptian women, whose liberation entailed the overthrow of backward conventions as a prerequisite to national progress. Writing in the weekly magazine *Akhir Saʿa*, journalist Saʿid Naʿmatullah narrated the entrance of girls into the factory as an erosion of the social norms and practices that kept the Egyptian woman "imprisoned in the walls of her home and restricted her from participating with man in his struggles and the building of his nation."[5] Coverage of the girls noted approvingly that the factory girls of Qina, who like all Egyptian women had lived concealed for centuries behind the *harim* (harem) and the *hijab*, had "demolished worn out traditions" and had taken their rightful place in the public realm side by side with their male colleagues.[6] Representations of Qina's female factory workers, structured around the dual narratives of women's liberation and national progress, were virtually interchangeable with hundreds of others extolling the successes of Egyptian women in the labor force.[7]

Pamphlets and tracts produced by the Ministry of National Guidance and the Ministry of Social Affairs in the early 1960s, chronicling the achievements of Arab Socialism, celebrated the participation of women in public life (*al-hayyat al-ʿamma*) through statistical surveys of female participation in the workforce and elaboration of the legislation and social service measures that guaranteed that participation.[8] Popular films such as *The Dreams of Girls*, *For Men Only*, and *My Wife Is a General Director* depicted the issues raised by the presence of women professionals in formerly male work environments.[9] Lavish photo spreads of women working in factories and laboratories were frequently used to illustrate triumphalist articles with titles like "Your Life in the New Society" or "New Aswan."[10] Cartoons lampooned the inevitable missteps caused by the introduction of women into formerly male work spaces. Editorials raised questions about the effects that women's labor would have on family life, gender relations, and workplace culture.

And yet, the figure of the *al-marʾa al-ʿamila* (the working woman), ubiquitous in the press and popular culture and within the regime's self-presentation, was out of proportion to the number of women who were actually working. Despite the passage of extensive legal provisions aimed at guaranteeing women's right to work, and economic and social policies that opened opportunities for women in the expanding state bureaucracy and newly nationalized industries, the Nasser regime's attempts at mobilizing women did not result in a massive influx of female workers into the workforce. While the gendered composition of the labor force was certainly changing during this period, particularly in urban centers where women were coming to make up an increasing percentage of professional and office workers, overall female labor participation remained strikingly low.

The disjuncture between women's literal presence in the workplace and their symbolic presence within public discourse forces us to ask a different set of questions than those that are commonly posed about women and work in Egypt. The intention of this chapter, therefore, is not to try to provide a definitive answer to the question of why women's labor force participation remained low despite state efforts. Nor will it raise questions about how the focus on formal waged labor has consistently underestimated the productive capacity of Egypt's women by ignoring their participation in the "informal economy."[11] Rather, I ask what other sorts of labor did women perform in the context of state socialism, other than (or in addition to) material labor? What kind of ideological work did the figure of the working woman perform?[12] What groups were charged with carrying out this symbolic labor on behalf of working women? What lay at the heart of the anxieties and conceptions of women's work as a social problem, particularly by the culture producers, intellectuals, and women activists who were themselves staunch advocates and beneficiaries of the state's efforts to mobilize female labor? How was the social figure of the modern working woman constructed in Nasserist Egypt?

I argue that the figure of "the working woman" was critical in mapping out the contours of a socialist, postcolonial public sphere. It was the unveiled and active presence of women in an outer sphere of progress that marked the Nasserist public sphere as modern, secular, and socialist. The linkage between gender visibility, the progress of the nation-state, and new notions of publicness had earlier corollaries, both in Egypt and elsewhere.[13] What was different in the Nasserist case was that the state now claimed new responsibilities for ensuring both the inclusion and the regulation of women in the newly defined spaces of revolutionary public life.

Legal regulations pertaining to women's work, social policy, propaganda, popular culture, and debates over women's and men's roles at home and at work signaled a redrawing of the gender boundaries of the political and social order in ways that called established notions of equality and difference, and their spatial corollaries "public" and "private," into question. While state feminism thus built on older understandings of the public as a sphere of progress and the domestic as a sphere of women's activity and gendered difference, it also attempted to redefine and transform both spaces in ways consistent with new notions of citizenship, inclusion, and socialist development.

THE PREREVOLUTIONARY POLITICS OF WOMEN'S WORK

There was nothing inherently revolutionary in the idea of Egyptian women engaging in waged labor. Beginning in the mid–nineteenth century, Egypt's transition to an export economy based on cotton cultivation created an increasing seasonal demand for female agricultural workers; peasant women largely engaged in wage labor alongside the work they performed on small family holdings, although such labor was counted inconsistently in official statistics. The early growth of female education and the expansion of public health institutions in the first decades of the twentieth century brought small numbers of women into the labor force. In the 1920s, the expansion of the Egyptian textile industry brought thousands more women into factories in the giant industrial complexes of al-Mahalla al-Kubra and Shubra al-Khayma. During the 1930s, the presence of women in the workforce—in textile manufacturing, education, health care, and trade—increased, and wartime production during the Second World War created more factory jobs for women. The 1930s also saw very small numbers of professional women—among them lawyers, journalists, and doctors—graduating from Egyptian universities. Much harder to gauge is the precise numbers of women working in domestic service or who worked for themselves—as midwives, peddlers, seamstresses, Qur'an readers, and others—although they must have numbered in the thousands. By 1947, official demographic reports and social scientists generally agree that women composed between 4 and 6 percent of the formal waged workforce.[14]

Within prerevolutionary nationalist discourses, women's labor, although hardly a novelty, took on new gendered and classed meanings. The emergence of a debate around women's work at the turn of the century situated the issue of women's labor within the context of emerging notions of nationalist womanhood that delineated the domestic sphere as the proper space of women's activity. As elite women pushed for greater acceptance of women in the workforce, they recast middle-class women's labor from the application of caretaking roles in the home to such roles in the social body.

By most accounts, female workers, particularly those working in low or unskilled factory or service work, suffered from low pay, long hours, and lack of legal protections. Legal protections advocated by Egyptian feminists, realized in the 1930s, both conceptualized "the working woman" as a unified category with rights and responsibilities distinct from those of male workers, and defined working-class women as particular objects of regulation and tutelage.[15]

The single largest article of the law enumerated the types of work forbidden to women, including labor considered physically taxing or dangerous, work that was considered polluting, or most work performed at night.[16] Other provisions included fixing the workday for women at nine hours and mandating that pregnant women be given one month of maternity leave prior to giving birth.

The actions and positions taken by the EFU and other social reformers with regard to the issue of women's labor were thus simultaneously class-consolidating and custodial. They reformulated the meanings of women's labor in ways intended to extend bourgeois nationalist ideals of domesticity and, in doing so, recast class differences between elite, middle-, and working-class women. While Egyptian women as a whole needed to be made ready to take up gendered duties in the service of the nation, to be protected from the potentially corrupting influences of work, and made more able to fulfill their individual duties as mothers and wives in healthy, reformed households, it was clear that working-class women needed more protection and tutelage than their educated middle-class sisters.

The social and political displacements of the postwar period brought greater labor militancy, the emergence of an independent trade movement, and new formulations of women as workers.[17] The programs and publications of labor organizations—and of communist and other leftist organizations—which played a key role in the outpouring of trade union activity during this time, conceptualized the struggle of working-class women as indivisible from the struggle of workers (and the struggle of the nation) as a whole. Calls for improvements in working conditions, limiting the work week, better wages, the provision of social services to workers, and more political representation were made by labor unions on behalf of "the Egyptian worker," and the problems of working-class women began to figure in a newly radicalized workers' press. Some women, like Hikmat al-Ghazali, leader of the Association of Egyptian Working Women, which was the first organization of women workers in Egypt, took active leadership roles in the labor movement. By the late 1940s the platforms of many communist and labor organizations displayed an abstract commitment to women's political and economic rights, including the right to vote, to work, and to receive equal pay.[18]

As in the interwar debates on women and work, however, the labor moment and communists reproduced the notion of working women in ways that affirmed both their inclusion in the category of "worker" and their essential differences within it, albeit within a very different political framework. While leftist and labor discourses affirmed the right of women to work and leftist women rejected notions of tutelage asserted by elite women's organizations, female workers figured most often in the labor press in ways that affirmed their essential differences from male workers. Whereas male workers were portrayed as active historical agents, women largely appeared as workers who had to be protected by male-dominated labor unions or as tragic victims of capitalist exploitation, or were valorized for the nurturing and supporting roles they provided as mothers and wives of politically active male workers.[19] While working women (and working-class women in particular) were thus envisioned as rights-bearing subjects within the wider category of "worker," they also remained gendered subjects whose agency was mediated through their relationships with politically active male family members, through the protections offered by male trade unionists, and through their domestic roles.

STATE FEMINISM AND THE MOBILIZATION OF FEMALE LABOR

Beginning in 1952, the Nasser regime embarked on a series of programs (including the redistribution of agricultural land, the nationalization of industries, the creation of state-run consumer cooperatives, and import substitution) aimed at replacing the agriculturally based economy with industrialization and at redistributing income.[20] As a necessary prerequisite to development, the state also created new public sector institutions that would both mobilize Egypt's "popular working forces"—defined by the National Charter as peasants, workers, and the intelligentsia—and expand social services. Following the publication of the National Charter in 1961, the regime launched a series of employment drives aimed at providing employment for thousands of recent high school and college graduates, and staff for the burgeoning public sector.[21]

Viewing women as an underutilized source of labor, the regime took steps in the late 1950s and early 1960s to mobilize women into the workforce and to redefine "the working woman" as a legal category. Article 52 of the 1956 constitution stated that all Egyptians had the right to work and the state was committed to providing work for its citizens.[22] The 1956 constitution and the National Charter formally recognized women's status as equal citizens with the right and duty to work alongside men in building a new socialist nation. A series of labor laws and administrative decisions passed between 1958 and 1959 accorded female workers de facto equality with men by removing gender as a basis of discrimination in wages and hiring. At the same time, other forms of gender-specific protective legislation aimed at "protecting womanhood" by making the "role of the working woman . . . compatible with her role as wife and mother."[23]

Law 91 established provisions for maternity leave and mandated the establishment of day care centers for businesses with more than one hundred workers. Other regulations prohibited women from working at jobs that were identified as being hazardous to their health or moral standing. Proscriptions covered work performed between 8 PM and 7 AM (exceptions were made for performers, nurses, and those who worked in hotels and restaurants), work in nightclubs that featured gambling or sold alcohol, and jobs that required "heavy labor" such as work in mines and foundries. Other categories of labor were phased out completely. Prostitution, which had been legal in Egypt, was criminalized in 1952.[24]

The conceptualization of women as both ungendered laboring agents in the task of building state socialism and gendered subjects with differentiated rights and responsibilities had gender and class ramifications for the composition of the workforce. The prime beneficiaries of state efforts to increase the size of the female labor force were educated middle-class women.[25] The dramatic expansion of the national education system, particularly the establishment of free, compulsory elementary education, increased demand for elementary school teachers.[26] State attempts to expand access to health care created a need for women trained as doctors, nurses, pharmacists, and lab technicians, and the emphasis on social engineering required social workers and researchers trained in the gathering of sociological data. The expansion of higher education and the increase in female college graduates, along with the state's promise in 1964 to provide employment for all those with a university degree, increased the pool of professional women.[27] Finally, the nationalization of Egyptian industries and the proliferation of state bureaucratic institutions created new civil service positions at the middle and lower levels of the bureaucracy, where the bulk of female civil servants were concentrated.[28]

In some ways, these measures facilitated the advancement of educated professional women by allowing them access to the higher ranks of professions that had been heavily feminized during the prerevolutionary period—professions such as education, health care, and social services. In other ways, however, Nasserist labor policy preserved the gendered division of labor apparent prior to the revolution. While Nasserist era newspapers and magazines prominently featured interviews with women who had achieved in "non-traditional fields"—often when they were the first to do so—these women remained relatively exceptional. At the same time, upper-level positions in other fields remained barred to women.[29] These included judgeships, diplomatic postings, and managerial positions at the Ministry of Agriculture. And while the salaries of men and women working at the same job were roughly equal, the sectors in which women were largely employed—clerical work, for example—were lower paying than other, predominantly male sectors.[30]

There was also a relatively small increase in women working in factories. Egypt's drive to industrialization resulted in expansion of light industry and goods for popular consumption (food stuffs, electronics, textiles). Women were seen as particularly suited for the delicate manual work of assembling televisions and refrigerators, although heavy industry remained largely a male endeavor.

Women's labor in the countryside is more difficult to assess, in large part because official Egyptian statistics often underestimate women's contribution to agricultural production.[31] While such statistics generally reflect a decline in the number of women in waged agriculture, they must be treated with a certain amount of suspicion.[32] As James Toth has suggested, the use of male migrant labor by the state throughout the 1960s in large-scale building projects, like the Aswan Dam, created overwhelming seasonal demand for women and children in agricultural labor. Official statistics do not include such seasonal, often temporary, labor in the category "work."[33] In addition, Egyptian census data consistently underreported the number of women working in agriculture, in part because enumerators frequently counted peasant women's agricultural activities as housework. Legal provisions didn't regulate the employment of agricultural workers (whether they were male or female) beyond setting minimum wage guidelines. Such guidelines established a wage hierarchy based on perceptions about the traditional gender division of labor in the countryside. Land reform measures in 1952 fixed the minimum wage for women and children in waged agriculture at two-thirds of that of male workers on the grounds that the tasks women and children most often performed traditionally paid less.

While statistical representations of women's labor varied widely and excluded many categories of economically productive labor as work, rendering some forms of labor as visible and others invisible, they nevertheless give a rough sense of the kinds of labor some women were performing. Answering the question of why women themselves worked is much more elusive. With all caveats about the dangers of overgeneralization aside, it is probably not inaccurate to conclude that for the majority of Egyptian women wage labor was a means of economic survival and a material contribution to the family economy. It may also have been, in many cases, a temporary strategy—a response to sudden changes in economic circumstances or social need. Aspirations of upward social mobility may also have played a part, as discourses on consumption and social progress held out the promise that even for families on a limited income, the benefits of modern life were within reach with the increased purchasing power brought by an additional salary. The reasons that women took up waged work were also shaped by age, generation, and stage of life. Young Egyptian women who could afford to do so often left the labor market temporarily or permanently after marriage or the birth of a child. Nonetheless, it also appears that in the 1950s and 1960s, as public sector work opportunities and higher education for women expanded, some educated middle-class women were beginning to develop professional identities that overlapped with or transcended economic need and family welfare.

SPACE, MODERNITY, AND THE PROBLEM OF WOMEN'S WORK

Despite state rhetoric and the regime's legal commitment to increasing the number of women engaged in waged work, women never made up as significant a percentage of the formal waged workforce as they did in other contemporaneous state socialist projects.[34] While the percentage of professional women increased quite dramatically (31.1%) in the eight years following the publication of the National Charter, the overall number of women in the formal waged labor force during this period remained relatively low.[35] By 1969, women still composed only about one tenth of the formal wage labor market.[36]

Drawing from a wider body of theoretical literature attempting to trace the engineered exclusion of women from the public sphere, some scholars have explained the seeming disjuncture between the regime's commitment to increasing workforce participation and the actual numbers of women working as a conflict between "public" and "private."[37] Selma Botman and Mervat Hatem (in some of her earlier work) have pointed out that while Nasserist state-building resulted in extensive legal commitments to female workers, and the extension of educational opportunities to women opened up many new avenues of employment for Egyptian women in the public sphere, the state's refusal to alter patriarchal relations in the private realm of the family remained a barrier to women's participation.[38] Others, focusing on the Arab world as a whole, have argued that women's work has been problematic precisely because it entails the circulation of women in public space. Building on notions of gendered space in Muslim societies as divided between the public male universe of the *umma* against a domestic female universe of sexuality, they argue that the presence of women in the public realm is ontologically problematic for Muslim societies.[39] What such accounts have in common is the assumption that the boundaries between the two spheres and their gendered content remain largely unchanging. They also view the problem of women's relationship to the public as primarily one of exclusion. The presence of women in the public sphere becomes problematic precisely because of gendered legal and social norms that confine them to a persistently retrogressive private. In contrast, I argue that the figure of the working woman became a site of debate, discussion, and intervention, not because traditional mechanisms and practices of exclusion made women's work problematic but in fact because state feminism was predicated upon women's inclusion and participation in public life.

The figure of the working woman was critical in mapping out the contours of a secular, postcolonial public sphere. Female workers, particularly those working in the new sites carved out by socialist development (the office, the factory, or the classroom), were represented in state feminist discourse not only as necessary to the economic success of state socialist policies but also as a critical symbol of the regime's successes in transforming Egypt into a modern socialist nation. This new public sphere, the space where *al-hayyat al-'amma* was enacted, was defined through the visible presence and active participation of women. In this, emerging definitions of publicness built on existing gendered notions of space as foundational to the construction and preservation of a modern Egyptian nation-state.

In the late nineteenth century Egyptian nationalist reformers singled out institutions and practices associated with women's seclusion—such as the veil and the harem—as both a cause and a symptom of the degraded nature of Muslim societies and their inhabitants.[40] Reformers argued that the physical separation of women and men, which confined women to the space of the household, left Egyptian women uneducated and illiterate. Such ignorance became endemic as these women transferred that ignorance to their children (see Chapter 1). Early nationalist reformers such as Qasim Amin called for the education of girls and the end of veiling and seclusion as a means both of reforming women (so they could be fit mothers to a new generation of Egyptian citizens) and of creating a new spatial and social order that would give testament to the modernity and civilization of the nation. As Timothy Mitchell has argued, the formation of an educated Egyptian motherhood was part of the process whereby the "inaccessible" and "invisible" world of women and the family would be rendered visible (and thus governable) by the institutions of modern power and the state.[41] The identification of "the new woman" with the reformed Egyptian home and a new bourgeois cult of domesticity based on monogamy, companionate marriage, and scientific child rearing and household management presumed rather than rejected women's presence and visibility within an emerging national sphere of public participation.

Drawing on the earlier reformist imagery of the *harim* as a barrier to women's liberation and inclusion, Nasser era advocates of women's work posited progress as the result of the outward movement of women from domestic confinement to public participation. Metaphors commonly employed to talk about women's participation suggest the spatial contours of this process. Phrases like "she has gone down into" (*nazalat*), "she has entered" (*dakhalat*), or "she has left the house" (*kharajat al-bayt*) were used ubiquitously to describe women's participation in the workforce and in public life more generally. In everyday conversation, such phrases were used to refer to the physical act of going outdoors. But in state feminist discourse, commentators on women's work employed this language to talk about not only the physical act of leaving the house but also the active engagement with and performance of the duties of citizenship.

A tract written in 1974, a few years after the period of this study, is emblematic of the ways in which space, gender, history, and the liberation of the nation came together in a narrative of the progress of the secular nation-state. Entitled "Egyptian Women: A Long March from the Veil to Oct. 6, 1973," the tract established a link between Egypt's "victory" in the 1973 war and the presence of unveiled Egyptian women outside of the home:

> Egypt, having suffered a long era of occupation and attempts to shut off any gleam of light or progress, it was natural that the weaker sex (women) should be subjected to the effects of injustice and constraint [sic]. It was also natural that foreign domination should fight the education of women and their participation in public life . . . confining women forever within the limitations of the home and the family.[42]

The pamphlet went on to present a narrative history of Egyptian women's progress. Using spatial and temporal metaphors for advancement, it tracked women's public visibility, as source and sign of their emancipation and as a defining element of the spatial and symbolic content of publicness. Women's unveiling and participation "in public life" in such depictions served as a rich trope, symbolizing the nation's arrival at the end of history—an overcoming of colonialism and backwardness, national strengthening, and eventually, of military victory over a trenchant and formidable enemy. Such progress narratives were universal in multiple senses. They situated Egypt on a universal trajectory of development, which all nation-states underwent in their transition from backwardness to modernity, and made gender central to it—the presence of Egyptian women in this evolving public sphere was a sign that *all* Egyptians had overcome their colonial and benighted past.

And yet, discourses of inclusion that stressed the necessity, indeed the inevitability, of women's entrance into the workforce had the effect of constituting women's labor as a social problem, not only for critics of the state's calls for women to take up work outside the home but also for its advocates. Articles and depictions of working women written by commentators on the subject of women's labor frequently raised concerns about the effects that women working could have on the health and stability of domestic life. This phenomenon was not new. As they had in the decades leading up to the revolution, nationalist ideals of domesticity continued to structure much of the public (and private) discussion over women (particularly middle-class women) working outside the home. Such ideals stressed the model of the nuclear family with a male breadwinner and an educated mother as household manager. But in a context in which state ideology made "the working woman" central to its vision of social and economic development, anxieties about preserving the home as a space of gendered labor and affectivity took on new salience.

Advocates of women's work did not question the widely held perception that biology and social norms constituted male and female as differently gendered subjects with correspondingly different duties. Nor did they challenge the notion that the domestic sphere was a privileged site for the expression of such differences. Prerevolutionary ideals of nationalist womanhood that had valorized the domestic realm as the appropriate sphere of women's participation were thus not abandoned by state feminism; rather, they were reconfigured, generating new tensions between the building of the state and the preservation of the nation.

In the case of Indian nationalism, Partha Chatterjee has argued that the identification of women with both the "inner" space of the home and the cultural sovereignty of the nation resolved this fundamental tension within "nationalist patriarchy," that is, the desire to modernize the nation and its subjects (including women) and the desire to preserve cultural authenticity. Identification of women as the bearers of the values of the timeless inner sanctum (which was immune from the potentially corrupting elements of modernity) ensured their relatively unproblematic participation in an "outer," public sphere of universal progress.[43]

Looking at the issues surrounding women's work in postcolonial Egypt provides a different picture. In the context of revolutionary change, neither the boundaries between "inner" and "outer" nor their gendered content could be taken for granted. For advocates of state feminism, the relationship between home and workplace was precisely what was at issue: if the domestic sphere was a legal and moral site of gendered norms and practices that had to be protected, as well as a potential barrier to equality and participation in public, how could the domestic realm be transformed to accommodate public duty? If the public was a masculine sphere of participation defined in opposition to the feminized space of the domestic, how would the workplace accommodate the influx of large numbers of women?

State efforts to transform both spheres consistently with its vision of socialist modernity raised new sorts of concerns and questions about spatial and social boundaries. For example, was it appropriate for a male coworker to call or visit a female coworker at home? How should women who worked only in order to attract a husband be dealt with? Would the stress and strain of work prevent women from fulfilling their duties as wives? How should boundaries between female subordinates and (largely) male bosses be negotiated? Were day care facilities a substitute for the care and affection of a mother? Women activists, intellectuals, culture producers, and other advocates of state feminism struggled with these issues in print, while Egyptian working women and their families struggled with them in their daily lives. These tensions reveal that the boundaries between home and public, between inner and outer, were neither fixed nor readily self-evident but in fact had to be continually reconstructed to suit new social realities, economic imperatives, and socialist visions of modernity.

SUCCESSFUL WIVES AND ENERGETIC WORKERS

The mobilization of female labor fueled concerns among commentators, state officials, and private citizens that women would ignore their maternal and wifely roles, and engendered fears that women working would blur gender boundaries, resulting in a breakdown of the social and moral order and the erosion of male authority. Questions about women going out to work were a regular subject of the advice column "*Is'aluni*" (Ask Me), which appeared in *Al-Musawwar*. One reader reported that some of his relatives opposed his marrying a working woman because "she would impose her authority upon me."[44] Another female reader who wrote in said that her fiancé had made their marriage conditional on her leaving her civil service position, so that he could support the family; doing so would provide her sufficient time to tend to the domestic needs of the household.[45] Amina Saʿid, the editor of Egypt's most important (and after 1957, sole) women's magazine, *Hawwa'*, received a letter from a bachelor who lived in the provincial city of Dumiyat, who said that he preferred to marry a housewife because women who worked were forced to "give up their soft, gentle disposition and gain the nature of a man."[46] Other concerns were that professional work for women risked undermining men's position as breadwinners within families and created competition for professional jobs. Appearing on the television program *Nur 'ala nur* in January 1962, Shaykh Abu Zahra, an Azhari cleric and popular writer on Islam and social issues, complained that the mobilization of women had created a "crisis" of unemployment among male college graduates.[47] It's important to point out that such objections coalesced largely around the labor of women who were married and for whom work was not an economic necessity. Abu Zahra, for example, pointed out that a woman working outside the home was acceptable if she had no other means of financial support or did not have a husband and children to care for.

Most advocates of state feminism dismissed such criticisms as having no place in a modern society. In a response to a reader complaining that Amina Saʿid's support for women working was endangering home life, Saʿid wrote, "In our opinion, [such views about] the issue of working women is one of multiple examples we place under reactionary thinking."[48] In the dozen or so articles that Saʿid wrote on the subject of women's labor, she justified work outside the home simultaneously as an imperative for socialist development and as a means of providing the accoutrements of modern life for families. In an editorial entitled "Why We Work," she wrote:

> The most prominent difference between a strong and a weak country, an advanced [*mutaqaddim*] country and a backward [*mutakhallif*] country, is the struggle of women in the public arena and her ability to share financially in

her life and the life of those around her. . . . We work for the sake of lessening the burdens on our husbands or our sons. We work to provide for the people closest to us . . . more food, cleaner clothes, a more beautiful house, a better education.[49]

While some portrayals of working women in the press did tend to situate their labor within the context of familial duty and sacrifice, discourses on women's work also stressed that labor was a means of personal fulfillment. In an article in *Hawwa'* entitled "Your Happiness in the Home and Your Success in Work," journalist Yusuf Jabara warned that liberation would occur only when women transcended their identity as wives and assumed the universalized status of laboring human beings:

> You will not be liberated as long as you are merely a wife who offers food and drink to her husband, fulfilling his desires and whims. You won't consent to a return to the age of the *harim*. . . . You went out into life to struggle and work, to build with young men and to assure that you are a human being with all of the rights of a human and all of his responsibilities . . . home is the place which fills your heart and your emotions and work is the thing which satisfies your ambition and your humanity.[50]

Jabara's article typified the didactic pieces the magazine *Hawwa'* addressed to working women about balancing their duties at work with their duties towards their families.

Such articles challenged the idea that women's only appropriate sphere of participation was in the home even as they valorized conventional domestic roles. In this they could be read as just another example of the ways in which Egyptian working women, like working women everywhere, were forced to take up "the double burden." And yet, the home represented an ambivalent and problematic space for Sa'id and other commentators on the issue of working women. On the one hand, domestic relationships and the gendered division of household labor between husbands and wives represented a barrier to women's emancipation. On the other, writers coupled critiques of the "reactionary" thinking that barred women from the workplace with a concurrent emphasis on the importance of being a good wife and mother.

The phrase "an energetic worker and a successful wife," which the women's press often used to describe the individual professional women portrayed on its pages, may have represented an accommodation to those who feared that women's work would result in the destruction of the family. But it also reflected attempts to elaborate a new professional identity for women, which foregrounded the home as a site of gendered labor and affectivity even as it posited the workplace as an important and necessary sphere of women's participation. The model of the exemplary working woman offered a vision of middle-class domesticity, marriage, and motherhood that structured much of the debate (and the normative solutions posed) over the problem of women reconciling the potentially conflicting demands of home and workplace.

The most famous model of the successful wife and energetic worker appeared not on the pages of *Hawwa'* but on the silver screen, in the screwball comedy *My Wife Is a General Director*, which starred two of the brightest lights of the 1960s-era Egyptian cinema, Shadia and Salah Zulficar.[51] The complicated and multiple tensions between women's duty to participate outside of the home and their continued centrality within it were the source of inspiration for many Nasser era culture producers.[52] The cinema, in particular, commonly narrated the increasing entrance of women into the workforce as a series of boundary crossings, role reversals, and passings, in which potential transgression was accommodated to the dictates of economic development and modern life. In the context of radical social change, such representations of women's roles often exercised a normalizing function.

The film opens with the now famous quote from the National Charter—"Woman must be regarded as equal to men and must therefore shed the remaining shackles that impede her free movement so that she might take a constructive and profound part in shaping life"—signaling the filmmaker's intention to engage with the debate over gender equality in the workplace.[53] Ismat and Husayn are a young upwardly mobile couple with civil service jobs. Ismat gets promoted to the position of director of Husayn's section. The couple tries to preserve the division between home and work by keeping Ismat's marital identity secret from other employees. At work, Ismat is a firm and demanding boss, pushing her employees (Husayn included) to fulfill production quotas. At home she is pictured as an affectionate and exemplary wife, cooking her husband's favorite dishes and sewing buttons on his shirts.

It does not take long, however, for the couple's carefully preserved division to break down. At home, Ismat's relationship with Husayn is suffering as a result of her authority in the workplace. One night, after a particularly trying day at the office, she tries to lure her husband upstairs to bed for a romantic interlude, but he rebuffs her saying that he has to work late. In another scene,

Ismat, bringing dinner to her employees, who are working late at the office to finish a project before a deadline, displays an affection and wifely concern for her male subordinates that she has increasingly failed to show her own husband. The couple's domestic relationship is revealed when one of the employees sees Ismat sitting in Husayn's lap wheedling him to eat more. Bringing their marital relationship into the workplace threatens both Ismat's authority as director and Husayn's masculinity. With her marriage in jeopardy, Ismat requests a transfer to another unit so that Husayn will no longer have to work under her. After tearfully bidding farewell to her employees, Ismat goes to her new office only to find Husayn there waiting for her. He has arranged secretly for a transfer so that he can continue to work with her. In a gesture of support, he announces, smiling, "My wife is the general director." The film closes with a scene of the couple pushing their perpetually broken-down car off into the sunset—a vision of cooperation in companionate marriage.

Much of the comedy within *My Wife Is a General Director*, as in other films that depicted gender relations in the professional workplace, lies in its satirization of gender role reversal and the challenges to authority in both the home and the workplace that such reversal threatened. It played on multiple common anxieties about women's work: men losing their authority as husbands and bosses, women losing their femininity as a result of their work identities spilling over into the home,[54] and the inability of men to accept new work roles for women. The film's ending suggests companionate marriage as a neat resolution to Husayn and Ismat's work-driven marital problems.

Yet the final scene cannot be arrived at without the two major characters undergoing a transformation in both their marital and their working identities. Ismat's professional ambitions are tempered by her desire to be a good wife; rather than jeopardize her marriage, she requests a transfer from a job in which she has been highly successful. Husayn is able to accept his wife's authority at work only when he accepts her as a full partner. Apologizing after a particularly nasty argument at work, he tells her, "I want a wife and a friend." The film suggests that successful marriage is a cooperative enterprise in which individual ambitions and ego must take second place to a commitment to the partnership. The view of women implied by companionate marriage itself—as friends, companions, and colleagues, as well as wives—is a necessary prerequisite for successful relations between the sexes in the workplace.

Part of what is interesting about *My Wife Is a General Director* as a commentary on state socialist mobilization of women into the workforce is not only its diagnosis of (and proposed solutions to) the potential tensions it engenders but what appears in the film as taken for granted. The couple lives in a spacious split-level villa of a type that throughout the 1930s and 1940s had been emblematic of upper middle-class status but that by the late 1950s was being adapted to less wealthy, more middle-class contexts as well. Ismat's kitchen has modern appliances, including a stove and a refrigerator, as well as an older female servant. The spatial context of Ismat's domestic labor, unremarkable within the film's narrative, presented a normative solution to a problem that was an important focus of social research and discussion within the press—that of women's labor productivity.

In the late 1950s and early 1960s, the productivity of female employees became, for the first time, an object of social analysis. State agencies conducted at least three major social surveys on working women, and in 1964 a national conference, devoted largely to discussing aspects of women workers' productivity, brought together leaders of industry and administrators from the Ministries of Education, Social Affairs, and Industry as well as social researchers from the National Center for Criminological and Social Research and the Center for Public Mobilization and Statistics.[55] Drawing on the methodology and findings of sociological studies from contexts ranging from the United States to Japan to Eastern Europe, social researchers framed their studies as investigations into how to help the working woman negotiate problems that came from "combining her burdens as an employee with the burdens which come with responsibilities to her home and the education of her children."[56]

Using statistical analyses and interviews with working women and their supervisors, studies found that female workers were less productive than their male counterparts, working fewer hours, taking more personal days, arriving late more often, and bringing domestic labor into the workplace. What one observer dubbed "the knitting complex" (after the practice of teachers and other female public sector employees knitting during working hours) became an oft-deployed metaphor for the purported failure of women to adequately juggle domestic and work obligations. [57]

The solution posed by social policy as well as didactic discourses aimed at working women was a transformation of the domestic as a space of reproductive labor. The modernization of domestic space promised a means of balancing gender-specific duties at home with purportedly ungendered duties at work. This included participation in modern regimes of consumption, rational household management, and time discipline through the use of labor-saving domestic technologies as well as transferring certain aspects of child care to the workplace through the establishment of day care centers. Thus, the physical transformation of the inner sphere of the domestic (and the gendered social relations in it) played a critical part in assuring women's visibility in the outer realm of material progress.

DAY CARE

"How can the teacher give the necessary care for the daughters of other people when her own child is at home neglected?" was the lament of one Cairo elementary school teacher interviewed by Amina Sa'id, not coincidentally, on Mother's Day in 1962.[58] It was a lament that was replicated in the dry language of statistics reproduced in public policy papers, the didactic voices that pronounced on the unsuitability of neighbors and maids as caretakers for impressionable and vulnerable children, and in the exhausted and worried tones of thousands of working mothers facing the problem of what to do with preschool-aged children while they were at work. They reflected what was widely perceived to be a "crisis" in day care—identified in the press, interviews with policy makers, and forums devoted to treating the problems caused by the influx of women into the labor force—as perhaps the single biggest challenge facing working women.

Prior to 1958, day care facilities were run primarily by social service and women's charitable organizations as an extension of their general efforts to improve maternal and child health (although a few could be found in some of the larger textile factory complexes). But as the state exhorted more women to enter the workforce, it soon became abundantly clear that demand was outstripping supply. When state officials announced in 1958 that the Majlis Umma would take up the task of modifying the existing labor code to make it more consistent with the regime's vision of development, female labor leaders successfully pushed for the provision of subsidized day care facilities for the children of working women.[59] The new, unified labor code passed in 1959 mandated that all businesses, factories, and government ministries having more than one hundred female workers provide day care facilities at prices determined by the Ministry of Social Affairs; a year later, an administrative decree mandated that these facilities be located in or adjacent to the workplace.

Despite the legal assertion that day care was a "right" of working women, critical day care shortages remained, particularly in urban areas.[60] By 1962, there were only twenty-six day care centers in Cairo to serve the needs of over

57,000 female workers.[61] Lawyer Mufida 'Abd al-Rahman reported on widespread noncompliance with day care regulations and "tricks" engaged in by employers (such as keeping the number of women employed under one hundred) to avoid providing subsidized day care services. Other difficulties included the inability of many lower middle-class and working-class women to pay the fees associated with existing day care services offered by charitable organizations, and the costs of transporting children across the city to day care facilities located far from their homes. In an interview in *Akhir Sa'a*, Minister of Social Affairs Hikmat Abu Zayd admitted that the system of subsidized child care envisioned by state policy makers "lacked planning."[62]

The issue, however, was framed not only as one of quantity but of quality. According to the final report issued by the Conference of the Working Woman, held in 1964, the purpose of day care was not only to provide a cheap, convenient place for women to leave their children; it had to "compensate the child for the care of his mother when she is not there. . . . being deprived of this care is harmful to the child and harmful to his sound upbringing."[63] What exactly did such compensation consist of? What were the practices of mothering and child rearing that day care was supposed to replicate? What values and attributes were ascribed to the alternative solutions working women had developed, in the absence of day care, to assure care for their children while they were away at work?

In many respects, notions about the caretaking roles that day care was meant to provide replicated earlier discourses on ideal mothering that stressed care, cleanliness, and structure as the key to proper child rearing.[64] In fact, the notion of what "compensation" for mothering would entail was seemingly so commonsensical that there was very little discussion among its advocates of what day care specifically would look like in practice. There was a great deal of discussion, however, on what kinds of child care day care was meant to replace. In the absence of day care, upper middle-class working women largely relied on paid domestic help, and less affluent working women on homosocial networks made up of female neighbors and extended family members. The day care "crisis," as it was produced in the press, called into question the fitness of such extramaternal figures as providers of care and safety to Egyptian children.

"Save This Generation from the Hands of Servants" was the subheading of an article that appeared in *Akhir Sa'a* in 1957 entitled "The Dangerous Problem Faced by the Children of 800,000 Female Public Servants and Workers," in which statistical information about the number of working women and the number of day care centers intermingled with personal experiences of women who, in the absence of other options, left their children with maids or female neighbors. Horror stories abounded, such as the mother who discovered that her maid had stabbed her son with a pin so that he would stop begging her to play with him, or the woman who found out that the maid she employed to take care of her child while she was at work had given him a piece of broken glass to play with.[65] Another working mother reported that she had come home one evening to find her daughter in "terror" after her young domestic servant had left her alone in the house unsupervised.[66] Somewhat less shocking stories included that of the working mother who left her children with a neighbor and came home to find them "dirty, hungry and exhausted," and the one who discovered that her maid was stealing much of the food she left for her young daughter.[67]

The point is not that such stories didn't happen, or that very real concerns a mother might have for the safety and well-being of a child have no validity, but that such narratives of danger, filth, and neglect were shaped by classed and gendered notions of the home as a heteronormal space in which mothers were ascribed the primary responsibility for ensuring the production of sound national citizens. The safety, hygiene, affection, and organized care that characterized the ideal environment for raising children were destroyed by the "ignorance," "cruelty," "caprice," and indifference of lower-class women.

Day cares, by contrast, would replicate as closely as possible an ordered domestic space where children could be free of the pernicious and neglectful influences of domestic servants, paid nursemaids, and female neighbors. A day care center opened by gynecologist Munira al-Ibrahim in the middle-class Cairo neighborhood of Qasr al-Aini was held up as a model for Egyptian day care provision by the press and by policy makers and social scientists at the Ministry of Education, who recommended in a 1957 report on the "Problems of Female Public Employees" that Ibrahim's day care provide a template for the expansion of child care services throughout Egypt.[68] Ibrahim had modeled her day care center on those she had seen during a trip to Denmark, where she reported being impressed with the "concern of the state with the education of children and the comfort of working women."[69] An article on the women's page of *Akhir Sa'a* chronicled the center's successes: "After today the working woman won't worry about her children. And the presence of children won't be a problem which shatters the nerves of husbands and wives.

You'll go to work in the morning and be sure that your child will eat clean food. And he will play and [thus] gain beneficial health and energy and will remain clean all day."[70] The article went on to describe the regimen at the day care, which included a defined schedule of meals, play, lessons, and downtime. After arriving at the day care, children were fed a breakfast of milk and a "croissant" followed by a structured play session outside on the playground, where teachers endeavored to instruct their charges in Arabic, English, and French vocabulary by pointing out objects and naming them in the various languages. Children were then given a session of free play time to build "character and independence" and a nutritious lunch of cheese or egg sandwiches, and afterwards took a nap so their bodies could benefit from the nutrition provided. The day care center also had defined areas for play, meals, and instruction and were tended by child care "specialists." Munira Ibrahim, whom the children referred to as "Mama," the article pointed out, personally oversaw every aspect of the center's operation, from food preparation to encouraging the children to eat properly, "safeguarding their health physically and psychologically."[71]

It must have been a comfort for many working women to envision their children in such a space, even as they fretted that such spaces were few and far between. Day care held out the promise of lightening the double burden and of lessening reliance on paid domestic servants and homosocial networks, which had already been challenged and perhaps frayed by notions of domesticity and social change foregrounding the nuclear household as primary site of affectivity and affiliation. But the greatest promise held out was that in the absence of a mother's care, day cares would provide the affection, structure, and sound upbringing to children that lower-class women were deemed unfit to provide.

DOMESTIC TECHNOLOGY: MAKING THE HOME HEAVEN

In addition to day care, the other social policy solution posed to the problem of female worker productivity was to increase the availability of labor-saving domestic technology. The findings of the Conference on the Affairs of the Working Woman included recommendations that the state facilitate the dissemination of household appliances—gas stoves, semiautomatic washing machines, refrigerators, and electric irons—and that more worker housing be built to accommodate them. The conference findings also suggested that training programs could be established, which would instruct working women in how to use such appliances properly.[72] By 1965, household management classes—which were mandatory for young Egyptian women in the public education system—had added lessons on how to properly use and maintain household appliances, like vacuum cleaners, as part of a curriculum intended to teach them how to be productive housewives.[73] In an article discussing some of the reasons behind women's lagging labor productivity, Amina Sa'id wrote:

> The state calls for the necessity of implementing the assistance necessary to help the working woman carry out her various responsibilities like increasing the number of daycare centers ... and flooding the markets with modern household appliances—refrigerators and washing machines and electric vacuum cleaners—and offering them at the cheapest prices which won't burden those who have small incomes and who need to benefit from these types of civilized tools.[74]

Until such financial assistance was widely available, Sa'id argued, women's work would continue to be negatively affected. The assumption that structured the calls for working women to be provided with modern domestic technology at affordable prices was that making women more efficient and productive in the home would help them become more efficient and productive in the workplace.

Imported domestic appliances had been available in Egypt since the early 1950s. American-produced Westinghouse refrigerators first appeared in 1955; other brands, like Tappan, Kelvinator, General Electric, and the French Miele, had arrived a few years earlier. In 1954, public sector companies began to manufacture household appliances as part of the Nasser regime's import substitution policies. The public sector Ideal Company produced gas stoves, metal kitchen sets, washing machines, and perhaps most famously, refrigerators, which were touted as being so good they were even being exported to Africa and East Germany.[75] Such household appliances were proudly featured at the 1966 Cairo Industrial Exhibition alongside tractors, farming equipment, and plastic dishes as examples of the successes of socialist economic planning and industrial self-sufficiency.[76]

Despite increasing availability, however, there was initially little demand for these new household appliances among most of the population. Elite families, who relied on servants to perform household labor, purchased imported appliances as status symbols, domestic accoutrements that demonstrated their ability to consume the most modern and scientifically advanced technology Europe and the United States had to offer.[77] For upper middle-class families, the widespread availability of cheap domestic labor frequently made paid domestic help a more affordable alternative. A 1959 *Ruz al-Yusuf* cartoon featured a well, but not ostentatiously, dressed woman and her be-suited husband standing in front of a store display window featuring a semi-automatic washing machine. The caption reads: "No, Mahmud, I don't want a washing machine, they're so expensive. Um Ibrahim the washerwoman and some bleach are enough, and the wash will turn out beautifully."[78] For the vast majority of working Egyptians, the price of a washing machine, shiny new Tappan stove, or even a locally produced Ideal refrigerator was far out of reach. According to a *New York Times* article, the price of an Egyptian-made washing machine in 1966 was $580 (263 LE), approximately ten times the price of an average civil servant's monthly salary.[79] In order to increase the initially tepid response of Egyptian consumers to homegrown domestic appliances, in 1962 the Ministry of Industry lowered prices on locally produced models, making them significantly cheaper than their imported counterparts, and in-stituted a purchase-on-installment plan for public sector employees. A 20 per-cent down payment at Omar Effendi, Sednaoui, or any of the other newly na-tionalized department stores and a modest monthly payment would allow the families of public sector employees to take home an air conditioner, electric vacuum cleaner, refrigerator, washing machine, or other "modern domestic tools."[80] While household appliances could still only be found in a minority of Egyptian households by the late 1960s, social science surveys suggest that some appliances, particularly gas stoves and refrigerators, were becoming an increasingly common feature within urban middle-class homes.[81]

As John Waterbury has pointed out, import substitution and the man-ufacture of domestic appliances were part of larger state efforts to increase standards of living and create a new, middle-class consumer culture. Income redistribution measures would expand the ranks of the urban middle class, whose growing demand for locally produced consumer goods would fuel in-dustrial growth and eventually allow Egypt to begin exporting. "The average Egyptian would have his own dwelling, a modest range of appliances, perhaps even a car. . . . While accepting modest consumerism on the part of the citi-zenry, the state would be able to tax the population's growing prosperity to generate investment for further growth. The process would eventually become self-sustaining."[82] The state-driven manufacture and promotion of domestic appliances was thus aimed not at working women alone; rather, it reflected

Figure 2.1 *Al-Ahram* contest: "Know the Products of Your Country." *Al-Ahram*, Aug. 6, 1962, 104–105.

the intersection of new regimes of consumption and new visions of efficient domesticity intended to benefit working and nonworking women alike.

In 1962, the daily *Al-Ahram* newspaper ran a reader contest to publicize the new household consumer goods being produced in state-owned Egyptian factories. It featured an elaborate two-page drawing of a home filled with an array of appliances and technologies. The house featured a well-appointed living room with a radio, television, air conditioner, and tape recorder, a fully equipped kitchen with a semiautomatic washing machine, refrigerator, gas stove, electric iron, and vacuum cleaner, and even a garage with a car (Figure 2.1). As the accompanying paragraph asserted: "The ten years since the revolution have brought great development in Egyptian industries and their ability to satisfy the needs of every citizen. The flag of Egyptian industry flies today in every home . . . in the bedroom, in the living room, in the kitchen and the bathroom and the garden."[83] Readers were invited to send in a list of all of the Egyptian-manufactured products in this "model home" to the newspaper—whoever was able to identify the greatest number of locally produced goods would win a prize of 50 Egyptian pounds (about twice the monthly salary for a midlevel civil servant).

The image of the model Egyptian home speaks to some of the ideological work images of domestic technology performed, even as it suggests some of their inconsistencies, disjunctures, and disconnects. The production of domestic appliances (and the creation of idealized domestic spaces of which they were an integral part), was linked to an explicitly nationalist, state-led development project that championed class-based mobilization and uplift. The point of the contest is to help citizens recognize the ways in which state modernization provides them with the means to realize the normative ideals and imperatives of modern living. The home itself replicates gendered divisions of space and social relations associated with older colonial and nationalist discourses on "the home" as a locus of Egyptian identity and prosperity—single family dwellings with functionally specific rooms filled with Egyptian products, the nuclear family, and an ethic of efficiency, hygiene, and rationalized housekeeping signaled by the appliances themselves.[84] There is, in fact, quite a lot in this image that is rather predictable to anyone familiar with earlier twentieth-century Egyptian discourses on domesticity. Within the context of the postrevolutionary period, however, one element, at closer glance, seems slightly out of place. Instead of one female figure there are two: a maid tucked away in the kitchen doing the ironing, and the lady of the house herself, standing in the bedroom admiring herself in a large mirror over a dresser-top filled with perfume bottles, powders, and other cosmetic goods (also being manufactured in Egypt during this period).

The most obvious interpretation would be that the ideal middle-class household included not only labor-saving appliances but also domestic help. And yet, the maid pictured would not have been easily recognizable to readers as a domestic servant without the simultaneous presence of the chicly dressed housewife in another room of the house. With her short dress, crisp white apron, and absent the *mandil* (kerchief), which female domestic servants and working-class women generally wore over their hair while doing housework, she could easily have been mistaken for the lady of the house and not the paid help. Attending to this disconnect between domestic laborers as historical and social agents and the pictured maid as an imagined figure present in an idealized domestic space suggests alternative interpretations.

The figure of the maid situates domestic technology firmly within the space of the feminine while simultaneously distancing housewives from the dirt and labor of household work. The kitchen, filled with labor-saving appliances that all families, ostensibly, would be able to benefit from with the advent of import substitution and installment plans, appears spatially walled off from the rest of the house. The housewife, the purported beneficiary of the revolution in domestic technology, remains at far-remove, almost on the other end of the home. While the pictured home is spotless, the housewife herself is unburdened of physical labor, free to busy herself with other sorts of gendered tasks—putting on makeup, choosing the right sort of dress, and creating a happy, calm, aesthetically beautiful domestic atmosphere for her husband and children.

The image of the labor-free housewife presented in the *Al-Ahram* contest was replicated in advertisements for stoves, refrigerators, and washing machines that began to appear in *Hawwa'* and on the pages of general interest magazines in the late 1950s and early 1960s. For middle-class readers, these advertisements offered the promise that technology would lighten the heavy burdens of housework. For the less affluent, they provided a gendered vision of the benefits of modern domestic living to be derived from consumption, perhaps made possible by the additional income a working woman's salary could provide. Appliance advertisements thus built on existing messages of hygiene, domesticity, class, and consumption, as well as notions of female empowerment, and recast them in new ways.

Advertisements for household appliances stressed their aesthetic and material benefits. An ad for Kelvinator refrigerator, the "exemplary refrigerator of 1957," declared that it was both "elegant" and "economical."[85] The French Miele company promised that its semiautomatic washing machine was "cheap, economic and quick . . . [it] saves effort, time and money."[86] An advertisement for Vim cleaning powder, one of the few that pictured a woman and domestic technology in the same textual space, featured an immaculately dressed housewife in an apron and high heels standing next to her now spotless stove, under the caption "Vim: cleans everything quickly."[87] All of these devices promised to produce a cleaner home, one metaphorically distant from the dirt and intensive labor associated with poverty, a home now available to all Egyptian families thanks to the wonders of Egyptian industry and the regime's commitment to social uplift, which drew on the widely held sentiment that purchasing domestic appliances would make life much easier—homes could be cleaner for less time, work, and effort and with less household expenditure. At the same time, advertisements and images of household appliances focused on the affective and emotional benefits that domestic appliances could bring to every household. The emphasis on cleanliness, thrift, and beauty, as well as ease, also contained the message that domestic technology would "permit a happy home life."[88] An advertisement for the public sector Nasr Trading Company urged women to come to the opening of the company's new branch in downtown Cairo, where they would be treated to displays of the "most modern" refrigerators, stoves, hot water heaters, chandeliers, and radios. "Nasr trading company takes care that its offerings are in reach of the lady of every household. . . . a housewife can have a complete kitchen which will transform her house into a heaven."[89]

Where did the working woman fit into such images? Certainly the truth-claims asserted by such advertisements, spoken in the language of efficiency, economy, as well as beauty and comfort, intended to address the desires of working women and housewives alike as custodians of the domestic realm. But the promise that housework would no longer entail back-breaking labor but could be achieved with a minimum amount of money and effort and with maximum results affirmed the wider social policy message that domestic technology could free women from labor-intensive housework so they could enter the labor market, get an education, or spend extra time in activities that would serve the nation. Articles on working women pointed out that modern appliances had become "a big help" to the working woman, "allowing her to carry out her duties quickly and perfectly."[90]

Such representations worked to efface certain forms of labor and social relations. The "liberation" from housework that allowed many upper middle-class women to enter the workforce, gain additional education, or enjoy other opportunities for personal fulfillment was often as much dependent upon the underpaid and undervalued domestic work performed by lower-class women as it was on household technology. John Waterbury estimates that in 1960 as many as a fifth of the urban employed were household servants, whose wages accounted for only 5 percent of urban incomes.[91]

Moreover, while profiles in the press of working women, particularly educated, professional women, often pictured them in domestic spaces that reflected the aesthetic and consumer ideals demanded by socialist society—spaces that looked a great deal like the *Al-Ahram* drawing described previously—these did not include picturing them with the labor-saving devices that were meant to help them work or to be the fruits of their additional salary contributions to the household. In fact, such images, often juxtaposed with pictures of women hard at work in their offices, conveyed a sense of ease and companionate domesticity rather than labor. Working women were pictured sitting on living room couches with their husbands and children, or presiding gracefully over the family dinner table, not laboring in the kitchen, images that were also replicated in photographic depictions of housewives.

Historians of domestic technology have often pointed out that the dissemination of household appliances marked the ascription of new value to the affective components of housework and a subsequent reallocation of women's domestic labor.[92] Because domestic appliances reduced the amount of physical housework, housewives were expected to allocate more time to the "caring" aspects of housework—making the home beautiful, spending more time with husbands and children, cooking more varied and complicated meals, and so on. The nonpresence of domestic appliances in idealized images of Egyptian family life, coupled with the focus in the press on appliances as a means to creating a happy home life, suggests a similar shift.

An article in *Hawwa'* compared the "virtues" of marriage between a working woman and a stay-at-home wife, arguing that it was easier for housewives to create an atmosphere of domestic comfort and leisure (*raha*) for their husbands and children.[93] As for the working wife, she came home from work tired to find housework still waiting for her. Able to spend the time their husbands were out of the home and their children were at school on the completion of household tasks, housewives could better create an idealized domestic space seemingly free of toil and effort in which dirty and time-consuming labor processes were effaced. Even Amina Sa'id admitted that women who worked outside the home could not as easily achieve the same effects of effortless comfort and ease as could full-time housewives.[94]

And yet, what made the housewife a potentially superior mate was not the amount of time she was able to devote to performing domestic work. Many commentators on the problem of the "second shift" pointed out that the difference in the amount of time housewives and working women spent on household duties was negligible, particularly since domestic appliances now made it possible to carry out those duties more quickly and efficiently. Educational administrator Su'ad Nur al-Din, who was profiled with her husband in the pages of *Hawwa'* as an example of a successful working mother, pointed out that the ease of domestic affairs in the modern age no longer required all of women's time be spent at home. "The preparation of meals doesn't take more than a few hours, and with refrigerators food can be preserved for days and gas stoves cut [cooking] time in half. As for cleaning, sweeping and ironing, a servant can do that and she's present in the home of working women and housewives alike."[95]

What was at issue was not the amount of time spent on household labor but the ability to make the home appear as a space of peace and leisure.

Discussions of housework, modern labor-saving devices, and the challenges faced by working women thus invested the home with affective content and delineated new standards of comfort and effortlessness that all Egyptian women were now expected to achieve in their own homes and families. Paradoxically, housework—whether performed by domestic appliances, servants, housewives, or working women—would require the mastering of new skills of rational household management that would ultimately allow women to be better wives and mothers.

While many of the professional working women interviewed by *Hawwa'* stressed that domestic appliances were what allowed them to take up new roles outside the home, they spoke far more frequently about how the skills they acquired through outside work allowed them to effectively budget time and organize household tasks, to provide emotional support and empathy to their husbands and a sound upbringing to their children. 'Aida Tahir, wife of noted visual artist Salih Tahir, who had been both a stay-at-home housewife and a working woman, pointed out that work taught women responsibility and accustomed them to organization.[96] According to actress Madiha Yussry, quoted in an article that provided portraits of successful working women and their husbands, "the working wife knows how to organize her affairs and to evaluate her time down to the last minute and second." An ethic of time discipline and efficiency was, she argued, what saved working women from falling into the "messy confusion" (*al-lakhbata*) that was the common fate of less disciplined housewives.[97] Failure to complete household tasks, like having dinner prepared when husbands came home from work and having clean clothing for children to wear to school, and being absent from the home when other family members were present were most often attributed to wasting time in unproductive tasks like gossiping with female neighbors.

Such assertions speak to the complex and contradictory relationship between the introduction of domestic technology and the real and imagined social context of gendered household labor during this period. Advertisements targeted housewives as the primary beneficiaries of labor-saving devices, but families who could afford such appliances often employed domestics to take care of much of the heaviest and most time-consuming household tasks. Appliances promised freedom from physical domestic labor even as changing notions of domesticity ascribed new value to the caretaking aspects of gendered domestic work. In such a context, the assertions that professional working women made about the need for efficiency, time discipline, and

organization—skills highly prized in a society devoted to socialist planning—appear simultaneously as didactic, effacing, and, perhaps, as a form
of resistance. While professional working women who spoke about their experiences contributed to a vision of domestic life where care, comfort, and
affection were intertwined with new forms of disciplined practice, they also
insisted that the ideal home didn't resemble the magical, labor-free space envisioned by discourses on housework. In such a context, the words of professional working women can perhaps be read as an attempt to invest seemingly
effortless, domestic labor with affective value.

FOR MEN ONLY? THE PERILS AND PROMISES
OF THE CO-ED WORKPLACE

The problems that women's influx into the labor force posed for the balancing of work and domestic roles were not the only subject of commentary in
debates about and portrayals of working women and their potentially destabilizing effects on social boundaries. The changing gender composition of the
workforce occasioned new social and cultural commentary on the integration
of women into the formerly male-dominated, homosocial space of the workplace—the subject of the other major film that, in addition to *My Wife Is a
General Director*, offered moviegoers a vision of working women in new spaces
of socialist development.

Li-l-Rijal Faqat (For Men Only) was a comedy that revolved around the
transition from gender-segregated work spaces to co-ed ones.[98] Movie stars
Nadia Lutfi and Suad Husni play two geologists who apply for positions on an
oil exploration project in the Sinai administered by a public sector oil company. Salwa (Husni) and Hind (Lutfi) are rejected for the positions on the
grounds that the site is "for men only." After Salwa delivers an impassioned
speech declaring that women can do any work that a man can do, two male
applicants for the position arrive at the Cairo office. Salwa and Hind steal
the applicants' credentials and take their places at the work camp, dressed in
the guise of male engineers. Upon arrival, Salwa and Hind are immediately
attracted to two drilling technicians named Fawzi and Ahmad. Comedic high
jinks ensue as the two women must control their sexual attraction and continue to act as men, their passing as men made increasingly difficult by the
close quarters of the work camp—shared bedrooms, shared bathrooms, and
the rough-and-tumble camaraderie of their fellow workers. It is not only the
presence of women in male space that is portrayed as potentially transgressive,

however. The homosocial space of the work camp, and the bonds between men it engenders, are themselves potentially endangering to the boundaries of appropriate sexuality. When Salwa and Hind arrive at the work camp's mess hall, the men are gathered together, dancing cheek to cheek to Western-style romantic music. Fawzi asks Salwa to dance, and an argument ensues over who is going to lead. In drag, Salwa protests, "I'm a man," and Fawzi agrees to be the passive partner. The gendered and hinted-at sexual transgressions are accommodated through the two heroines' eventual unmasking. Hind and Salwa reveal their identity as women and pair off as appropriate heterosexual couples with Fawzi and Ahmad.

In an article on homosexuality in Egyptian film, Garay Menicucci points out that in the 1960s, female transvestism in the Egyptian cinema often served a didactic function intended to provide ideological justification for the crossing of gender boundaries.[99] By the end of the film, the potential tensions engendered by Salwa and Hind's forays into the homosocial space of the labor camp—the blurring of gender boundaries, the specter of unrestrained male and female sexuality outside the confines of heterosexual pair bonding, inappropriate performances of both masculinity and femininity—are neatly resolved through the reestablishment of heteronormative marital relationships. The co-ed workplace, which began as a site of potential transgression, ends as a site for the disciplining of inappropriate gender and sexual displays for men and women alike.

How such a transformation was to be enacted in real life was the subject of many commentaries on women's work that dealt with the comportment of women in newly gender-mixed workplaces.

The presence of middle-class women in the professional workplace in the late 1950s and 1960s occasioned new discussions over etiquette, femininity, fashion, and bodily deportment. How the working woman should dress, speak, and behave in the office, how she should negotiate social boundaries with male coworkers, decorate her office space, and provide appropriate support to (largely) male bosses became the subject of editorials in the press, prescriptive articles in women's magazines, proposed social policy, and not infrequently, social satire. These discussions advocated a metaphorical reveiling, based not on the covering of the body but on modest deportment and conduct. Veiling as a sartorial practice stood as a symbol of backwardness and outmoded traditionalism. The veiling of conduct, on the other hand, was posed as a necessary solution to the tensions engendered by women's integration into formerly homosocial work spaces at a time when most urban upper- and middle-class women had stopped veiling and donned Western-inspired fashions.

Conversations about fashion, femininity, and workplace relationships not only sprang from the physical, uncovered presence of women in formerly homosocial workspaces but also reflected anxieties prompted by the movement of activities, practices, and social relationships formerly associated with the home to new public spaces of sociability. A 1959 *Ruz al-Yusuf* article chronicling the growing prevalence of female secretaries in Egyptian offices elaborated the qualities and skills that made a good secretary: strong character, cleverness, good taste, knowledge of general culture, and a sense of fashion and elegance, qualities that largely replicated those found in the middle-class ideal of the proper wife.[100] The article pointed out that the old saying "Behind every great man is a woman" has now come to be "Behind every great man there are two women, his wife and his secretary." The assertion was intended to be a positive one, stressing the professionalism and contributions of female office workers. But the homology between wives and secretaries as supportive (and subordinate) intimates to figures of male authority also played to the sexual and moral transgressions that might be occasioned by new configurations of social space that blurred boundaries between home and work. A cartoon appearing in *Ruz al-Yusuf* in 1959 depicted two businessmen walking together on a windy day. Across the street, the wind has blown up the skirts of two women, concealing their faces but revealing their garter-clad legs and underwear. Pointing at the woman on the right, one man says to the other, "Look, there's my secretary."[101]

Where families had played a pivotal role in choosing and securing marriage partners for their daughters, now the workplace and university became potential sources of spouses, chosen by young women themselves on the basis of mutual affection and compatibility. Whereas women in the context of the household may have been subject in various ways to the masculine authority of husbands, fathers, brothers, and other male family members, in the workplace they also became subject to the authority of male bosses. The caretaking roles that women had performed in the domestic realm were increasingly reproduced in spaces of labor, particularly in lower-level service jobs such as clerical work, nursing, teaching, and waitressing, where much of the urban female workforce was concentrated.

FROM THE VEIL TO ETIQUETTE: FEMININITY
AND DEPORTMENT IN THE WORKPLACE

In his contribution to the debate on what should constitute Egyptian national culture after the revolution, prominent journalist Ahmad Baha al-Din wrote: "The citizen who clothes himself in a British suit made of American textile for which he pays a few pounds does not have grave consequences . . . but the citizen who acquires a British or American mind we have lost forever."[102] For al-Din and other secular intellectuals who took up the project of defining Egyptian national culture after the revolution, the project was one of "Egyptianizing" modernity, of developing a notion of Egyptian national culture derived from the nation's own heritage (*turath*) and adapted to the universal conditions of development and progress.[103] The markers of Egyptian cultural authenticity would reside not in external markers like clothing but were to be internalized in mentality and practice. Such ideas were embodied in a popular government slogan, *Al-badla al-sh'abiyya ahsan min al-galabiyya* (the popular suit is better than the *galabiyya*).[104] They were also evident in the illustration, featured prominently in Egyptian textbooks from the 1960s, of feminist Huda Sha'rawi's dramatic unveiling in the Cairo Central train station upon her return from an international conference in Rome in 1923. Egyptian nationalist narratives trace the gradual disappearance of the veil among the elite and the middle classes to this historical moment. The movement to remove the veil was elite, linked with upper-class women's participation in the nationalist struggle against colonialism.[105] Some women, however, had already begun to unveil in the two decades prior to Sha'rawi's public act of protest. During the 1930s and 1940s, urban middle- and upper-class women (as well as upper- and middle-class men) began wearing "Westernized" fashion as a matter of course.

By the 1960s, the prototypical college girl or female civil servant wore knee-length skirts.[106] Many middle-class women purchased the German *Burda* magazine for the sewing patterns of the latest European fashions it included.[107] The great Egyptian department stores, like Cicurel, Sednaoui, and Omar Effendi, which had been nationalized in 1958, carried dresses, skirts, stockings, and high-heeled shoes at prices affordable to the urban middle classes. Egyptian magazines featured models in dresses and provided tips on the latest fashion trends. A fashion column in *Ruz al-Yusuf* called "Give My Regards to Your Dear Husband" provided fashion tips that detailed where the latest European clothes and accessories (or local knockoffs) could be found for the cheapest prices. Egyptian writer Ahdaf Soueif, who was a teenager in

Cairo in the 1960s, recalled in an article she wrote for *The Guardian* newspaper that dress was a telling signifier, not only of class status but also of professional affiliation, level of education, marital status, place of origin (urban or rural), and neighborhood of residence:

> Until the early 1970s, if you sat in the café Riche on Qasr el-Nil street watching the world go by, you could tell fairly accurately what a person was by their clothes. And, generally, the more affluent a person was, the more westernized they were. That woman there, the slim one in the well cut suit with the skirt just above the knee, in sunglasses, she might be an engineer/doctor/lawyer or married to one. . . . That child hurrying across the street in slippers and an ill-fitting dress with a white kerchief binding her hair is a servant girl, sent out to fetch something in a hurry. And here come two women deep in conversation—one has her hair covered in a kind of filigree bonnet, the other wears hers in a bun; they walk slowly in their sensible shoes, they wear what most Cairene women wear: a straight, dark gabardine skirt ending just below the knee and over it a shirt in a floral or geometric pattern with an open collar and sleeves just above the elbow. They are (or married to) minor civil servants, school teachers or legal workers, but they might also be the wives of men in trade, or workers in large public sector factories: textiles, pharmaceuticals, food, steel and so on. In other words, they are either the petty bourgeoisie or upwardly mobile working class. As for that comely, plump woman hurrying along, her long, black overdress similar to that of the peasant woman, her head covered in a loose, black, transparent *tarha* over the flowered scarf which binds her hair, she might be married to a butcher or a grocer's assistant, she might work as a cleaner in a school or a hospital or a government office.[108]

Soueif's depiction indicates far more complexity in dress styles and the meanings associated with sartorial choices than a simple dichotomy between "traditional" and "Western" fashions would imply. Her observations, nevertheless, suggest that women's visibility—both in the absolute sense of their circulation in this most public of urban thoroughfares, and in relative degrees of being covered and uncovered—was a critical marker of social prestige and privilege.

Afsaneh Najmabadi has traced the ways in which women's visibility (in both senses) was critical to marking out the contours of a public sphere in late nineteenth- and early twentieth-century Iran. As women's unveiled presence outside of the household came to define the meanings of "publicness" and modernity for Iranians, the transition from older notions of homosocial separate private spheres to a single heterosocial public sphere marked a simultaneous change in gendered bodily practice and comportment. "Before the physical veil was discarded, it was replaced by a metaphoric veil, not as some object, a piece of cloth external to the female body, but a veil to be acquired through modern education, as some internal quality of self, a new modern self, a disciplined, modern body that obscured women's sexuality, obliterated its bodily presence."[109]

I would argue that a similar move towards the cultivation of disciplined bodies, a sort of "reveiling" in 1960s Egypt, can be read in discussions of the problems that might arise from women's presence in the formal workplace. Here, the notion of the *hijab* functioned as a metaphor for female modesty. In August 1961, the weekly magazine *Akhir Sa'a* ran a series of articles called "Frank Recollections of a Working Girl," which chronicled the search of an anonymous recent university graduate for an office job. After a protracted search, she gains "a respectable position" in the accounting department of a well-known company. On her first day of work, she meets Nawal, an older female employee who advises her how to conduct herself within the workplace: "I want to advise you from the beginning, don't enjoy yourself with the male employees," Nawal warns. "Put a heavy veil [*hijab kathif*] between yourself and them so that your relations with all of your colleagues will be on the same level."[110]

In Nawal's advice to her young colleague, *hijab* is meant to function as a performative boundary between male and female employees. It achieves a leveling effect by allowing for equitable relations between men and women in the workplace. In Nawal's meaning, veiling is explicitly inclusionary rather than exclusionary, ensuring the integration of her colleague into the professional life of the office. At the same time, Nawal's injunction that the young woman not "enjoy herself" signals that this performative veil is intended to "cover" and thus exclude manifestations of female desire.

While this pleasure is not identified as explicitly sexual, the use of the word *hijab* calls forth a complex web of signification in which both male and female sexual desire, bodily discipline, notions of honor, and history converge. In an article in *Ruz al-Yusuf*, journalist Muhammad al-Ghazali Harb examined the historical connection between veiling and the notion of *fitna*.[111] The word *fitna* means, variously, attractiveness, temptation, and fascination, as well as chaos and discord. According to Fatima Mernissi, it refers to the "chaos provoked by sexual disorder and initiated by women."[112] Harb wrote to several

Azhari *shaykhs* to request religious opinions (*fatawa*) about the permissibility of women wearing bathing suits. According to the article, the requested *fatawa* called for return to the *hijab shar'i* (religiously prescribed veil). "What is this so-called *hijab shar'i*?" Harb asks. "They have known it as the covering of all of the body of the woman including her face and her hands to protect against '*fitna*.'"

Harb criticized religious officials and others who asserted that the veil was a "sacred emblem" of Islamic or Egyptian national culture. Veiling as the covering of parts of a woman's body, he pointed out, was a historical practice that predated the appearance of Islam and later became common among non-Muslim communities.[113] While there were strict injunctions against Muslim women stepping outside their homes uncovered during the first century of Islam, Harb argued, such restrictions were in the process of disappearing in Egypt. According to Harb, the coming of "modern civilization" eliminated much of the "oppressions" associated with the *hijab*, except in some of the Arab (Gulf) countries.

In his criticism of calls to return to the *hijab shar'i*, Harb rejected neither the existence of *fitna* as inherent in relations between men and women, nor "the veil" as a means to protect against *fitna*. He contrasted the idea of the veil as a physical covering with the veil as a description of female comportment. Harb viewed the *hijab* as something temporal—a mere piece of clothing. "As for the visible *hijab* which the men of religion mean, it's nothing but a historical phase in the life of women in the world." Moreover, according to Harb, physical veiling was no guarantee of the prevention of *fitna*. Harb viewed *fitna*, in fact, as a natural attribute of male and female behavior, arguing that the necessary and inevitable mixing of men and women in public is the "true" *hijab*, which is defined by appropriate female comportment and the cultivation of a disciplined, modest demeanor.

Potential displays of female sexuality in the workplace, manifested in dress, were a concern not only of male writers, such as Harb, but of feminist advocates of women's work. Latifa al-Zayyat, although she had discontinued political activism by the mid-1950s, remained active as a writer and commentator in the press on gender issues. In her occasional column for *Hawwa'* she condemned women who misused their femininity in the workplace as no better than prostitutes. In the column entitled "The Working Woman and the Weapon of Femininity," al-Zayyat argued that women's presence in the workplace assumed certain notions of gender equality. These demanded that the laboring female subject separate her characteristics as a female from her attributes as a working woman. "When a woman goes out to work she stands on the same ground as a man and she must use the same weapons as a man," she argued. "In other words, she must leave her femininity at home before she descends into the street."[114] Sexualized femininity gave women an unfair advantage over the males with whom they worked, since it was a "weapon" that men could not use. The public space of the office and the wider sphere of participation, al-Zayyat argued, must be governed by universal characteristics of humanity (*insaniyya*), such as self-discipline, patience, force of personality, rational deliberation, and debate. Al-Zayyat did not view such attributes as ontologically male but rather as human qualities that transcended gender and whose display was incumbent upon men and women alike within public spaces. While al-Zayyat adopted a critical stance to displays of femaleness that were sexualized and praised seemingly gender-neutral characteristics as the basis for workplace interaction between the sexes, she didn't reject the idea of the workplace itself as a gendered space. Thus, she writes:

> I don't mean to turn women into men or for her to make the workplace void of her elegance, her delicacy or her feminine characteristics. In fact the opposite is true: Every working woman should exalt her femininity just as a man exalts his masculinity. . . . They must deem their femininity sacrosanct and hold it above all material or spiritual gain, being ashamed of its use in a realm it was not created for.[115]

What did this "exalted" notion of femininity specifically consist of for al-Zayyat and others who commented on the deportment and conduct of the working woman? Which bodily practices and sartorial choices did it embrace, and which did it exclude? An article appearing in *Hawwa'* asked, "Is it necessary for a women who works in an office . . . to become masculinized and put aside toiletries and make-up and a charming smile, everything which increases her elegance or gives proof of her femininity?"[116] One of the more august lights of the Egyptian intellectual scene to take up this question was Salama Musa. Musa, a Copt Christian and Fabian socialist, whose writings on Egyptian science and culture had helped define interwar political and intellectual discourse, influenced secular writers and thinkers such as Naguib Mahfouz and Taha Hussein. In 1956, Musa turned his pen to the subject of the new revolutionary woman; his book *Woman Is Not the Plaything of Man* was a typically unabashed treatise in defense of women's rights and a critique of prevailing gender norms.[117] Taking up the issue of femininity in the book's chapter on women's work, Musa rejected the notion that work blurred gender boundaries by making women too much like men, or the idea that women must give up their feminine characteristics in order to enter the workplace. Instead, a female worker should "remain conservative in her appearance, appropriate to her position and her obligations." Musa listed numerous objects that he felt had no place in the office: cologne, chic dresses, high heels, laughing, and raised voices. Describing the female employees working in the reception area of a government office he found himself in one afternoon, Musa praised their appearance and conduct:

> I didn't find on a single one of them the *tabarruj* [showy adornments articulated in a combination of dress and behavior] which you know in many housewives. I mean adornment of face make-up or adornments in chic clothing which make the woman half-naked, and adornments in words and gestures. Likewise, you don't find one of them who smokes or who raise her voice in the harsh tones we hear from a man. No. No delicacy and no roughness. She does her work in dignity and beauty together. I found the question boring into my mind: Why don't they adorn themselves since all of them are still young? And I found an answer. The woman, when she works, finds *karama* [honor] . . . and she knows that her *karama* and her life and her happiness don't depend on her physical beauty alone. . . . The concern with adornments is a signal that she has hung her ambitions on home and marriage.[118]

In Musa's rendering, excessive adornment becomes at once a marker of bourgeois frivolity and inappropriate feminine display. Musa's ideal female worker, who does not flaunt her body by wearing makeup and revealing clothing, nor call attention to herself by raising her voice, resembles Harb's metaphorically veiled woman who covers her sexuality with modest behavior. Like al-Zayyat, he insists that dignity, beauty, and honor must necessarily provide the basis for a gendered performance that was eminently feminine but desexualized, a femininity appropriate for display in a co-ed workplace. Musa, however, introduces a discussion of class into his treatment of women and work that is absent from Harb's and al-Zayyat's work. Musa connects housewives who can afford not to work with particular patterns of consumption, such as buying makeup and chic fashions that reveal the body. By making such a connection, Musa includes these women as part of the "decadent" Egyptian bourgeoisie, whose excesses ran counter to the ethic of socialist economic planning and austerity.

How did working women themselves experience and negotiate prescriptions for appropriate workplace comportment? Interviews and opinion surveys that magazines conducted with working women throughout the 1960s suggest that professional working women were highly conscious of such representations and the expectations that surrounded their presence in the workplace. This is particularly evident in the reasons many of these women gave for preferring a co-ed workplace. (In one survey, this preference was as high as 90%.)[119] Some women employees complained that in a workplace staffed only with women they would spend all of their time talking about "fashion," trading gossip about other employees, or talking about their husbands. They argued that the presence of male coworkers would, in the words of one, "make women immediately attentive" to the work at hand, instead of wasting time talking about subjects that respondents described as frivolous.[120] They also cited the problem of competition between women over who had the nicest clothes, as well as the jealousy and pettiness women displayed when confronted with the presence of a younger, more attractive and fashionably dressed woman.

Qadriyya al-Suyufi, a teacher at the Higher Institute of Home Economics, however, complained that "a woman who works with male colleagues is ordinarily shackled [*muqayyida*] and doesn't behave freely. She will measure every word and movement so she doesn't risk misunderstanding or mis-interpretation."[121] Another woman, an employee in the Ministry of Agriculture, described the co-ed workplace as a "prison" that provided for the *tahzib* (correction) of morals.[122] Despite the parallels that this anonymous woman drew between a mixed workplace and prison, she went on to state her preference for the mixed workplace precisely because of its disciplinary effects, not only on women but also on men. Aliyya Afifi, a teacher, said, "Civility, understanding and good behavior are the weapons that the Eastern working woman uses in vanquishing the problem of worn out traditions [problems arising from mixing at work]."[123]

Afifi's words suggest how women adopted the terms of discussion concerning their position in public in order to critique prevailing gender norms and to carve out a space for their own participation in the workforce. Being around male coworkers would force working women to be modest, but their presence would also exert a disciplining influence on men. By rearticulating gendered prescriptions of etiquette and embodied performance, working women claimed space in public and criticized the masculine behaviors that rendered that presence problematic. The modest behavior of women in public would civilize men, making them more able to accommodate the changes dictated by the process of modernization.

CONCLUSION

The emancipation promised by women's participation in public life was predicated on relatively new sorts of disciplined practice within the newly formed nation-state's revolutionary project. State feminist solutions to the problem of how best to ensure the incorporation of women into the labor force recast the home and the workplace as classed and gendered spaces. Emphasis on the need to modernize domestic spaces (and the relationships in them) in order to help women manage the multiple burdens of work and family not only reinforced the bourgeois home as a privileged location of gender difference but also provided solutions that were largely available only to middle-class women. The often elaborate prescriptions for how women were to behave in public, particularly in the workplace (how to deal with coworkers, how to dress, how to organize time productively), were not simply residual products of persistent older views of appropriate gender relations. Instead, they were integral to a new vision of the revolutionary woman and new spaces of public sociability.

3 LAW, SECULARISM, AND INTIMACY

Debating the Personal Status Laws

DURING THE NASSER PERIOD, debates over *al-ahwal al-shakhsiyya* (personal status laws) were a key site for fashioning the relationship between state feminism and the family. These laws formed what Marnia Lazreg has termed "a dual legal system," which includes both secular codes of law and ones inspired by religion.[1] In the Egyptian legal system, based largely on secular codes, the personal status laws that governed marriage, divorce, child custody, financial support, and inheritance were the last remaining province of religious law. It was this dual legal system that provided the gendered framework of rights and duties within which family matters were adjudicated in Nasserist Egypt, settling conflicts over who could marry and divorce whom, who got custody of children, and the meaning of the legal terms "obedience" (*ta'a*) and "support" (*nafaqa*).

In the period following the nationalization of the courts and the abolition of the religious court system, which had adjudicated family law since the late nineteenth century, women activists and their supporters launched a campaign to redress what they saw as fundamental gender inequalities within the existing laws. Drawing on a new discourse of citizenship rights, they called upon the state to regulate the rights of men under *shari'a* law in the interests of protecting the family and its most vulnerable members: women and children. The calls for reform met with vocal opposition from members of the official religious establishment and its supporters, who championed the existing laws as adequate to the task of maintaining the family as the pillar of revolutionary society, and argued that reform was antithetical to the gender-specific conceptualization of rights and duties embodied in Islam and the existing legislation. Ultimately the reform campaign failed because reformers' strategies depended on the will of state functionaries and institutions to take a more active role in regulating domestic relations and curbing the authority of religious officials, a role the state proved reluctant to accept. The personal status laws remained in their prerevolutionary form until 1979.

Assessments of women's citizenship in the Arab world and Iran have frequently argued that the provisions of personal status codes impinge on the rights and freedoms of Muslim women guaranteed to them by national constitutions. In particular, scholars have pointed to the continuing institutional role of religion in governing gender relations in the family as somehow incompatible with a secular nation-state project, and the primary reason the progressive promise of emancipation and enfranchised citizenship for women in the region has not been realized.

The decade-long debate during the Nasser period over the personal status laws challenges the binary framing of that debate that places "Islam" and Westernization" at its center. It suggests that the ways in which the rights of women were delineated by the state both enabled and limited the new sorts of claims reformers could make, and also calls into question the easy identification of the conflict as one between the modernizing, Westernizing impulses of secular elites and the religious establishment, who formed its appeals to religious tradition over and against a monolithically constructed notion of "Westernization." Making sense of these debates necessarily entails reassessing how scholars understand secularism as well as a more historicized understanding of feminist struggle around it. Ultimately, women activists failed to achieve their goals, not because they used a language of secularism that was at odds with the religious foundations of family law, but because the laws were eminently compatible with the normative visions of gender roles and family relationships embodied in the Nasser regime's modernizing project.

BEFORE THE DUAL LEGAL SYSTEM

The legal system that the postrevolutionary government inherited had its roots in the colonial period and the legal reforms of the late nineteenth century. Prior to that time, personal status courts did not exist in Egypt or anywhere else in the Ottoman Empire. Legal matters, both civil and criminal, were adjudicated through the *shari'a* courts on the basis of Islamic law or, in the case of Christians and Jews, the *milliyya* (confessional) courts.[2] *'Urf* (customary law) also played a critical role in legal practices, influencing local preferences for particular schools of legal interpretation and strategic choices by plaintiffs on how and where particular sorts of cases were raised. Thus, although the Hanafi school of legal interpretation provided the basis of Ottoman executive law (*qanun*), plaintiffs had recourse to the other recognized schools of law that were practiced in the *shariʿa* courts.[3] In Egypt, the Shafiʿi school was favored in the Delta, and the Maliki in Upper Egypt, although in practice the Egyptian public could raise cases in front of a judge from the *madhhab* (school of legal interpretation) of their choice.[4] Decisions by jurists were interpretive, based on the practice of referencing and interpreting texts rather than on codes promulgated by the governing authority.

What did this mean for women and the adjudication of gender relations in the family? Recent works based on Ottoman court records have argued that the fluid nature of adjudication often (although not always) worked in the interests of women, who used the court system regularly as a way to assert their legal rights.[5] Judges, who were not bound by standardized codes of law, had greater room for interpretation and opted for "an approach that led away from confrontation and conflict and toward harmony in the community as well as the protection of its weaker members."[6] Thus, while the law privileged male power in the family by legitimizing the husband's authority and the wife's duty of marital obedience, emphasizing the primacy of male needs and desires in divorce and highlighting the role of the father as provider, protector, and transmitter of lineage, jurists and courts often elaborated and enforced the rights that women did have under the law in order to protect them from abuse and coercion. The legal system thus generally honored a woman's right to choose a husband, to enter marriage as a propertied person, to demand adequate support for herself, and to negotiate a divorce at her own initiative. Such courts, which were authorized to adjudicate the cases of all parties that came before them, were patronized not only by Muslims but also sometimes by Christians seeking to gain divorces or register marriages, which would then follow the principles of *shariʿa* law.[7]

Egyptian legal reforms of the late nineteenth century, the culmination of a legal reform process that started during the reign of Muhammad Ali Pasha, drastically altered the terrain of law and adjudication. In 1876, the establishment of the Mixed Courts ushered in a system of civil law based on the Napoleonic Code. These courts were confined to adjudicating disputes between Egyptians and foreigners. In 1883, however, one year after the British had occupied Egypt, a modified version of this civil code was compiled for the new

National (*ahliyya*) Courts. The new National Courts assumed jurisdiction over criminal and commercial matters. Matters related to marriage, divorce, custody, guardianship, and inheritance remained the judicial province of the *shariʿa* and *milliyya* courts.

SECULARISM, LEGAL REFORM, AND THE FAMILY

Relegation of *shariʿa* law to matters of "personal status" was integral to two related processes that shaped the emergence of modern nation-state institutions in Egypt during the first decades of the twentieth century: delineation of the parameters of Egyptian secularism, and elaboration of the family as a site to be regulated by public bodies and institutions. Unlike secular states in Europe, which confine religion (as a matter of faith, custom, and belief) to the realm of the private and relegate religious institutions to minor functions in the public sphere, Egyptian secularism entailed the engineered inclusion of Islam within the political and legal system rather than its exclusion.[8] The laws governing the family in Egypt are perhaps the most visible and publicly contested manifestation of this engineered inclusion. Restricting the jurisdiction of *shariʿa* to matters of "personal status" (*al-ahwal al-shakhsiyya*) served the function of defining a new public space for religion and religious authority within the framework of state law.[9] It also reflected a relatively new understanding of the family as a social unit and of its relationship to public politics and citizenship.

Confining *shariʿa* to domestic matters politicized the family both as a sphere of intimate, affective relations and as a repository of group identity of which religious affiliation was a defining legal and moral characteristic. A committee made up of religious leaders incorporated rules from the various *madhahib* to create a single, unified body of law and procedure, which was then reviewed by the minister of justice and approved by the prime minister. Such reforms institutionalized the authority of religious officials to legally regulate the shape and content of kin relations and the domestic realm, now enshrined in law as a privileged site for the preservation of religious identity underpinned by the sanction of secular state institutions.

Languages of privacy that entered the legal discourse around matters of personal status concurrently with the limiting of the *shariʿa*'s jurisdiction served to create "the family" as both a private space and one that was central to political order.[10] The subsequent codification of the Muslim personal status laws that occurred over the course of the 1920s was an integral part of defining the family as a legal category.

Such changes occurred in part because of an intensive campaign by the Egyptian Feminist Union, which had placed modification of the personal status laws at the top of its reform agenda. After an unsuccessful attempt in 1923 to gain voting rights for women, the EFU turned its attention to improving the status of women within the family. Using the rhetoric of liberal-nationalist feminism, reformers launched their critique of family law from within a maternalist framework and built their arguments around new ideals of domesticity to give women more rights as wives and mothers. They called for an increase in the minimum age of marriage, the expansion of women's right to divorce, the abolition of polygamy, and making divorce subject to a judge's approval.[11] They were partially successful. Later legal reforms raised the minimum age of marriage (to sixteen for girls, and eighteen for boys), made state registration of marriage a requirement, and rationalized male divorce pronouncements (*talaq*).[12] Amendments laid out provisions for judicial divorce by the wife on the basis of *darar*, or harm, making marital discord (*shiqaq*) grounds for divorce. Harm was defined broadly and could encompass not only physical deeds but also words, and by law was to be interpreted according to circumstances and social conditions.[13] In spite of the very different status of marriage within Coptic law, which recognized marriage as a holy sacrament sanctified by God rather than as a contract between two people, contemporaneous changes in Coptic family law mirrored the general trends toward reform in the Muslim personal status laws.

The codification of family law created a dual legal system that underpinned new sorts of gendered and confessional hierarchies both within individual families and within the new nation-state. Women became legal dependents of their husbands and of their confessional communities. In some respects this reified existing legal and social norms, which recognized women as dependents of their male kin. However, the recognition of women as legal individuals with rights that had to be protected by the state was new. In addition, the provisions of the law reflected a wholly new understanding of marriage as an intimate, affective relationship between husband and wife.

The codification of family law established the gendered roles of mother and wife and of husband and father as a legal basis of personhood and citizenship upon which rights and duties were accorded. While such rights and duties recognized generally prevailing social norms that viewed men and women as having complementary (and unequal) roles within Egyptian society, they also reflected new notions of the family and familial relationships that cut across religious divisions. The new personal status laws reflected an idealized construct of the bourgeois nuclear family, which privileged the relationship between husband and wife over other sorts of kin relationships. The idea of compatibility and intimacy as the basis of the marital bond informed provisions that made a husband's prolonged absence or incurable illness a basis for divorce, rationalized *talaq* pronouncements, raised the minimum age of marriage, and made *darar* (harm) a legitimate basis for a female-initiated divorce. Such measures were instituted on the basis that companionate marriage was the key to reforming Egyptian families, and the place of women in them, in a way that was consistent with the dictates of a "modern" and civilized society.

Despite the failure of the Egyptian Feminist Union to achieve key demands such as the abolition of polygamy and making divorce subject to judicial approval, the provisions of the law related to marriage and custody were largely compatible with turn-of-the-century modernizing discourses on the emancipation of women, which linked their rights and status within the family to the transformation of marital law and practice.[14] Thus, the personal status code laid out the conditions through which women could obtain a divorce, receive support from their husbands, retain custody of their children, and contest marriages concluded by their male guardians without their consent. It was precisely this recognition of rights, however, that constituted women as dependent legal subjects and emphasized male familial authority. The provisions of the new family law made wifely obedience and financial dependence the basis of the marital relationship.[15] A wife who had a judgment of disobedience against her could be returned forcibly to her husband's home by the police. The practice of legally enforcing a wife's residence within the marital household is known as *bayt al-ta'a*, or "house of obedience."[16] As wives and mothers, women were entitled to economic support and protection from "harm" in exchange for obedience, while unilateral divorce was rigidly enshrined as a male prerogative. At the same time, the legal delineation of the conditions under which either husbands or wives could obtain a divorce privileged new notions of companionate marriage based on the authority of the male breadwinner at the expense of wider male kin—and may actually have made divorce more difficult to obtain for both parties. Egyptian secularism thus presumed a particular form of family and a model of gendered citizenship consistent with it, both of which were strikingly apparent in the policies and legal provisions of the Nasser period.

UNIFICATION OF THE COURT SYSTEM

In 1955, the Nasser regime announced its intention to dismantle the existing religious courts, which included over fourteen recognized confessional legislative bodies and eight separate legal codes, and create a new, unified national court system (*al-mahkama al-wataniyya*).[17] The nationalization of the court system was one of a number of measures taken by the government over the course of the 1950s and early 1960s that aimed at curbing the political and economic autonomy of the *ulama* (the Muslim religious establishment) and other religious authorities in the interests of centralization and the consolidation of state control. These measures included the nationalization of *waqfs* (religious endowments) in 1952 and the 1961 reorganization of al-Azhar University, which transformed it into a state-controlled religious university.[18] Unlike *shari'a* courts, whose judiciary had come to be licensed and appointed by the state, within the preunification statutes confessional communities had retained jurisdiction to adjudicate their own personal status cases, run their own courts, and appoint their own judges. Whereas the personal status codes for Muslims were promulgated by the Egyptian legislature in conjunction with religious authorities and judges were government officials, the law courts of Christians and Jews were largely internally regulated by their respective communities. The existence of multiple courts thus structured gendered citizenship differently for different communities. Egyptian Muslim women seeking to obtain their rights in court entered into a direct relationship with the state, while women from other confessional communities were subject to the jurisdiction of their own communities. While the existence of these courts upheld the principle of the family as the receptacle of group identity, their different relationship to the state suggests that the overlaps between religious and national identity were legally hierarchical.

Within the new system, the judiciary of the *shari'a* courts were to be retained and absorbed into the new courts where they would share jurisdiction over family cases with civilly trained judges.[19] No such provision was made for the judiciary of the confessional courts.[20] The abolition of the *milliyya* courts provoked a tide of outrage from the Christian community. On October 3, 1955, leaders of Egypt's Christian communities sent a memorandum to Gamal Abdel Nasser arguing that unification of the court system did not effect the abolition of all religious courts on an equal footing but replaced confessional legal institutions with Islamic ones.[21] While legal reforms attempted to undermine the judicial autonomy of confessional communities, then, they also reaffirmed the rights of communities to preserve their cultural and religious distinctiveness within a system in which the centralizing state claimed full legal sovereignty. Rather than create a new, unified personal status code to go with the new, unified court system, the personal status codes of each confessional community, hammered out in the 1920s, remained the basis for the adjudication of family matters. In other words, though the structure of the court system changed, the actual laws did not.

Preserving the original personal status codes intact while at the same time abolishing the confessional court system constituted, in effect, a gendered legal compromise that attempted to balance between the authority of the state, individuals, and communities. The state privileged the rights of confessional communities to have their family matters adjudicated by their own laws over the institution of a uniform civil code (like that instituted in Turkey in 1926, and Tunisia in 1956), which would have (at least formally) recognized the rights of women and men from all confessional communities equally. At the same time, however, the unification itself was explicitly linked to the protection of citizens' rights by the national state. In the explanatory memorandum that accompanied the new law, officials stated that the law was designed to counteract the "anarchy" that accompanied the adjudication of family matters:

> The rules of public law require that the sovereignty of the state be complete and absolute in the interior and all those who live in it, without distinction of nationality, be submitted to the laws of the country, to its courts and to a single jurisdiction. . . . there should not remain in the country any vestige of an exceptional organization which would limit the power and sovereignty of the state vis a vis certain categories of citizens. . . . That sentences concerning the very status of a person be carried out by non-responsible jurisdictions acting without the intervention of the state . . . this is in opposition to national sovereignty.[22]

The memorandum went on to argue that the government, in abolishing the *shari'a* courts and the confessional courts, was establishing its commitment to "fulfilling its duties with regard to the judicial organization by facilitating the path to justice for all its citizens without distinction or partiality."[23] The potential conflict between the rights of communities to religious "freedom" and the rights of individuals to legal justice "without distinction" was avoided by reasserting the authority of religious law over families and the women in them. The hierarchies of gendered citizenship of the previous era were reconstituted under the new auspices of a unified, national court system, which now sanctioned those hierarchies as truly national rather than confessional.

Given the difficulties of accessing court records for the post-1955 period, it is hard to know the effects this unification might have had on individual women and the opportunities that legal reforms may have opened or closed for them. It is possible to speculate that such a move may have given women more space for negotiation vis-à-vis confessional communities while at the same time reducing the sorts of leverage they might bring to bear on the men in individual families. Without accounting for differences of class, religion, or location, however, such speculation is perhaps more useful in raising questions than providing answers.

CITIZENSHIP AND THE PERSONAL STATUS LAWS

The period following the unification of the court system and the promulgation of the 1956 constitution, which granted women the right to vote and hold public office, offered what seemed to be new opportunities for women activists to effect personal status reform. The representation of women in parliament (albeit highly limited) represented the opening of a new institutionalized space to women interested in advocating for social and legal change. Moreover, the climate seemed to suggest that progressive reform would meet with official support at the highest levels of government. The rhetoric of revolutionary change, coupled with the diminishing autonomy of the religious establishment, appeared to herald the promise that the continuing gendered inequalities enshrined in family law could be redressed. After a number of false starts, the Nasser regime announced, in 1961, that it was convening a committee to draw up recommendations for bringing personal status law in line with the requirements of a progressive Arab Socialist society.[24] And yet, despite the fact that personal status reform occupied a central place in public debate throughout the late 1950s and 1960s, there were no significant modifications to the personal status laws until 1979.[25]

Rereading from the vantage point of the successful campaign waged by Egyptian women activists, which resulted in significant legal reforms in 2000, scholars have tended to dismiss debates over personal status law during this period as a conflict between the liberal-secular aspirations of feminists and modernist reformers on the one hand, and on the other, the gender conservatism of male parliamentarians and the religious establishment, who for the most part, opposed reform. While such an explanation appeals from the vantage point of the present to commonsensical understandings of religion (represented by the religious establishment) and secularism (represented by feminists and other modernizing reformers) as dichotomous categories, I would suggest that leaving the concept of "the secular" and its relationship to state feminism uninvestigated and undefined risks eliding much of the complexity of both.

Nasserist constructs of citizenship both enabled and limited the sorts of claims that women activists could effectively make on the state. It enabled women to use a new language of rights to justify the necessity for legal change and made it difficult to dismiss out of hand calls for change, but it restricted the ways in which those struggles could be waged. Recourse to the languages and concepts of secular modernity were in this case particularly ineffective in securing changes, not only because they ran counter to appeals to religious authenticity but because the existing laws were themselves the product of a secularizing, modernizing process.

The Nasser regime's project of state feminism embodied both the concept of abstract individual rights, which accrued to citizens on the basis of their participation in national development, and the concept of gendered relational rights in the family. According to Suad Joseph, "In the liberal tradition, citizenship is an attribute of the individual and the individual is the bearer of rights."[26] By contrast, in many Middle Eastern countries, she argues, "a widely supported construct of self-hood is relational. This construct of self-hood is linked to a relational notion of rights. Relational rights are generated by and embedded in specific relationships (such as those between a daughter and father and between a husband and wife)."[27]

In Egypt (as in many Middle Eastern countries) the personal status laws were the most fundamental institutional expression of this notion of relational rights, but they were also spelled out in the 1956 constitution and later reaffirmed by the National Charter. While the 1956 constitution, the National Charter, and laws dealing with employment and education affirmed the rights that all Egyptians held as individuals, Article 18 of the constitution declared that the state was to secure, in accordance with the law, the support of the family and the protection of mothering (*al-ummuma*) and childhood (*al-tufula*).[28] The family, as the "base of society," was constituted by religion, ethics, and patriotism (*al-din, al-akhlaq wa al-wataniyya*).[29] The National Charter went on to affirm the family's status as the "first cell of society," which must be "afforded all means of protection so that it might be better able to preserve the national tradition and to reproduce its social fabric."[30] It was mothers and wives, as reproducers of future generations of Egyptian citizens, who were to bear the marks of Egyptian cultural difference.

Official discourses on state feminism did not, however, articulate individual rights and relational rights as mutually exclusive categories. The intent of the laws and social programs aimed at mobilizing women was explicitly couched as helping women fulfill their roles both as "mothers of the nation" and as equal citizens and participants in national development. The task of reconciling conflicts that might arise between the various rights and responsibilities that accrued to citizens was claimed as the purview solely of the state as the guardian and guarantor of "the public good."[31] Documents like the Constitution and the "Charter for National Action" explicitly recognized the sovereignty of the religious establishment over aspects of national culture and the family as the site of its reproduction. This sovereignty, however, did not exist in a vacuum. At any given historical moment there are multiple claimants to religious authority with competing claims to knowledge. The existence of these competing claims shapes not only the meaning and content of Egyptian secularism but also the possibilities of change and contestation.

The state's campaign to circumscribe the institutional authority of the official *ulama*, beginning in the 1950s, coupled with its suppression of independent religious institutions and the imprisonment of Islamist activists in 1954, might at first glance suggest that those seeking to further restrict the institutional power of religion over everyday life would be in a good position to succeed.[32] Paradoxically, the state's measures may have strengthened claims against reforming personal status law. Having co-opted the religious establishment by simultaneously reducing its autonomy, repressing dissenting voices and competing authorial claims, as well as giving it access to state funding, the state also accorded those within the official *ulama* who were willing to work within the new system an institutional monopoly over religious authority. In some cases, the state used its new control over religious institutions to garner support for its policies, as in the case of family planning (see Chapter 4), by promulgating *fatawas* (religious opinions) or by influencing the content of the Friday sermon (*khutba*) delivered in state-controlled mosques. But in the case of the personal status laws, the state's apparent reluctance to pressure the religious establishment to support modifications to the existing laws suggests a tacit bargain between the state and religious leaders; while the power of the religious establishment was reduced in some areas, in the case of family law the repression of competing claims may have strengthened the position of the official *ulama*, many of whom were antireform, who could now claim a privileged position as interpreters of what constituted legitimate religious practice and textual interpretation. In such a situation, female activists and their supporters were in a particularly disadvantaged position to effect changes that would address the gendered inequalities of the laws.

CAMPAIGNING FOR REFORM: DIVORCE AND *BAYT AL-TA'A*

The changes proposed by women activists and their supporters were not aimed at overturning the dual legal system or the framework of gendered relational rights that underpinned it. Among their demands were that child custody decisions be made by the court system, that the taking of a second wife be subject to a judges' permission, that divorce pronouncements be certified by a judge, that divorced wives be given compensation for ill-treatment or frivolous divorce petitions by their husbands, the abolition of compulsory obedience verdicts, and the abolition of a rule that automatically transferred custody of children to their father if their mother remarried. They challenged male rights to unilateral divorce and to take a second wife, the father's ownership in his children, and the legal principle of obedience as the foundation of women's marital rights.

The approach of proreform women put the formal legal regime at the forefront of the struggle for women's empowerment. It placed responsibility for women's status on the posture of the state, expressed in its laws, rather than on the women who lived within that legal system.[33] The professional women who were the most vocal and public in their calls for reform were the prime beneficiaries of state feminism: educated, middle-class women who held prominent positions in the public sector. Amina Sa'id, in addition to serving as the editor in chief of Egypt's leading women's magazine, *Hawwa'*, was also vice president of the press syndicate. Suhayr Qalamawi was a literary critic and head of the Department of Arabic Literature at Cairo University. 'Aisha 'Abd al-Rahman (known popularly by her pen name, Bint al-Shati') was the chair of the Arabic department at the girls' college at 'Ain Shams University; and 'Aziza Hussein was a prominent social reformer and Egypt's representative to the United Nations Commission on the Status of Women. Mufida 'Abd al-Rahman, the only woman to serve on the 1963 reform committee, was a member of the board of the lawyers' syndicate. As beneficiaries of Nasserist state-building, it is therefore not surprising that in their attempts to advocate for legal change, reformers focused less on gaining new rights for women within marriage (such as new grounds for female-initiated divorce or mothers' absolute right to custody of their children) than they did on trying to persuade the state to take a more active role in restricting the rights of men as husbands and fathers. Thus, their battle was fought largely over state regulation of the affective, intimate ties of family and kin relations.

What forms of state regulation were necessary to protect and police relations deemed to be both intimate and critical to national well-being and public welfare was a question that lay at the heart of discussions over two of the most contentious issues under consideration for reform by the committee: the "restriction" (*taqayid*) of divorce, which would have made husbands' rights to divorce their wives subject to judicial approval, and the legal constitution of wifely obedience as the foundation of marriage, specifically the compulsory enforcement of *bayt al-ta'a* (house of obedience) verdicts. According to a series of court decisions at the turn of the century, which were later institutionalized in the personal status codes, a disgruntled husband could have his wife declared "disobedient" (*nushuz*) by a judge and forcibly returned to the marital household by police if she had left it. Such a judgment was referred to as *bayt al-ta'a*.[34]

In discussions over divorce and *bayt al-ta'a*, the notion of companionate marriage was both a crucial focal point of debate and contestation, and a shared point of reference—particularly the concept of *mu'ashara*. *Mu'ashara* means, variously, "intimate association," "intimacy," "companionship," and "joint-ness." It was often used to depict the normative affective bonds of marital and familial life and evoked the constellation of subjectivities and practices associated with companionate marriage. In their contests to define the scope and content of state intervention into domestic relations, reformers and opponents of reform alike appealed to notions of trust, affection, and consent as the basis of the marital relationship. Moreover, both groups not only linked companionate marriage to the preservation of the social and political order but also saw it as integrally linked to issues of rights, freedom, and citizenship.

In arguing for more state regulation of divorce, reformers deployed a new language of rights, which argued that unions violating the tenets of marital intimacy were antithetical to women's status as enfranchised citizens in a modern nation-state. Amina Shafiq, a prominent journalist for *Al-Ahram*, pointed out that while working women held the same political and economic rights as men (such as the right to an equal wage and the right to safe working conditions), their rights within the family remained outside the realm of state protection. The Egyptian woman remained "restrict[ed] to her home with shackles which tie her to her husband."[35] From *Hawwa*'s editorial page Amina Sa'id helped spearhead the reform campaign, becoming one of its most public and recognizable faces. In a 1959 editorial, one of a series dedicated to the issue of legal reform, Sa'id wrote: "*Al-ahwal al-shakhsiyya* in our country was put in place 100 years ago and there have not been any fundamental modifications to it up to today. . . . The woman, who at that time was bought by a man at the slave market . . . has become today—with the constitution's recognition of her rights—a complete citizen."[36] Sa'id went on to argue that women made material contributions as wives and mothers to the well-being of their families. The Egyptian woman worked in fields and in factories or in other waged work; she washed clothes and raised children. However, unlike the material labor she had formerly performed under conditions of "subjugation," as a slave, her efforts now emanated from her desire to assist her husband in creating a shared future and a better life. It was thus the affective bonds between husbands and wives (as well as the labor she performed on that basis) that entitled her to live "honorably" in her home, a condition the existing legislation did not allow.

One of the more striking aspects of reformist discourses on legal reform was the extent to which women's political subjectivity was viewed as contingent on the legal policing and regulation of male behavior. Ali Hamdi al-Jamal, a columnist for *Al-Ahram* newspaper, wrote that reform was necessary to protect wives from the "deviant" behavior of some husbands.[37] Men who violated the tenets of intimacy (either by keeping a wife against her will or by cruelly and recklessly abandoning her) not only violated the "honor" of women but also violated the social and political order.

In a 1959 article, Suhayr Qalamawi disputed the characterization of *al-ahwal al-shakhsiyya* as a personal, private matter: "a thousand homes divided and threatened with collapse . . . doesn't count as a personal danger because from these homes the nation is created. . . . There are no laws of personal status, there are general laws of public social status and the status of the Islamic community [*umma*] bound by the good of the nation."[38] She went on to argue that Islam placed limits on the male right of divorce, by laying out provisions for arbitration by the families of the divorcing couple before the divorce was effected, and by making divorce irrevocable only after the third iteration of *talaq* was pronounced: "How to reconcile between this and the unruly, absolute freedom without fetters or conditions which is divorce under the law? . . .

We are in the second half of the 20th century. We are in a time in which the meaning of freedom has developed greatly. Freedom is not bound by limiting the harm to others alone. But it is limited today by the public good."[39] Just as the state was required to limit the freedoms of its citizens in public to preserve the public good, it was also required to limit the freedoms of men in the family in order to protect women and children from the effects of male tyranny. Such protection, reformers argued, was fundamental to the constitution of women as free political beings.

Those who were most vocal in their opposition to regulating divorce did not dispute reformers' characterization of divorce as a social problem, nor did they fundamentally challenge reformers' conceptualization of men as utilizing their rights irresponsibly. Moreover, while antireform arguments often did consist of monolithically constructed appeals to Islam or to the natural, ontological differences between men and women, the argument against reforming divorce provisions was most often constructed using the very terms of companionate marriage and conjugal intimacy that lay at the heart of modernist notions of proper family relations.

Those who opposed making divorce subject to a judge's ruling argued that just as women should have the freedom to choose a marriage partner on the basis of compatibility, men and women should also be free to divorce without recourse to the court system when such compatibility was no longer present. Munira Husni was an activist who had been involved in women's charitable organizations since the 1930s, and in the late 1940s had been a member of Duriyya Shafiq's organization, Bint al-Nil Union. Her book *Marriage and Divorce* was written as a response to the debates over personal status reform. According to Husni, the male right to divorce in Islam was not a "game or a whim" that men could exploit unconditionally but was already limited by religion. It was no secret, Husni argued, that the call for restricting divorce displayed all the marks of "European secularism," which was incompatible with national and religious identity.[40]

In spite of the specter of European secularism, which was not infrequently invoked by those who opposed amending the personal status laws, it would be a mistake to read that invocation as a defense of "tradition" or a rejection of "modern" forms of domestic relations. Husni also tied her opposition to restricting divorce to a notion of companionate marriage based on the mutual consent and affection of husbands and wives, which was itself a product of European constructions of secularism. "How can we women demand the freedom to choose a husband," she asked, "and then demand at the same time the absence of freedom to end the same marriage if its lack of soundness is established or the corruption of married life between the spouses is established?" She argued that regulating divorce would damage the trust and affection between men and women that constituted the basis of proper marital relations. "If we assume that all men trifle with marriage and aren't capable of fulfilling their responsibilities," she wrote, "doesn't that mean a lack of trust between men and women? For how can a woman feel safe with a man she has no trust in, just because the law safeguards her rights?"[41] Drawing on a similar notion of companionate marriage, *Al-Ahram* columnist Jamal al-Atayfi wrote that putting divorce in the hands of a judge risked creating *fitna* (chaos) in the family. If a judge refuses a husband's petition for divorce, he would be forced to continue in a marriage without "affection" or "love." In the absence of an abiding emotional tie between the spouses, "the marital relation becomes based not on consent but on subjugation."[42]

Others, such as Shaykh al-Azhar Muhammad Shaltut argued that penalties against frivolous use of divorce already existed in the law. He went on to argue that courts had to be more consistent in leveling penalties against men who had misused their marital rights or failed in their marital duties as prescribed by *shari'a*. If the courts were more diligent in implementing Islamic law, he wrote, "then divorce would be virtually unknown in families" and there would be no need to discuss modifying the existing legislation.[43]

One of the most often voiced criticisms of restricting divorce was that it would undermine the intimacy of marital and familial bonds by exposing them to public gaze. A well-known fashion commentator who wrote under the pen name "Mediha" devoted one installment of her long-standing fashion column in *Ruz al-yusuf* to the subject under the headline "Restricting Divorce Won't Prevent Its Occurrence."[44] "There are divorces which occur for reasons of moral [lapse], whether by the husband or the wife, and if they happen in front of a judge, they will inevitably disclose family secrets which could inflict pain upon the children and shatter their feelings toward one of their two parents." Such concerns were paramount to the eventual absence of judicial divorce from the reform package. According to Muhammad Faraj al-Sanhuri, the chair of the reform committee, the committee's decision not to restrict divorce was based in part on the imperative to protect the "family secrets" of Egyptian citizens from the public scrutiny a court case might bring. Even if family court proceedings remained closed, he argued, the details of cases would remain in the files and reports related to the case as a matter of public record. Children, he said, might then be able to read the damning testimony given by their parents. Thus it was not only the public performance of going to court and giving testimony that constituted a violation of privacy but the very existence of information, recorded for the purposes of adjudication and governance, that constituted a violation of the intimate bonds of marriage and the authority—of husbands over wives, and parents over children—on which the reproduction of those bonds was based.

It's important to note that opponents of reform were not monolithic in their advocacy of limiting the state's jurisdiction over marital relationships, nor were reform proponents always in favor of extending state authority. Unlike the case of judicial divorce, in which reformers called for the state to more actively intervene in marital disputes, in the case of *bayt al-ta'a* they appealed to notions of intimacy and companionate marriage to define the desired *limits* of state regulation. This suggests the extent to which the concept of marital intimacy was foundational to debates but also flexible: it was appropriated in multiple ways and deployed by various groups to articulate competing visions of family law and its role in regulating marital relations.

Reformers argued that police enforcement of *ta'a* rulings was both damaging to the dignity of women and inconsistent with notions of companionate marriage. 'Aisha 'Abdel Rahman, a writer and professor of Arabic literature known more popularly by her pen name "Bint al-Shati'," argued that just as the Qur'an stated there was no compulsion in religion, there was also no compulsion in a marriage concluded according to correct Islamic principles. Without consent, marriage was reduced to a form of bondage little different from feudal relations of slavery.[45] The equation of *bayt al-ta'a* with feudal relations of slavery was a common trope utilized by its opponents. Jundi al-Munqabadi, an agricultural engineer who was interviewed as part of a reader survey conducted by *Al-Ahram* on the proposed personal status laws, argued that compulsory *bayt al-ta'a* judgments should be abolished on the grounds that it was inconsistent for a husband to compel his wife to live with him by force "in a time when all laws guarantee the freedom of the individual and absence of bondage and slavery."[46]

As in debates over divorce, normative visions of what constituted appropriate male behavior within marriage were a formative part of these reformist discourses. The "house of obedience," its opponents argued, constituted not only a violation of the dignity of women but a violation of the tenets of

manliness upon which companionate marriage was based. *Al-Ahram* columnist Ali Hamdi al-Jamal, an outspoken advocate of personal status reforms,
wrote: "In my opinion, merely the transfer of the wife to the house of obedience is a threat not only to the honor of the woman but to her existence
as a human being. It's not proper for a husband to impose upon a woman
who doesn't want to live with him."[47] Ibrahim Gadalla, dean of the Mansura Religious Institute, argued that the absence of companionable relations
between husbands and wives "sullied" the marital relationship, making the
marital home a source of corruption that undermined male claims to authority. "There's nothing in masculinity where the man brings fault/uncleanliness
into his home," he wrote in an editorial.[48]

What was clear in such discussions was that opponents of compulsory execution of *ta'a* judgments saw a particular kind of masculinity (one that relied
on force to exact compliance from wives) as antithetical to a vision of marriage based on cooperation and intimacy. What was perhaps more ambiguous
was reformers' stance on the principle of wifely obedience. Most reformers
didn't condemn the principle that a wife owed obedience to her husband, but
they were concerned about how that obedience was to be obtained—through
consent or through subjugation. In reformers' attacks on *ta'a*, what appears
is a vision of marriage based on marital intimacy that didn't ultimately question a husband's authority, merely the means by which authority was to be
enforced.

Its defenders, however, characterized *bayt al-ta'a* not as something that
underpinned unrestrained and despotic male familial authority but as the
institutionalization of the principle of wifely obedience, which was a cornerstone of marriage and the gendered rights and duties that were its foundation. They rejected the characterization of state enforcement of *ta'a* verdicts as
compulsion, arguing instead that it constituted the protection of marriage as
a legal and moral institution. Ali 'Abd al-Wahid wrote in an opinion piece in
Al-Ahram: "Husbands and wives both have rights and responsibilities. [Laws]
are for achieving balance between the two . . . and for stabilizing of the life of
the family. One of the most important of these duties for the husband is the
financial maintenance of the family and fulfilling these duties stands as the
counterpoint to his rights over his wife and the duties she has towards him."[49]
He argued that there was nothing "backward" or unique to Islamic law about
the principle of obedience: it was also a guiding principle of marriage as a
moral and legal institution in civilized (*mutahadira*) countries generally. In

France, he pointed out, the husband was legally required to provide for the upkeep and maintenance of his wife, to provide for her all the necessities of life, and thus was entitled to obedience from his wife.[50] The role of the court, as Wahid and others argued, was to uphold the precepts of relational rights, which entailed maintaining a balance between gender-specific rights and duties. Shaykh Abu Zahra, a professor of Islamic law at Cairo University, who published widely on issues surrounding Islam and the family, pointed out that "Islam, pursuant to its basic rules imposes support on the husband and obedience upon the wife."[51] Thus, if a judge could legally compel a husband to provide financial support to his wife, he was also fully justified in ruling against the wife on the grounds of disobedience.

In 1967, compulsory enforcement of *ta'a* verdicts was ended by an executive order issued by the minister of justice. The principle of wifely obedience, however, remained a component of family law. While women would no longer be forcibly returned to their husband's home by the police, a woman judged "disobedient" by the court forfeited her economic right to support by her husband. According to Egyptian Grand Mufti Hasan Ma'mun, *bayt al-ta'a* would remain in the draft law on the principle that

> the wife is legally responsible to be in the home of her husband, participating with him in married life and to co-operate in its stability. . . . The husband has the right to present his problem to the court if the wife leaves the home. The law clearly articulates that the wife's right to support [*nafaqa*] which is the duty of her husband becomes null and void if she opposes a judge's order to return to the home of her husband."[52]

The official position thus did not constitute a rejection of the state's responsibility to regulate family life nor an uncomplicated rearticulation of bourgeois European notions of the domestic as a private realm. The limits placed on the abilities of husbands to exercise their rights to obedience were not to emanate from the state in its role as the arbiter of freedoms in the civic realm (as they did in reformist discourses) but instead from its role of maintaining the family as the terrain of religious law and the site of communal identity. In fact, the stated reason for the 1967 abolition of compulsory enforcement of "house of obedience" judgments was because it undermined the Islamically prescribed system of rights and duties that lay at the heart of the family. According to al-Sanhuri, "Our decision was not to abolish *bayt al-ta'a* because it was contrary to human expression, but in fact because it was established that verdicts of obedience had become a way to nullify judgments of support . . . the woman who doesn't comply with a verdict of obedience doesn't deserve any regard because she is bound by the judgments of her religion and the law and the courts."[53]

CONCLUSION

In the 1950s and 1960s, at a time in Egyptian history when there was an explicit government commitment to improving women's status, why didn't family law reform proponents achieve their goals? One reason is that the vision of marriage contained within the personal status laws was eminently compatible with the model of family promoted by the state—which stressed the male individual authority over women as breadwinners, companionate marriage as the basis of the marital relationship, and the obedience of wives to that authority on the basis of consent, obtained within the rubric of companionate unions. The one instance in which this was not the case was compulsory *ta'a* judgments, which were abolished in 1967. The vision of gender-specific relational rights embedded in family law was thus not antithetical to state feminism (or the model of citizenship that underpinned it) but was, in fact, an integral part of it.

4 THE FAMILY IS A FACTORY
Regulating Reproduction

> *The lane was teaming with youngsters scattered like breadcrumbs*
> *tumbling about in all directions, and getting in his way. They*
> *pulled at his shawl, knocked against him . . . all he could do was*
> *lash out at them, vituperating furiously against their fathers and*
> *forefathers, the rotten seed that gave them life, and the midwife*
> *who brought them into existence. Shaking with rage he cursed*
> *and swore and snorted and spat on the wretched town where brats*
> *sprouted out of the ground in greater numbers than the hairs on*
> *one's head.*[1]

IN HIS 1954 SHORT STORY "THE CHEAPEST NIGHTS," Yusuf Idris tells the story of
Abdel Karim, a peasant struggling to make ends meet in a small village in
the Egyptian Delta. The story revolves around Abdel Karim's attempts to fill
the hours in the evening after his work in the fields is done. With six children
he can barely feed and no money, even the simplest evening amusements of
the village—drinking tea, smoking a water pipe, sitting in a coffee shop—are
beyond his reach. "The Cheapest Nights" of the title are the long winter nights
of darkness when he turns to his wife for comfort with the inevitable result of
another child every year whom he is unable to support.

Two decades later, a cartoon appearing in the popular magazine *Ruz al-
Yusuf* offered a solution to the problem of the impoverished Egyptian couple,
living in squalor, crammed in a single room with too many children and with
nothing to fill their leisure time except sexual intercourse. It shows a woman
in bed while her brood of children sleep piled up on the floor surrounding her
(Figure 4.1). The caption quotes the words of one child: "Mama, we are too
many. Please don't listen to Daddy anymore!!!" This seemingly straightfor-
ward illustration of Egypt's "population problem" sent multiple, overlapping
messages: that women should feel empowered to take more control of their
reproductive agency vis-à-vis demanding husbands, that they should be more

Figure 4.1. Family planning cartoon: "Mama, we are too many." *Ruz al-Yusuf,* Jan. 27, 1969.

attentive to the material and physical well-being of their families when negotiating that most intimate of marital activities, and that reproduction (and
by extension sexuality itself) was a matter of female self-control, a message
underlined in the cartoon by the absence of the husband, whose purportedly
unrestrained impulses had led to the problem in the first place. The cartoon's
various messages are emblematic of how solving the relatively new problem of
"overpopulation" came to rest in the regulation of individual female bodies.

This chapter examines Egypt's establishment of a national family planning program in the late 1950s and 1960s. It considers how one aspect of secular
modernization, that of making reproduction a matter of public policy, placed
the intimate affairs and domestic arrangements of Egyptian citizens at the
forefront of public discussion and made them central to the objectives and
aspirations of state technocrats, religious officials, women activists, midwives,
and patients. I argue that the Egyptian family planning program was a normalizing project aimed at creating modernized families, bodies, and gendered
subjects as a means to social, economic, and political transformation.

Established in 1966, Egypt's national family planning program was a cornerstone of the Nasser regime's state-building program and plan for the development of a society based on the principles of Arab Socialism. Its primary aim was to combat what the government perceived as a crisis of overpopulation caused by declining infant mortality and elevated fertility rates among rural and working-class urban women. In its attempts to arrive at a solution to "the population problem," the Nasser regime drew both on prerevolutionary discourses that linked the reform of motherhood to social welfare, and on international shifts in demographic theory that posited the regulation of individual bodies as the key to controlling demographic growth. The establishment of a national family planning program in many respects relegated the management of reproduction to men in their capacities as heads of household and as policy makers and state functionaries. However, the adoption of a population program based on contraception also entailed the recognition of Egyptian women as reproductive subjects for whom using birth control was to constitute part of the duties of citizenship, even as it simultaneously delineated the normative parameters within which reproductive choice could be exercised. Egyptian women themselves, far from being passive objects of such policies, negotiated the reproductive politics of state family planning in ways that both challenged and reaffirmed its normative assumptions about gender, the body, and modernity.

THE PROBLEM OF OVERPOPULATION

In his book *Egypt's Destiny*, written in 1955 (barely a year after he had been ousted from office), former president Muhammad Neguib laid out what was then the unofficial Egyptian government line on combating overpopulation:

> Contraception has been suggested as the answer to Egypt's runaway population. In spite of religious objections, Christian as well as Moslem, the Council of the Revolution favors the control of births by every accepted means. But birth control by means of contraception is hardly feasible in villages where homes lack running water, toilets and electric lights. A more effective means of controlling births, we feel, is to provide the villages with the rudiments of modern civilization. The mere introduction of electric lights in certain Indian villages has tended to reduce the rate of their increase in population. There is no reason to believe that the introduction of electric lights in Egyptian villages will not have the same effect.[2]

Egypt's "runaway population" became a pressing concern for Egypt's new leaders almost as soon as they had taken power. As early as 1953 'Abbas 'Ammar, the minister of social affairs, had submitted a memorandum to the newly formed Permanent Council of Public Services highlighting the dangers of population growth to the health and well-being of the Egyptian people. 'Ammar called for the formation of a National Commission for Population Problems, charged with studying population trends and presenting recommendations for influencing demographic outcomes in a way that was consistent with Egyptian national planning.[3]

Largely discussed as an issue of rural reform in the pre-1952 era (see Chapter 1), overpopulation was taken up by the new revolutionary government as a problem to be remedied by state-driven development. Egyptian demographers and technocrats maintained that the primary reason for Egypt's low standard of living and the general misery of the lower classes was not unrestrained reproduction in and of itself but misdistribution of wealth and lack of development. Rejecting contraception as the solution to reducing birth rates, the regime adopted a socioeconomic approach which held that development and modernization would eventually result in a decrease in fertility rates. Egypt's new leaders were certainly not unique in this respect: this was the preferred strategy employed by many leaders in the newly postcolonial world and the global South who sought remedies for social and economic ills in smaller populations.[4]

Whereas proponents of birth control argued that use of contraception was a prerequisite for social and economic development, the unofficial Egyptian government position on decreasing population was that declining fertility (whether through contraceptive use or through other means) was a "natural" outcome of the historical process that all nations eventually underwent. Through state provision of the basic accoutrements of "modern civilization"—running water, toilets, electric lights—the rate of Egyptian peasant reproduction was expected to drop, further improving standards of living and aiding the process of Egypt's "transition" from a backward agricultural economy to a modern industrialized one, as had happened in Europe a hundred years previously. Transition theory was the 1940s brainchild of demographers at Princeton's influential Center for Population Research led by American demographer Frank Notestein. It offered a general historical model that tied fertility decline to Western-style modernization and political liberalization where the ingredients for demographic success included urbanization, industrialization, rising standards of living, education, the lessening influence of traditional religious and cultural institutions, and popular participation in political life.[5]

FROM TRANSITION TO CONTRACEPTION

The late 1950s and early 1960s saw a decisive shift from a socioeconomic approach to overpopulation to one based on family planning leading to the official announcement in 1962 that the regime would establish a national family planning program. This shift was due in part to the results of the 1960 census, which showed the highest recorded increases in fertility in the country's history.[6] According to census figures, by 1960 Egypt's population had reached twenty-six million and was growing at an annual rate of 2.34 percent. This was a significant increase over the 1.41 percent growth rate measured in the 1947 census.[7] It was not simply that Egypt's population was continuing to increase; it was that the rate of growth recorded by the census was the highest rate of growth ever recorded in the history of Egypt. But while the failure of large-scale development projects to halt Egypt's rapid population growth explains why policy makers eventually abandoned their reliance on the light bulb as a cure for Egypt's social ills, it does not explain why family planning in particular came to be (and remains) the centerpiece of Egyptian population policy.

To understand why family planning became the almost universally adopted solution to the problem of overpopulation, not only in Egypt but in much of the global South, requires a brief examination of post–Second World War developments in demographic theory and the global political shifts that underpinned them. Following the end of the war, demographers began to reject transition-based theories in favor of those that mandated active and direct forms of intervention in reproductive practices. The period immediately following the Second World War saw a proliferation of demographic studies among the countries of the global South, which were used as a testing ground for the validity of American demographic theories. Major fertility studies undertaken in India, Taiwan, Malaya, Egypt, Indonesia, the Philippines, Korea, and China indicated that despite improvements brought about by modernization, population growth rates continued to increase. Within the context of the emerging cold war global order, the demographic community and American and European policy makers reviewed the results of these studies with alarm.[8] Policy makers feared that the potential economic and social destabilization caused by runaway population increases in the "Third World" could upset the emerging global balance of power by making nations in Asia and Africa vulnerable to communist influence.[9] The political and ideological struggles of the immediate postwar period created a context for the rethinking of demographic theory and the emergence of demography as a "policy science" intimately related to US cold war strategies.[10] Increasingly, demographers argued that the only solution to the rising threat of population explosions in the developing parts of the world lay in the establishment of national family planning programs throughout the global South. Massive increases in funding for demographic research and the related creation of organizations such as the International Planned Parenthood Federation (IPPF) and the Population Council (both founded in 1952) gave these new forms of demographic knowledge a global, institutional basis.

Egypt had been a key case study for American demographers, both as a newly postcolonial nation and because of its potential to become a key US ally in the Middle East. The international assessment of Egypt's demographic situation was that the country was facing a population crisis of unprecedented levels. Princeton demographer Clyde Kiser, who presented the findings of a study he had conducted on Egypt at the 1944 Milbank Memorial Fund annual conference, concluded, "Egypt is in a demographic jam." He warned that its population would reach twenty-four million in 1970 if growth rates continued to increase.[11] Egyptian policy makers would certainly have been cognizant of such assessments; there was an Egyptian delegation present at both the IPPF's 1952 Bombay conference and its conference in Tokyo in 1955, which consisted of, among others, 'Abbas 'Ammar and demographer Hana Rizk, the head of the newly established Social Research Center at the American University in Cairo.

Echoing Kiser's conclusions, Rizk pointed out in his talk at the IPPF Tokyo conference that it had taken Egypt only half a century to double its population. If the current rate of national increase continued, he argued, it would take only another quarter century for Egypt to double its population again.[12] Such statistics were quoted in the Egyptian press with increasing frequency by policy makers and members of Egypt's intelligentsia. As Salah Namiq, a professor at the faculty of commerce at Cairo University, pointed out in an article that appeared in *Hawwa'*, the "language of numbers" was becoming a persuasive and oft deployed argument for the need to make birth control more widely available in Egypt.[13]

The official arguments for birth control not only were couched in statistical terms but were also linked to the regime's commitment to social transformation and construction of a socialist state. Drawing on the revolutionary rhetoric of social justice that stressed the "common welfare" and "basic needs" of Egypt's citizens, the Nasser era technocrats came to assert that the provision of birth control, like its provision of other social services, was part of its role in providing for its citizens and protecting the weaker members of society, particularly women and children. In 1960, the Egyptian Association for Population Studies, a quasi–state body made up of government officials, demographers, and medical personnel devoted to the study of "the population problem" and its possible cure, published a book about its recent activities.

The frontispiece of the book contained a picture of President Nasser and a quote underneath that read, "I want every child in the United Arab Republic to have a better life."[14] The book went on to link family planning with the state's responsibility to ensure the "basic constituents of a Socialist, Democratic and Cooperative Society":

> The state is to make available for all citizens an adequate level of living with regard to provision of food and dwelling as well as hygienic, cultural and social services. In accordance with the law, the state is to ensure the consolidation of the family and protection of motherhood and childhood. The state is to protect youth from exploitation as well as from moral, physical and spiritual negligence.[15]

In an interview several years later, Nasser defended the state's decision to adopt a population policy based on contraceptive provision, arguing that without a national family planning program, the state would be unable to provide "a decent standard of living" to Egypt's families."[16] Furthermore, birth control would improve the physical condition of Egyptian mothers, who often bore a large number of children at the expense of their own health.[17]

Nasserist notions of citizenship thus reinscribed interwar, liberal notions about social welfare within a new language of rights and obligations. As in the previous period, Nasserist discourses conceptualized the institution of measures aimed at promoting social well-being as a necessary component of the project of national uplift. What was new were the ways in which social welfare became the purview solely of the state in its capacity as guardian and protector of "the people." The state premised its legitimacy on its ability to provide the accoutrements of social and material well-being—clean water, sufficient food, sanitary houses, better health care—to all Egyptian citizens, particularly its most benighted, victimized, and excluded members.

Moreover, the adoption of family planning signaled not only new conceptions of citizenship but also a new approach to state-building. Whereas previous attempts to solve the population problem had focused on large social structures and their transformation, now state technocrats would focus on the transformation of individual behavior and the medical management of individual bodies.

ESTABLISHING AND IMPLEMENTING
A NATIONAL PROGRAM

In the 1961 "Charter for National Action," which laid out the Nasser regime's emerging plan for the development of an Arab Socialist society to benefit all Egyptian citizens, the state signaled its intention, for the first time, to develop a family planning program on the national level. In the section that addressed scientific planning, the document pointed out that population increase constituted "the most dangerous obstacle that faces the Egyptian people in their drive towards raising the standard of production in their country in an effective and efficient way. Attempts at family planning deserve the most sincere efforts by modern scientific methods."[18]

From the publication of the National Charter onward, family planning ceased to have the status of a "field experiment" and became a matter of national policy at the forefront of public attention.[19] In 1966, after four years of intensive planning, Egypt's National Family Planning Program was officially launched and 1,991 clinics—in government health bureaus, rural health units and combined centers, maternal and child health clinics, and outpatient departments of major hospitals—opened their doors three afternoons a week and provided contraception to Egyptian women on demand.[20] By far the most commonly distributed method of contraception was the birth control pill. For 10 piasters, clinic respondents received a monthly cycle of pills and a special "family planning stamp" on her national identification card. Other methods had been tried during the experimental phases of contraceptive nationalization. The diaphragm, despite positive results in the early days of the program, was not adopted because it was thought to be difficult for poor people to use because of the lack of running water and other sanitary facilities as well as privacy. This was also reported to be a problem with contraceptive suppositories and foam during the experimental phase of the program. Also, the prescription of pills, unlike the IUD (intrauterine device), could be done by a trained nurse or clinical practitioner, and did not require the presence of a doctor.[21]

The majority of clinics were attached to government health facilities: hospitals, mother-child health units, and rural health centers. Whether the clinic was run by the government or by a participating voluntary organization, the doctors and nurse practitioners (*hakimat*) who staffed the clinics were largely drawn from the staff of the Ministry of Public Health, who were farmed out to the family planning program.[22] Every clinic was also staffed by a social worker employed by the Ministry of Social Affairs who was charged not only with providing counseling about the benefits of family planning to clinic respondents but also with keeping statistics on the number of women served by the clinic and the social background of respondents, including age, number of children, education, and economic status. By April 1968, the number of clinics had grown to 2,631 and provided contraception to over 230,000 women.[23]

NEW FAMILIES, NEW CITIZENS

While the immediate aim of family planning, according to policy makers, was to reduce the average number of children being born to the target population (married Egyptian women between the ages of twenty and thirty-five) to three, it was also clear that the program was very explicitly about more than just limiting births.[24] According to Dr. Muhammad Raziq, general director of child health at the Ministry of Health and a pioneer in family planning efforts since the 1930s, "The basic goal of these units [which offer family planning services] is not to prevent pregnancy or to control births. The goal is to encourage, secure and organize it and thus to guarantee the production of happy, stable families ... which are in a position to conceive children who will grow up in complete health and will become, in the future, the youth of a healthy nation."[25] Raziq's focus on the qualitative benefits of using birth control—happier families and healthier children—was not in itself revolutionary. The idea that Egyptians, to paraphrase Ann Anagnost's work on China, should reproduce less to reproduce better was foundational to interwar discourses on population (see Chapter 1).[26] What was new was the emphasis on rationalization and scientific planning as a means to producing a new kind of family and a new kind of citizen. New definitions of inclusion and the regime's attempts to create a radically transformed social and political system legitimated a whole range of state interventions into the most intimate domains of life in the name of progress and social welfare.[27] Family planning was only one of many state measures that aimed at reshaping the spaces, practices, and affective bonds of Egyptian family life in a manner that was unprecedented in Egyptian history. The management of reproduction, like the inclusion of courses in personal hygiene in the newly expanded public school system, the subsidizing of household appliances like refrigerators, and the licensing of village midwives, was an attempt to create new sorts of families as a means to creating a modern society.

At a conference in 1964 on the Egyptian family, Minister of Social Affairs Hikmat Abu Zayd pointed out the importance of the Egyptian family as a site not only of physical but of social reproduction:

> The family is not merely the first cell of society where the connection of the man to the woman occurs to realize the operation of the perpetuation of life . . . but it has become an institute where the child learns the traditions of his people and their customs and their inclinations. . . . It is a factory in which the generations of the future are manufactured and through it the operation of social fusion of future generations begins.[28]

As her words suggest, the domestic sphere—defined as a space embodying particular kinds of subjectivities, social relationships, spatial organizations, and practices—was the site where national subjects were produced. The industrial language used by Abu Zayd, consistent with the ethos of social engineering that was a hallmark of Nasserist state-building, spoke to the underlying goals of state family planning. Organizing reproduction, making it more rational and efficient, in the same way that factory production makes the production of goods more efficient, was the means not only to limiting population but also to producing a better product.[29] The desire to create a fit population implied not only the creation of a particular kind of individual but also the creation of a particular kind of family. Indeed, cultivating modern citizens and creating modern families were seen as overlapping and mutually reinforcing projects.

The nuclear family, with no more than two or three healthy, educated offspring, a household containing the amenities and division of space that signified modern living and that observed the proper balance between work and leisure time, provided a normative model against which all households were judged. It was not enough for couples just to use contraception. According to program planners, they had to be convinced of the desirability of the goals—the creation of nuclear families, educated children, and the accoutrements of a middle-class lifestyle—that family planning made possible. Creating such families, reforming domestic space, uplifting society, and strengthening the nation came to mean not only rendering mothers fit to rear enlightened children through education (as these had during the first part of the century) but also the application of modern medical technology to lower-class female bodies, now localized as sources of health risks and unrationalized, unrestricted fertility.

Idealized images of nuclear families, long a staple of *effendiyya* political and cultural discourses, were now linked to messages about the importance of using contraception to produce smaller families. By 1967, discussions about the problems faced by large families were included in textbooks at the elementary and intermediate levels of education. In *The Student and His Local Environment,* a social studies textbook for first-year intermediate school students, "too many people in the family" was identified as the number one problem faced by Egyptian families: "This problem appears clearly among the peasantry and many times among workers. Among the most important reasons for it is ignorance which makes the married couple unable to provide the money and effort required to care for children."[30] In 1965, the yearly "Pick the Exemplary Mother" (*al-umm al-mithaliyya*) contest run by the Ministry of Social Affairs in conjunction with *Al-Ahram* newspaper to mark the occasion of Mother's Day was incorporated into the campaign to raise awareness about family planning. The exemplary Egyptian mother, according to the contest definition, was "a woman who has depended on herself in producing a generation which honors its nation." Excluded from eligibility were women who were divorced and those who had more than three children.[31]

A poster developed by the Egyptian Higher Council for Family Planning attempted to convey both the benefits and risks of having larger families by presenting a visual comparison between families that used birth control and those that did not (Figure 4.2). Depicted under the heading "The Unplanned Family" is a family with seven children. Their clothing marks them as rural, or perhaps as a working-class family recently migrated from the countryside to a nearby city. Parents and children alike are dressed in rags. The children are standing around idly, and are grouped so closely together that it is difficult to distinguish how many of them there actually are. One of the children holds her hand out imploringly to her mother, who ignores her. The mother's eyes are downcast and focused away from the mass of children around her, while the composition of the father's body is vaguely aggressive, suggesting that he is berating her. "The

Figure 4.2. *Al-Ahram*, Mar. 27, 1966, 7; *Ruz al Yusuf,* May 5, 1965.

Planned Family," on the other hand, is depicted not only as having fewer children but as an exemplar of the practices and orientations that signify more appropriate models of domesticity. While their clothes also mark them as rural or working class, their *gallabiyyas* are neat and clean. The three children appear alert and industrious: one boy is carrying a book; the other is playing with a ball at the feet of his parents.[32] The sole girl stands next to her mother, whose arm gently pulls her daughter closer to her. The daughter gazes up at her parents, who appear to be engaged in friendly conversation. Unlike the father in the "Unplanned Family," the father in the "Planned Family" is depicted as relaxed and attentive to his wife, around whom he has draped an affectionate arm. The accompanying caption reads, "There's a big difference in how far a salary, food and housing go." This was the message that was replicated over and over in family planning propaganda, in press coverage of the family planning program, and in social scientific works about the Egyptian family. Smaller families were better, not just because they had fewer children but because their members had successfully cultivated the habits and values of modernity. Hygiene, industry, an ethic of economy in which consumption was balanced with income and production was balanced with reproduction, engaged parenting, and marital relations based on care and affection rather than coercion—these were preconditions for both the prosperity of the individual family and the development and progress of the nation itself.

OVERLAPPING DISCOURSES: SECULAR AND RELIGIOUS
RENDERINGS OF REPRODUCTIVE BODIES

Secular modernizing discourses were not the only discourses to assert that an ethos of planning was necessary to creating better families. The subject of birth control was taken up in a number of *fatawi* (religious opinions) and works by religious scholars and theologians during the 1950s and 1960s. One of the regime's strategies to boost acceptance of contraception among Egyptian families was in fact to enlist religious support for family planning. In 1964, the daily newspaper *Akhbar al-Yawm* published a statement on Islam and birth control by the Grand Shaykh al-Azhar, Hasan Mamun, in support of family planning as a means to ensure the health and prosperity of the Muslim family.[33] Ahmad el-Sharabassy, a professor at Al-Azhar University, wrote a book endorsing family planning, which was distributed in pamphlet form in villages and at clinics providing family planning services.[34] Government officials at the district level instructed local religious leaders to promote family planning as Islamically permissible, at Friday sermons in village and neighborhood mosques. Such attempts to enlist religious sanction were not, however, uncontested.

Some public commentators on family planning opposed it, arguing that the unrestricted availability of contraception was an incitement to female promiscuity and the corruption of morals. Public opposition to birth control often invoked the specter of unrestrained female sexuality outside the boundaries of marriage and family. Shaykh Abu Zahra, a religious scholar who was considered the major opponent to family planning in Egypt at the time, believed that widespread contraception provision would undermine public morality and encourage promiscuity, a concern shared by opponents of family planning outside the religious establishment.[35] *Akhbar al-Yawm* newspaper columnist Sami Dawud called for the removal of the birth control pill from the market on the grounds that in countries where it was easily available, its main consumers were adolescents and unmarried women who were thus protected by the pill from the consequences of moral lapses.[36] Interestingly, other birth control methods had been available on the Egyptian market since the 1930s through private pharmacies and could be readily purchased in cities. Thus, fears about moral lapses may have reflected not only concern about the increased availability of birth control but also concerns specifically about the pill as a technology that gave women more control over their reproductive choices.

Other, more frequently voiced objections to family planning were that it undermined the purpose of marriage according to Islam, which was to bring up children. Doctor and health writer Hamid al-Ghawabi, for example, criticized birth control as a means by which couples dodged the responsibilities of bringing up children. In doing so, he argued, they undermined the socially binding basis of marriage, living only for their own individual fun and pleasure.[37] According to such critiques, the pill worked not simply to prevent conception but as the means by which subjects enmeshed in gendered social relations were transformed into individuals whose proliferating desires threatened to overflow the confines of the social and moral order.

In response to such charges, supporters of family planning, both inside and outside policy circles and the religious establishment, were adamant that family planning was not about selfish individualism or promoting sexual freedom but was about ensuring the health and well-being of the family and the nation. Amina Sa'id cited the threat of increasing population to public welfare and national development, calling family planning "among the most sacred of duties to ourselves . . . to our hopes, our nation . . . and the honor of our country."[38] Countering fears of female sexual promiscuity, she argued that "corrupt morals" came not from the presence of birth control but from a particular culture and lifestyle. Unmarried European and American women used contraception because social mores made such a practice possible. Young Egyptian women, however, as members of an "Eastern" society, adhered to the values of modesty and chastity, not because they were afraid of pregnancy but out of religious faith and adherence to social custom.

Other birth control advocates argued against criticisms that the family planning program was antinatalist and thus antithetical to social and religious mores. In a 1959 *fatwa*, the Shaykh al-Azhar Muhammad Shaltut argued that family planning was an "individual"—and temporary—choice made by those suffering from physical or social "sicknesses," such as maternal ill-health from repeated childbearing, or inability to provide financially for children. Distinguishing between *tahdid al-nasl* (birth control) and *tanzim al-usra* (family planning), he argued that the term "birth control" implied the attempt by the state to legislatively restrict births at a certain limit and was thus "repugnant to the natural law of the universe which is for growth." It carried connotations of sterilization or the permanent medical removal of the capacity to reproduce, which the Egyptian religious establishment condemned as outside the dictates of acceptable Islamic practice. Family planning, on the other hand, referred, he wrote, to the "planning and regulating [of] births for women who conceive quickly, who have hereditary illnesses and in such sporadic cases that cannot bear the responsibilities of children . . . [and] in this case is not unnatural. It is not disliked by the conscience of the nation and is not prohibited by religion."[39] It was religiously permissible so that "a healthy generation may issue."[40] Likewise, Shaykh Ahmed Sharabassy wrote in *Islam and Family Planning* that the use of birth control "should be abandoned once the necessities are removed. It should be voluntary and optional and not achieved by compulsion. It is a personal matter left entirely to the choice of the individuals concerned."[41]

Despite their often radical differences on the permissibility and advisability of contraceptive use and its provision by the state, most advocates and opponents of family planning shared a common normative conception of women's bodies as relational and reproductive. The "individual choice" that according to Sharabassy, Shaltout, Sa'id, and others who shared their views was the basis for contraception's sanction by Islam and by the national state was not a choice to be made by a rational, self-aware subject in her own bounded self-interest. Choice instead was to be exercised within the boundaries of marital, heterosexual relations and in the interest of the health and well-being of the family and the nation.

EMANCIPATED WOMEN, ENLIGHTENED MEN

The assertion that family planning was a national duty signaled an important shift from prerevolutionary discussions of birth control. Whereas social reformers had discussed women as objects of population policy, now policy planners, public figures, and the press began to talk of gendered national subjects for whom the use of birth control constituted the performance of the duties of citizenship. Women were recognized as having an important role to play in determining their own and, more importantly, the nation's reproductive destinies. Using contraception, like maintaining a household budget, undergoing civil defense training, and working in the service of the republic, became yet another way in which Egyptian women demonstrated their worthiness for inclusion in the revolutionary project. But not all women were equally recognized as being able to act as responsible reproductive subjects. Rural women were particular targets of family planning efforts, not only because statistically rural families were larger but because modernizing dis-

courses constituted gender relations in rural families as a particular impedi-
ment to the success of state development programs.

Drawing on modernization theory, which linked early marriage, polygamy, the preference for male children, and the view of children as wealth to
systems of labor that necessitated larger family sizes, Egyptian social scientists
argued that poor sanitation and the lack of modern medical technologies had
resulted in high rates of infant mortality, which made it necessary for women
to bear many children in order to preserve the family's labor capacity.[42]

As production increasingly moved out of the household and technological
innovation resulted in less labor-intensive work, there would no longer be any
economic imperative for large families. Tribal kinship and the extended family models on which it was based would in the modern world decline in favor
of smaller nuclear households.

Despite arguments for birth control, which were built on assumptions
about the inevitable triumph of the nuclear family, there was widespread acknowledgment that traditional gender relations and structures of male dominance were still alive and well in the Egyptian countryside.

An array of social and cultural practices and norms, reified in family planning discourses as persistent tradition, combined to make the Egyptian peasant woman, as one Egyptian demographer put it, "the most fertile woman
on earth."[43] Statistical data collected in villages in the Egyptian Delta and in
the Sa'id (Upper Egypt) correlated early marriage, the preference for male
children, the prevalence of extended kinship networks, and notions of gender
that viewed the production of many children as a sign of female health and
masculine vigor to large family sizes and women's illiteracy.[44] Commentators
on the family planning program argued that peasant women, entrenched in a
culture that perpetuated ignorant religious beliefs, fatalism, and male superiority, were unlikely to be persuaded to use birth control, even if they desired
fewer children.[45]

It wasn't just state bureaucrats and social scientists who made the argument
that peasant women and other lower-class women were enmeshed in family
forms that rendered them incapable of exercising reproductive agency. Similar
arguments were also made by middle-class women activists who linked family planning to improving women's status. Many of these activists, such as Zahya Marzuq, vice president the Alexandria Family Planning Association and
one-time undersecretary in the Ministry of Social Affairs; and Aziza Hussein,
head of the Cairo Women's Club and vice president of the Middle East and

North Africa Region for the International Planned Parenthood Federation, had a history of birth control advocacy that predated the national family planning program by several decades.[46] In their capacities as social reformers and heads of women's voluntary organizations aimed at providing maternal and child health services to the poor during the interwar period, they had pushed for greater recognition of the need to make contraception more available as a means to freeing women from the burden of unwanted children, so that they could be better mothers.

Over the course of the 1950s and 1960s, Egyptian feminists increasingly tied family planning to wider visions of liberation and participation in the public realm. They argued that freedom of reproduction was both the means and the necessary precondition for Egyptian women to enter the workforce, gain an education, and at the same time successfully undertake marital and maternal duties. At a public forum convened by the National Center of Social and Criminological Research to debate the population problem in 1963, Suhayr Qalamawi, invited to represent "the woman's perspective," pointed out that it was unfair to expect women to be both good mothers and good citizens without giving them access to birth control. "The woman today is not like the woman of yesterday. She's entered the workforce and shares with men the burdens of public life," she said. "So how do we ask the working woman to conceive and give birth repeatedly and then above that bear the efforts of work and the demands of home and children?"[47] Working women, she argued, should not have to shoulder the multiple burdens of caring for unwanted children and working in the nation's interest. At the same time, women activists argued that participation in the public space of the nation would also make women less vulnerable to the social, economic, and cultural structures that might prevent them from using birth control.

Feminist supporters of family planning maintained that in the context of traditional male patriarchal control over the family, social attitudes that demanded large family sizes produced a system of gender inequality where women's status and power were tied solely to the production of children. They argued that such conditions of unfreedom made it particularly unlikely that women in the countryside or the traditional quarters of Egypt's cities would be able to make the kinds of reproductive choices that would lead to smaller families and, consequently, an improvement in their status. "In the implementation of the family planning program, the vulnerability of poor, illiterate women is still a major obstacle and the independence of educated women is the greatest hope for success," Aziza Hussein wrote. "Thus, it is important that the cause of women's emancipation and family planning move forward together."[48]

Of particular issue to women activists who advocated female empowerment as a solution to the population problem were the laws and practices that governed marriage and divorce. An article that appeared on the Women's Page of *Al-Ahram* blamed population increases on the government's failure to reform the personal status laws that allowed men to divorce their wives without restrictions and to marry multiple wives and that encouraged early marriages.[49] (For an in-depth account of debates over reform of the personal status laws, see Chapter 3.) The ease of divorce and the possibility that husbands could take another wife meant that women produced children simply to ensure their continued position of favor within the family and with their husband. In an interview with *Al-Musawwar*, Hikmat Abu Zayd recommended that education about the benefits of the family planning program should target primarily men because they were apt to divorce women who failed to produce more than three or four children in rapid succession. Such a practice, she argued, led to uncontrolled population growth and the dehumanization of women, who were reduced to the status of "rabbits," existing solely to comply with the reproductive dictates of husbands and traditional social mores.[50]

Suhayr Qalamawi, one of the most outspoken public advocates of personal status law reform, underlined the economic vulnerability of poor women, who were trapped between dependence on their husbands' salaries to survive and marriage laws that allowed men to easily divorce women who didn't bear them enough children.[51] Qalamawi's solution lay not only in reforming the personal status laws so that women would be empowered to have fewer children, but also the more radical step, rejected by most other feminists and birth control activists, of placing legal limitations on the number of children women could bear, on the grounds that the social and economic dangers posed by large peasant families—unemployment, the influx of the rural poor into urban centers, and children whose moral upbringing was damaged by being crammed into a single-room dwelling with their parents and vast numbers of siblings—were too great to trust to a family planning program based on voluntary compliance.[52] Her position indicates some of the complexities of Egyptian feminist positions on birth control.

Feminist discourses on birth control reiterated statist discourses about small family sizes, the backwardness of lower-class women and men, and the public as the sphere of women's liberation, in complicated ways. On the one hand, female activists could be quite critical of state approaches to family planning. Aziza Hussein criticized state policy makers for being too "top down" in their approach to family planning and inattentive to the need for a program that would foreground women's needs and desires.[53] Amina Sa'id, though never outwardly critical of the state's program, used her position as editor in chief of *Hawwa'* to advocate making abortion legal, so that women who found themselves burdened with unwanted pregnancies could have safer alternatives than unhealthy back-alley terminations or unwanted children. Publishing articles on abortion that recounted the voices of women themselves in her editorials, she helped to conceptualize abortion not only as a medical issue but as one intimately related to the life experiences of women and the economic and other challenges they faced in raising families.[54] On the other hand, women activists shared development goals with the state, including the desire to reduce population growth and improve maternal health as well as the notion that using birth control constituted one of the obligations of citizenship.

Thus, while state policy makers tended to rely on the language of numbers and population targets to demonstrate the objective risks that lower-class women's bodies held for economic and social development, feminists used the subjective languages of injury, empowerment, obligation, and rescue to argue that birth control was necessary to improve lower-class women's lives.[55] What feminists and state policy makers shared was a normative conception of the kind of gender relations that were a precondition for women to be able to exercise reproductive agency consistently with their own interests as well as the interests of the nation itself. Modern families, formed on the basis of consent and companionability—in which the health of mothers and children was protected and women were able to regulate their births—were the solution, while rural and lower-class family forms, with their attendant notions of unrestrained male authority and unrestrained female fecundity, were the problem. Where technocratic discourses on family planning tended to objectify lower-class women as targets of state intervention, feminist discourses painted them as victims of backwardness who needed to be empowered to make the right kinds of choices. In both instances the assumption was that lower-class women were incapable of acting as responsible reproductive agents in part because lower-class men prevented them from becoming educated, modern subjects.

Such arguments are suggestive of the importance of looking not only at how definitions of womanhood were being transformed by state feminism but also at how notions of masculinity were also being reconfigured to suit Nasserist state-building. Like most contemporaneous family planning programs in other parts of the global South, the Egyptian family planning program targeted women as the primary recipients of services. The Egyptian program was largely based on the pill (and later the IUD), and male methods such as condoms and vasectomies were scarcely discussed during the 1950s and 1960s.

While the Egyptian family planning program didn't begin to systemically target men as recipients of family planning services until the 1990s, images of fatherhood and the role that men played in helping or hindering the goals of family planning were a significant part of family planning propaganda during the first decades of the program's operation. Coverage of the issues surrounding family planning in the popular press often featured representations—many of them satirical—of fatherhood and the role that fathers played in the success or failure of the government's program. Editorial cartoons frequently depicted subaltern men whose notions of manhood caused them to misread the family planning messages aimed at them by middle-class technocrats. A cartoon drawn by Salah Jahin, the renowned poet, artist, and satirist who was one of the intellectual figures most associated with helping to craft Nasserism as a cultural project, poked fun at the seeming disconnect between family planning messages and peasant notions of masculine vigor (Figure 4.3). Entitled "A Satirical Consideration of the Issue of Family Planning," it features an encounter in front of a family planning clinic between an Upper Egyptian peasant couple and a doctor. The man, clad in typical Upper Egyptian garb and sporting an impressive-looking mustache (also a marker of Upper Egyptian-ness), angrily confronts the white-coated doctor, as his wife, her face partially covered by a long, black garment that drapes her from head to toe, stands silently behind him. The caption reads, "Take this broad and regulate her births. She keeps having girls and boys and I want only boys!" In this cartoon, male desire for large families and the preference for sons play on stereotypes about Upper Egyptian male violence and the oppression of Upper Egyptian women. It suggests that subaltern masculinity itself is the problem, and not simply wanting more children, a view that was replicated in accounts of family planning that discussed how to promote birth control in the countryside and among lower-class couples in the city.

Figure 4.3. "A Satirical Consideration of the Issue of Family
Planning." *Al-Ahram*, Mar. 27, 1966, 7.

Fathers who desired large families thus stood in contrast to the responsible, enlightened heads of household who ensured the health and well-being of
their wives and children through rationality, economic planning, and benev-
olent, if firm, control over household members. Pamphlets and posters used
by the Cairo Family Planning Association to target men contained the pitch
that rationalized reproduction, and an ethic of care for family well-being was
what separated men from animals:

> It is part of manliness to be concerned with the health of the family.
> Any creature can conceive.
> Rabbits conceive by the tens.
> Fish conceive by the million.
> Humans alone are able to control
> The numbers of their children
> By means of Family Planning.[56]

Contrasting notions of gendered authority that were built on a man's ability to father (and a woman's ability to bear) many children, family planning advocates asserted that men's ability to provide the benefits of modern living—education, health care, a clean, well-maintained home, nutritional meals, and proper clothing—to their wives and children was a pillar of masculine national identity. A primary justification for the institution of a national family planning program was that without it, the basis of this new kind of male authority would be undermined.

FAMILY PLANNING AND LOCAL
MEDICAL KNOWLEDGE: MIDWIVES

As Faye Ginsburg and Rayna Rapp have pointed out, the medicalization of reproduction has often undermined the power and authority of local knowledge passed between generations of women.[57] Egypt was no exception in this regard. The adoption of family planning signaled an attempt to relegate reproductive management away from individual women and pre-existing female social networks to (largely) male policy makers and state functionaries. Existing alongside the state medical establishment, such local networks had an uneasy relationship with the Egyptian family planning program. On the one hand, state family planning was meant to displace and delegitimize older, gendered forms of contraceptive knowledge and practice. Traditional methods of birth control and abortifactants—obtained through *daya*s (midwives) or through knowledge passed on by other women in the community, such as neighbors and family members—were targeted by policy planners as a source of gynecological pathology and increased maternal morbidity. On the other hand, the state medical establishment found itself forced to make some accommodations with the local networks that embodied this older medical knowledge.

A case in point is that of the *daya* or local midwife. Since the nineteenth century, some *daya*s had been incorporated into the state's health delivery system as it expanded to encompass increasing sectors of the Egyptian population.[58] *Daya* training in the early part of the twentieth century consisted of a two-to-six-week course on theoretical midwifery at general hospitals and several months of practical training.[59] In 1932, the Department of Public Health expanded its instruction for *daya*s when it opened maternity training schools in Cairo, Alexandria, Tanta, Zagazig, Sohag, and Mansura. After training, *daya*s were licensed, and the most promising pupils were employed as birthing assistants in the maternal and child health clinics in each district. As the Arab Socialist state increased its commitment to the dissemination of medical care to encompass all Egyptian citizens, it became quickly clear that the state lacked the personnel and the infrastructure to deal with projected maternal health needs. One solution to the problem of scarce resources and expanding needs was to incorporate existing health networks and local practitioners, such as *daya*s, further into its health delivery system. In the late 1950s, existing midwife training plans were expanded for this reason.[60]

In the provision of maternal health care services, the relationship between *daya*s and the public health establishment was mutually beneficial. By incorporating *daya*s into its health delivery service, the public health establishment was able to extend its reach—through registration of births, referrals of patients by midwives to maternal and child health clinics, and notifications about newly expectant mothers—farther into the populations under its control. By undergoing the training required for licensing, *daya*s received the scientific medical knowledge on which they based their authority vis-à-vis other midwives and the local community. According to Egyptian anthropologist Leila el-Hamamsy, a midwifery license was a desirable commodity among younger *daya*s. In her 1968 ethnography of midwifery in an Egyptian village, el-Hamamsy recounted that the licensed *daya*s she interviewed stressed the superiority of their "modern" training. Umm Sa'id, one of the fourteen midwives in the village where el-Hamamsy conducted her research, had worked for several years in the school health center in the provincial capital of Shabin. She boasted of having worked alongside doctors and referred to unlicensed *daya*s as "this ignorant woman, this uncouth peasant."[61] Moreover, according to el-Hamamsy, younger *daya*s who had received training had often been sent by female family members who themselves were midwives who had not received training.

In the case of family planning, a service also provided by maternal and child health clinics, the relationship between *daya*s and the state was more conflictual. Many midwives were opposed to state provision of birth control over concerns about health, religious sanction, notions of family, and personal interest. El-Hamamsy recounted that the *daya*s she interviewed criticized the birth control methods provided by government programs on the grounds that they were not only ineffective but also harmful to women's health, causing hemorrhaging and general illness without preventing pregnancy. One linked the ill-effects of pills to divine predestination:

Procreation is by God's order. One woman gets one child and it never gets registered [it dies] but another gets ten then twenty. The number for each woman and man is predetermined and it is God who determines all. As for these pills, I know a woman who had a baby every year until she had eight children. She was in a terrible state; her house was filthy and she could not provide for these children. So she decided to take pills. She took them for a year but she had a hemorrhage; she stopped and became pregnant again . . . I don't approve of birth control; it is sinful to oppose God.[62]

The pronatalist sentiments expressed by one *daya* were fairly typical: "Procreation is a good thing and can never be abhorred. Children can be a burden at first, but later on when they grow up they will benefit us."[63]

In addition to concerns about health, religious sanction, and ideas about family size, midwives viewed family planning as inimical to their financial interests. The potential income a *daya* could derive from referring her patients to the family planning program was easily surpassed by the amount she could earn by participating in the activities surrounding the birth of a new child.[64] Also, although most of the *daya*s interviewed for el-Hamamsy's study declared that they were resolutely opposed to aiding a woman to induce abortions, several admitted they had done so, in part because the financial compensation was high—as much as two times what a *daya* would receive for a normal delivery. Because abortion was (and continues to be) illegal in Egypt, this was a highly remunerated service, which *daya*s could potentially monopolize.[65]

Thus, *daya*s and the family planning program competed for patients, the stakes being the successful implementation of the regime's development plans and the translation of its visions of modernity into a working project for the development of the nation, on the one hand, and the livelihood of midwives, on the other. One *daya* complained, "I had only three deliveries last month. . . . You see the pills have had a terrible effect on our trade."[66] Another told an interviewer, "You family planning people are taking the bread from our mouths."[67]

The opposition of local midwives to birth control coupled with their importance within local health networks made the *daya* both a figure of condemnation among family planning advocates and a target of co-optation by the family planning program. Articles in the press frequently blamed midwives for spreading false rumors about birth control, such as the article that recounted the story of a *daya* from Assiyut who told women that if they used IUDs, they would give birth to plastic dolls.[68] Another described midwives as "the new danger to family planning."[69] As an article in *Akhir Sa'a*, about a midwife in the village of Abi Namrus who told her patients that IUDs caused cancer, pointed out: "One woman in the village of Abi Namrus hinders the great campaign which the state is carrying out for family planning. . . . One woman is able to stand in the way of the efforts of a large group of doctors."[70]

But it was precisely the ability of midwives to influence the family planning program's target populations that also made them potentially important allies in the government's efforts to promote contraceptive use. At the same time as they charged *daya*s with spreading ignorance, corruption, and injurious health practices, articles in the press also stressed the important and potentially beneficial role the *daya* could play in the family planning program.[71] There were some attempts by the family planning program to enlist the cooperation of local midwives. One organization, the Society for Happy Childhood, which ran three family planning clinics in Cairo, offered *daya*s staple goods such as sugar and milk for referring women after childbirth.[72] Such measures, however, were limited, partial, and largely ineffective. The relationship of *daya*s to the national family planning program remained contentious.

The *daya*'s relationship with Egypt's public health establishment and the family planning program is suggestive of the ways in which the state incorporated local networks while simultaneously delegitimizing the local medical knowledge that formed the basis for those networks. In the case of midwives, that process was highly gendered; the local knowledge the state sought to exclude was exchanged between communities of women. Midwives could be integrated into the public health establishment but only if they engaged in an institutionalized, scientific practice of medicine consistent with the interests of the state. In 1969, the Ministry of Public Health announced that it was revoking its policy of training and licensing *daya*s on the grounds that there were now enough licensed nurse practitioners and nurses' assistants for the state to meet local demands for medical care. From the perspective of the national health bureaucracy, the *daya* had become redundant.[73]

NEGOTIATING REPRODUCTION: WOMEN'S EXPERIENCES WITH FAMILY PLANNING

By the early 1970s, the great experiment in family planning that had been widely touted in the press and political speeches as a centerpiece of the regime's state-building project was generally acknowledged to have been a failure. The fanfare surrounding the establishment of the family planning program and the almost weekly publication of newspaper articles chronicling the opening of yet another clinic, the implementation of yet another measure to bring family planning to even the remotest and most resistant segments of the Egyptian population, and the photo spreads in weekly magazines of women lined up to receive contraceptive services from concerned medical personnel hard at work in the interests of the nation and its citizens, all belied the banal reality of poor program administration, poorly trained clinical staff, and a target population that was largely indifferent if not outright resistant to government dictates about population control.[74]

While countless studies, newspaper articles, and program assessments have attempted to delineate the reasons for the program's quantitatively poor performance, the complex issues surrounding women's choice not to use (or to use) government family planning services render the issue of women's agency considerably more problematic. It has become a truism that texts, by their nature, are representational and the statistics, interviews, studies, and policy evaluations through which the story of family planning in Egypt is narrated tell us more about the producers of those texts than they do about the lives and choices (however circumscribed) of the individual women they claim to represent.

A failure to consider issues of women's motivation and agency, however, renders the effects of state and other, perhaps more unwitting forms of power as totalizing and one-dimensional. As Laura Briggs has pointed out in her work on sterilization in Puerto Rico, American feminist scholars (and feminist activists) have foregrounded the coercive aspects of sterilization policy without accounting for the voices and perspectives of Puerto Rican women, many of whom welcomed sterilization as a way to exercise more effective control over their lives and bodies. She suggests that for scholars to fail to account for the complexities that women face in making reproductive decisions is yet another way in which women from the global South are made to stand as "proof texts" for First World feminist debates about reproductive politics in Europe and the United States.[75]

With this in mind, it is important to acknowledge that Egyptian women could and did have their own complex reasons for participating in family planning. While trying to posit women's choices about their own reproduction as individual and outside the social, political, and economic structures in which they're made is a hazardous undertaking, not accounting for them at all risks overlooking the everyday practices, attitudes, and self-awareness through which the outlines (and contradictions) of the new Arab Socialist society manifested themselves. Attempting to reconstruct, however partially and imperfectly, the reactions women had to the program and their motivations in deciding whether to use family planning suggests something about how Egyptian citizens negotiated the revolutionary project in their daily lives.

Women's experiences with the family planning program were filtered and processed through their own positions within overlapping structures of class and gender with their attendant notions of self and community. Such a fact was not lost on observers of the family planning program. According to an article in *Ruz al-Yusuf,* messages intended to promote family planning and small family sizes were frequently interpreted by their target audiences in ways antithetical to the intentions of program planners.[76] At a rural social center in Manufiyya, a poster featuring the "ideal" family of three children contrasted with a family of seven children pictured in ragged clothing was shown to local women during an outreach session.[77] When asked for their interpretation of the picture, women pointed to the smaller family as the family that was "*mazluma*" (oppressed), and to the larger family as the happy family. This scene and ones like it were reportedly repeated throughout the country. A film shown to a male audience at one village presented two families, each with a monthly income of 40LE, one of which practiced family planning and the other which did not. The film apparently met with great favor by the viewers, who joked that if they earned 40LE a month, they too could afford to have ten children.[78] Another, which featured a bourgeois family of three children sitting down in their chicly furnished living room lined with bookcases as the "model" of a family that practiced family planning, was so removed from the reality of its peasant audience that it generated little reaction at all.[79] What I want to suggest here is not that complex issues of reproductive choice and desirable family size can be reduced to a (mis)reading of family planning discourses and the nationalist and state discourses on parenthood and domesticity that underpinned them, but that such discourses are never transparent or coherent, and can be read and interpreted through multiple lenses and deployed in contradictory ways.

The social importance of childbearing for families, and for women in particular, is certainly one of these lenses. For most Egyptian families, childbirth was, and remains, a cherished goal and a celebrated event.[80] It is the fulfillment of the idealized feminine role, which was underpinned not only by local so-cial practice but by nationalist assertions of the importance of motherhood as a component of normative definitions of femininity. As Marcia Inhorn has shown in her study of infertility among Egyptian women, the family planning program's insistence on birth control may be totally at odds with the desires of women themselves, for whom having a child is a blessing, and infertility a social stigma and a major source of anxiety.[81]

The physical experience of taking birth control and its relation to gen-dered notions of self and the body also played a role in whether women par-ticipated in the family planning program, and how long they continued with it. Side effects were a common complaint of pill users and contributed to high program dropout rates; a two-year study of pill usage in the Muharram Bey public housing project in Alexandria, conducted on 260 women, showed that 90.8 percent of women reported side effects.[82] These included dizziness, lassi-tude, headache, nausea, weight gain, and breakthrough bleeding, which were exacerbated by illnesses endemic to Egypt such as hepatitis C and bilharzia, cardiovascular disease, and nutritional deficiencies such as anemia. IUDs, for their part, could also cause breakthrough bleeding and infections that produced vaginal discharge. Not only did such side effects produce physical discomfort and, occasionally, serious health risks; but they could impinge on a woman's sense of self and bodily normalcy. In Assiyut, for example, reports of side effects made some women reluctant to take contraceptive pills because they feared that using birth control would disrupt their natural bodily func-tions, impairing their ability to work and bring in income.[83] Also, the pres-ence of breakthrough bleeding can hinder the performance of religious du-ties—since Muslim women are enjoined not to pray or fast during Ramadan while menstruating—which can thus injure women's sense of themselves as believers. Further, menstrual blood is widely connected to notions of pol-lution and bodily openness among Egypt's rural population, states that are viewed as rendering women more vulnerable to affliction and ill health.[84] The state of women's bodies during periods of openness—after childbirth, loss of virginity, and during certain periods of breast-feeding—was seen as par-ticularly endangered by the presence of another female body rendered "open" by menstruation or vaginal bleeding, which could cause infertility and the cessation of lactation in new mothers.[85] As Kamran Ali argues, such concep-tions of health, dependent as they are on the socially interconnected relation-ship between bodies, reveal gendered notions of the body as relational and socially inscribed, notions that do not correspond to the individual, medically normalized body of the family planning program. These bodily perceptions could affect whether a woman chose to use birth control in the first place, and whether she chose to discontinue contraception either temporarily or permanently at different stages of her reproductive life.

In the absence of oral histories or detailed studies that present the experiences of Egyptian women themselves with family planning, narrated in their own words, it is difficult to pinpoint in any systematic way exactly who was using clinics and the reasons that motivated women to use birth control at particular times. The question is further complicated by the ways in which forms of birth control that predated family planning were delegitimized by policy planners, medical personnel, and family planning advocates as gynecological pathology.

Egyptian women were not without the means and knowledge to prevent pregnancy prior to the establishment of a national family planning program and the widespread availability of methods such as the pill and the IUD. Derived from local knowledges about health, illness, and the body that predated the spread of modern contraceptive technologies, knowledge of such "*baladi*" methods (as they were commonly referred to in the press, policy statements, and research surveys) was exchanged between communities of women: mothers, daughters, neighbors, and midwives.[86] These included use of materials that were believed to hinder the movement of sperm and were inserted into the vagina, materials such as a piece of cotton wool saturated with salt dissolved in lemon juice, honey, or mint. Conventional medical pharmaceuticals, either alone or mixed with other substances, often figured prominently in home contraceptive remedies. Aspirin was a common ingredient in a host of preparations, as was quinine powder.[87] Studies indicate that such methods were not only widely known by those most targeted by family planning policies—rural women and the urban poor—but also commonly used. Research carried out in 1963 on attitudes towards contraception among 4,500 families in Alexandria reported that over half of them (2,417) used such methods of birth control. Another study done in the late 1960s of families living in the working-class Alexandria neighborhood of al-Liban established that many women still used *baladi* methods either instead of or in addition to scientific medical methods.[88]

It is difficult to know just how effective and safe such methods were. According to Aziza Hussein, one of the reasons that private charitable organizations began offering contraceptive services in the interwar period was that women coming to the clinics had requested birth control either after *baladi* methods had failed or after they had used traditional abortifactants to terminate a pregnancy.[89] On the other hand, Zahya Marzuq, who cited the results of the Alexandria studies in her article "Social Studies in Fertility and Contraception in Alexandria," pointed out that such concoctions did have some effect on reducing the mobility of sperm and were likely somewhat successful in helping to prevent unwanted pregnancies. Moreover, according to Marzuq, "Although women who used the above mentioned methods knew they could get the oral contraceptives or intrauterine devices free of charge in the birth control clinics, they were not willing to change their traditional methods. None of them was curious enough to try the new methods or even accept casual advice."[90] Marzuq went on to recommend that family planning propaganda address the issue of "primitive" contraceptives when trying to persuade potential family planning patients of the benefits of modern birth control. "It may be too late to try and convince old fashioned mothers of the importance of modern medical care," she wrote, "but it is never too late to concentrate on younger mothers, to convince them to . . . seek advice and guidance toward healthier and more effective methods of family planning."[91]

Whether the traditional methods of birth control and knowledge exchanged among communities of women were safe and effective is not an unimportant question. But addressing this question shouldn't prevent scholars from asking additional questions about how medical and social science discourses on family planning delegitimized forms of reproductive agency. The salient point here is that prior to the establishment of the family planning program and afterwards, Egyptian women could and did take an active role in determining their own reproductive destinies. When viewed through the lens of medicalized family planning discourse, however, whatever complex desires and calculations went into women's decisions to use traditional contraception (or to forego birth control altogether) were rendered illegible, reduced to overarching explanations of persistent ignorance and backwardness, which stood in the way of maternal health and progress.

What about the thousands of women who did make the trip to their local family planning clinics to request birth control? What little and partial evidence there is suggests equally complex desires and calculations. Women who were interviewed in the Egyptian press told stories of decisions they made based on health, family economies, and beliefs about modernity in

complicated ways that both diverged from and overlapped with state discourses on family planning. First, evidence suggests that patrons of family
planning clinics were primarily rural, urban lower-class, and lower middle-
class women. Women who could afford it tended to get their contraceptives
from family physicians or from private pharmacies. Second, the women who
were most likely to use family planning services were those who had already
had a number of children and were in the middle or at the end of their reproductive lives.

A magazine article presented interviews with women who attended a meeting about family planning services held at a government sugar-processing factory for its female workers and the wives of workers. One of the attendees was
a mother with ten girls and a boy; another was a woman with seven children,
the oldest five of whom were still in school. According to the article, all of
the women at the meeting already had at least five or six children.[92] Another
article presented an interview with Samira Muhammad Radwan, the wife of
a farmer and the mother of twelve sons and a daughter, the oldest of whom
was twenty-one.[93] According to Radwan, she and her husband didn't consider
family planning services until after they had a number of children. Fahima
Ibrahim Guda, who was interviewed at a family planning clinic in Minya,
was thirty-two and had been pregnant twelve times. When asked why she had
come to the clinic, she replied that she wanted a rest from the "drudgery" of
repeated pregnancies and so that her husband, a farmer and milkman, could
better support their existing children. He had agreed that she should use birth
control in order to take a rest, but saw this as a temporary measure.[94]

Feelings of fatigue and illness were commonly cited reasons by women for
why they had decided to use contraception, as was the need to "rest" from repeated pregnancies. Hafiza al-'Id, a mother of seven, had been married twenty
years to a civil servant whose monthly salary was 15LE. His salary was "not
sufficient to buy bread or meat for the family." Her oldest child was eighteen
and had left school but was unable to find work. Her other children, except
her youngest, a three-year-old, were still in school. She described the family's financial circumstances as "troubled" and said that her husband had
great difficulty providing all of the things her children needed: schoolbooks,
shoes, clothing, money for school fees, and general expenses. She had come
to the family planning center in Imbaba, a working-class district in Cairo,
in the hope of obtaining birth control pills.[95] Part of what these women's
stories suggest is that using birth control, for many women, was a strategic,

often temporary decision motivated by particular health concerns or socio-economic circumstances, and not necessarily motivated by agreement with the wider goal of the family planning program, which was to have smaller families.

But Hafiza al-ʻId's words also suggest that part of women's motivations for using birth control was formed through their active engagement with and investment in the social contract between the state and Egyptian citizens that lay at its heart—in particular, the importance stressed by al-ʻId and other women of being able to provide an education to their children as a means of ensuring prosperity and upward mobility. Workers and workers' wives who attended the family planning meeting at the government sugar factory worried that with every additional child, the opportunity for education and thus a prosperous future decreased.[96] Reproducing the rhetoric of the revolutionary state, which held that universal public education was a key to national rejuvenation and, as a mechanism of inclusion and social equality, a right held by all Egyptian citizens, one woman contrasted the Egyptian past with its present saying, "Now it is necessary to educate children."[97] Another women, a forty-year-old mother of fourteen whose taxi driver husband was unable to make enough money to educate their children, said, "We have been in need of a family planning plan for many years."[98] Such statements, while hardly unmediated, suggest how the complex web of rights and duties underpinning the Nasser regime's state-building project was understood and negotiated by Egyptians in everyday contexts. It was every Egyptian's right to have an education and to work, thus sharing in the benefits of the revolutionary project. It was also, however, all parents' duty to ensure that their children had access to the benefits and services provided by the state. The words of some of the women who used family planning services during this time suggest that they were willing to invest in family planning, as one component of Egyptian socialist planning, in order that their children could reap the benefits of Egyptian citizenship. This latter point is perhaps best exemplified in the statement of a thirty-five-year-old mother of six who visited a family planning clinic in Manufiyya. As she put it, "We must plan our families so that our children can get work with the state."[99]

CONCLUSION

The history of the Egyptian family planning program highlights the complexities of assessing the possibilities that Nasserist state-building both opened and foreclosed for Egyptian women. Family planning was an outcome of a more inclusive vision of citizenship and a more expansive definition of the responsibility of the state to provide social welfare, particularly to groups that had historically been excluded from access to medical and other social services. Egyptian women themselves, far from either passively embracing or resisting statist dictates about population and birth control, negotiated their relationship to the reproductive politics of Nasserism in ways that were shaped by class, gender, religion, location, notions of self, personal circumstances, and aspirations for the future. Female activists argued that family planning would help to free women from structures of male dominance in the family so that they could enter a public sphere of empowerment. Village midwives both operated within and contested the expanding public health bureaucracy and the medicalized conceptions of health and body they represented. And thousands of women perceived that there were potential benefits—to their lives, to their futures, and to the futures of their children—to availing themselves of family planning services.

Yet, the history of this program also clearly demonstrates how the state's attempts to fashion a new sort of family and to provide for its welfare may actually have created new structures of dependence, social hierarchies, and male dominance. Languages of liberation, modernity, and inclusion, used by policy makers, demographers, and women activists alike, converged to produce normative definitions of the family, gender, and self that subjected the most intimate practices of Egyptians to scrutiny and intervention. Lower-class female bodies were localized by elite discourses as both a source of risk and a means to national uplift even as women were being recognized as reproductive subjects in new ways. This was not a contradiction: the dual construction of women as both objects and agents of national transformation was an integral part of the operations of the postcolonial Egyptian state and the notions of agency, belonging, and gendered citizenship they were predicated upon.

5 OUR SISTERS IN STRUGGLE
State Feminism and Third World Imaginaries

FOUR YEARS AFTER THE BANDUNG CONFERENCE, the historic 1955 meeting that signaled the intentions of the colonized and formerly colonized world to challenge the emerging cold war global order by uniting under the banner of national liberation and anti-imperialism, the February issue of *Hawwa'* featured an interview with Sakina Kusima, a leading figure in the Indonesian women's movement. Kusima was in town at the invitation of Nahid Sirri, head of the women's committee of the Egyptian state-sponsored Arab Socialist Union.

According to the article, her mission was to bring to life the spirit of Bandung by promoting ties of sisterhood and solidarity between the women of Africa and Asia. In the interview, Kusima spoke of contemporary challenges for Indonesian women and invoked historical struggle and sacrifices. She responded to questions ranging from her views on women combining political and domestic duties, to the extent of Indonesian women's advancement in comparison to Western women, to the role of the "Eastern Woman" in the fight against imperialism.

> These advances are counted not only as a victory for Indonesian women, but for Eastern women in general . . . [However] the woman of the East must exert all of her power in taking up another battle to squash this great prison she has fallen into . . . the prison of decrepit tradition, which allows men to marry whom they will and divorce when they will. . . . The Western woman is, without a doubt, advanced, but she's not more advanced than the educated Eastern woman.

154

She concluded the interview by praising the example that Egyptian women provided for other women in the colonized and formerly colonized world as agents of modernization and participants in postcolonial nation-building.[1]

The interview with Kusima was one of hundreds of articles that appeared in the Egyptian mainstream and women's press that focused on non-Egyptian women in the decades following the 1952 revolution. Linked to the Nasser regime's attempts to forge a new social and political order at home and new alliances with formerly colonized nations abroad, the proliferation of articles on women in China, India, Vietnam, Thailand, Algeria, Germany, the Soviet Union, Cameroon, and elsewhere during this period suggests that the project of fashioning a modern Egyptian woman was not confined to the geographical borders of the nation-state alone. Rather, the political space of postcolonial nation-building overlapped with new political spaces in an era of transnational, anti-imperialist struggle. Such new spaces provided the context for Egyptian state elites of both genders to articulate new, gendered visions of identity and solidarity, as well as ascribe new political meanings to state feminism as a universalizing project.

This chapter examines the ways in which Egyptian state feminism shaped and was shaped by the emergence of the "Third World" as an imaginative space and political project, by looking at Egyptian women's transnational activism during the Nasser period and the depictions of non-Egyptian women in the Egyptian press that grew out of that involvement. These images were multivalent and often contradictory; they could be examples to readers of the promise that becoming modern held for a recently decolonized nation, or expressions of anxiety about the effects such a process could have on gender roles and on society in general. They could be used to assert the liberated status of Egyptian women under socialist rule in comparison to the condition of women in more "backward" nations. Depictions of "other" women played a part in the construction of an idea of "global sisterhood" even as they highlighted the tensions inherent in such constructions. Finally, they allowed their mostly educated, middle-class Egyptian female readership to imagine certain roles and lives for themselves while foreclosing others. Articles about "other women" were a vehicle through which the Egyptian women who were the most likely beneficiaries of Nasserist policies fashioned (and contested) state feminism as a project that was simultaneously local, national, and transnational in scope.

THIRD WORLD POLITICAL IMAGINARIES

The Bandung Conference was an inaugural moment in the formation of the "Third World," not as a place on a map but as a project, a political imaginary, that linked "the darker nations" of the world in common struggle for freedom.[2] The first large-scale meeting of Asian and African states in history, it brought together delegates and leaders from twenty-nine countries representing over half the world's population. Many of these were nations that, like host country Indonesia, were newly independent of colonial control.[3] The stated aims of the conference were to promote Afro-Asian economic and cultural cooperation and to oppose colonialism and imperialism, particularly attempts by the United States and the Soviet Union to extend their influence over the global South in the postwar global order. More than that, however, Bandung was an attempt to forge a common ideology among anticolonial nations that could supersede the cold war system dominated by the ideological conflict between communism and capitalism and the superpowers that were their standard bearers.[4] In his now famous address to conference delegates, Indonesian leader Sukarno laid out the basis of unity and cooperation between the disparate nations that made up the conference:

> All of us, I am certain, are united by more important things than those which superficially divide us. We are united by a common detestation of colonialism in whatever form it appears. We are united by a common detestation of racialism. And we are united by a common determination to preserve and stabilize peace in the world. . . . Relatively speaking, all of us gathered here today are neighbors. Almost all of us have ties of common experience, the experience of colonialism. Many of us have a common religion. Many of us have common cultural roots. Many of us, the so-called "underdeveloped" nations have similar economic problems, so that each can profit by the others' experience and help. And I think I may say that we all hold dear the ideals of national independence and freedom.[5]

These then were the elements of the "Bandung spirit" that came to define the Third World as an imagined political space of solidarity: support for national independence movements, opposition to the continued pernicious effects of colonialism in all of its postcolonial guises—intellectual and economic control, cultural influence, and indirect political interference—and mutual exchange and cooperation to address shared problems of economic, technological, and cultural underdevelopment. The Third World imaginary was thus based neither on a rejection of national differences nor on the articulation of essentialist claims to racial, cultural, or geographic commonalities, but on a recognition that the boundaries between national self-definition and transnational unity were mutually reinforcing. In his opening statements to the 1957 Afro-Asian Solidarity Conference held in Cairo two years after Bandung, then vice president Anwar Sadat echoed Sukarno's sentiments at Bandung:

> Your gathering today on Egyptian soil portrays one more aspect of [our] freedom. We have all been partners in one specific, common fate of imperialism and exploitation, partners in a common struggle and in a future common to us all. . . . The Bandung conference was not a haphazard event, but rather a *national, psychological factor* which led to the awakening of the peoples of Asia and Africa and roused them from their slumber . . . to resume the struggle for the recovery of liberty and freedom.[6] (emphasis mine)

The types of political movements and solidarities that Bandung enabled and inspired, as well as its symbolic relationship (in Egypt and elsewhere) to national and transnational struggles for liberation from European rule, suggest that the crafting of independent postcolonial nations also entailed the formation of other sorts of political imaginaries. The Nasser regime's attempts to contribute to the forging of a new world political order under the rubric of nonalignment, socialism, and Arab nationalism were an integral part of its self-definition as a progressive, anti-imperialist nation in a newly postcolonial world. With the 1956 nationalization of the Suez Canal, which stripped away the last vestiges of British colonial control, Egypt placed itself at the forefront of global opposition to Western hegemony over the formerly colonized world. Egypt's participation in the nonaligned movement, its increasingly close ties with the Soviet bloc, and its attempts to bring other progressive Arab regimes together under the rubric of Arab nationalism were intimately tied to domestic efforts to envision and create a new society that was both socialist and authentically Egyptian. The range and types of communities and solidarities invoked by depictions of non-Egyptian women both reflected and gave meaning to this project.

Bandung, in which Egypt had played a leading role, gave rise to a number of distinct but overlapping movements, including the Non-Aligned Movement, the Afro-Asian People's Solidarity Movement, and the African People's Summit. The Non-Aligned Movement, officially started in Belgrade in 1961 with twenty-five member states, was an outgrowth of the alliances made at

Bandung. It was founded by Indian prime minister Jawaharlal Nehru, Josip Broz Tito, the leader of Yugoslavia, Ghanaian leader Kwame Nkrumah, Sukarno, and Nasser. Its founding principles included peace and disarmament, independence and the right to self-determination of all colonial peoples, and multilateralism as well as economic and cultural autonomy and resistance to American and European imperialism. The Afro-Asian People's Solidarity Committee (AAPSC), the institutional body of the eponymous movement, initially made up primarily of Asian countries, was founded in 1955; in 1956 it transferred its headquarters to Cairo, and Egyptian author Yusuf Siba'i assumed the post of secretary-general. The choice of Cairo owed something to Nasser's status as an international symbol of anticolonial resistance to Western imperialism. More importantly, however, the move signaled the AAPSC's attempts to assume a more truly Afro-Asian orientation reflecting the increasingly important role that African nations were coming to play as frontline states in the battle against colonialism and global imperialism.

As the center of these various transnational movements was beginning to shift from Asia to Africa, Egypt was positioned to become an increasingly key player. Egyptian participation in pan-African conferences, like the second Conference of Independent African Nations held in Addis Ababa in 1960, played an important role in cementing transnational alliances between Arabs and sub-Saharan Africa, linking these nations for the first time as combatants in a common struggle for the liberation and development of the African continent. At the same time, the unification of Egypt with Syria in 1958 and the creation of the United Arab Republic (UAR) gave impetus to pan-Arab aspirations in the region and gave Nasser the status of standard-bearer of Arab nationalism.[7] The Nasser regime successfully worked to portray Egypt (both geographically and politically) as a crossroads connecting Asia, Africa, and the Arab world, thus further bolstering Egyptian claims to leadership within the emerging postcolonial global order.

The attention paid in the domestic Egyptian women's press to women in postcolonial Asia and Africa, the Arab world, and socialist countries such as Yugoslavia was partly a product of such shifts in Egypt's ideological and political orientation. But it was also produced by the creation of new spaces within the sphere of global politics within which people, ideas, and discourses circulated. This was perhaps one of the most lasting aspects of Bandung and the movements that followed it.[8] As new alliances were forged in the international arena, groups of women activists, writers, students, and politicians circulated within the milieu of international conferences, visiting delegations, summits, and committee meetings. The resulting exchanges and networks were part of what made possible the sorts of imaginings that overflowed the boundaries of the nation-state.

EGYPTIAN WOMEN'S ENGAGEMENT
WITH INTERNATIONAL FEMINISM

By 1952, Egyptian women already had a long history of participation in transnational activism, particularly through their involvement in various overlapping movements and organizations comprised in the heart of a flourishing international women's movement in the first half of the twentieth century. Members of the Egyptian Feminist Union (EFU) had been active members of a number of international organizations and congresses, including the International League of Mothers and Educators for Peace, Women's International League for Peace and Freedom, the International League for the Suppression of Traffic in Women and Children, and most prominently, the International Alliance of Women for Equal Suffrage and Citizenship (IAW) since the 1920s.[9] The EFU had joined the IAW when it changed its name from the International Woman Suffrage Alliance in 1923. The change in name signaled the IAW's shift from a narrow focus on suffrage to a multitiered platform that encompassed multiple rights and fully enfranchised citizenship.[10] Egyptian women's engagement with international feminism, however, was a story of disjuncture between the nationalist feminism of the colonized and the "universalism" of Western-dominated international feminism that masked the movement's imperial genealogy.[11]

The rhetoric of international feminism, as it developed in Britain and the United States, rejected ethnic and national differences between women in favor of a notion of solidarity on the basis of biological sex and a shared experience of oppression and disenfranchisement. A song of the International Women's Suffrage Alliance summed it up: "Whatever our race or country be . . . we are one nation / Womanhood."[12] Carrie Chapman Catt, the leader of the IWSA, rejected "local" (nation-specific) patriotism as a male phenomenon. National feeling had to be sacrificed for the sake of female solidarity so that the suffrage movement could present a united front to the world. The inclusion of non-Western women within the movement was key if it was to be considered a truly global enterprise. In 1923, for example, along with the EFU, the IAW also admitted the Woman's Indian Association, the Jewish Women's

Equal Rights Association from Palestine, and a Japanese women's association, which joined the ranks of women's organizations from countries like Greece and Turkey.

On the other hand, the ways in which non-Western women were included reveal the colonial assumptions on which "global sisterhood" functioned within the context of empire. In a letter written to an American magazine about the Egyptian women's movement in 1912, Catt praised the women of Egypt for "daring to refuse marriage" and demanding the right to education. She attributed the beginnings of a women's movement in Egypt to the influence of British colonial control. "Great Britain has created a new Egypt," she declared. "It has awakened a sleeping race and held before it the dazzling achievements of Western progress."[13] Thus, non-Western women were to be absorbed into international feminism in a position of subordination, not as leaders or equal partners with their Western "sisters" but as objects of tutelage. As Antoinette Burton points out, "British feminist internationalism—and more specifically, Anglo-American suffrage—was predicated on the assumption that Western women would lead the women of the East to freedom and British and American women would spearhead the charge."[14]

The rejection of nationalism as the antithesis of universalist female solidarity, and the absorption of colonized and formerly colonized women into the IAW as objects of Western reform and tutelage remained defining features of international feminism throughout the 1920s, 1930s, and 1940s, even as the movement challenged colonialism in other ways. Membership in the IAW was country-based, so although most Asian and African territories remained under colonial control, the IAW deemed them countries as opposed to colonial possessions so that they would be eligible for IAW membership.[15] In spite of its inclusion of women from colonized territories, however, the 1939 meeting of the IAW in Copenhagen graphically revealed the tensions in international feminism and lack of consensus between Western and non-Western women on what constituted feminism and gender solidarity. In its declaration of principles, IAW proposed to observe "absolute neutrality on all questions that were strictly national."[16] One of the issues of concern to Egyptian activists that was eschewed by IAW as "national" was Palestine. Saiza Nabarawi, writing in the EFU's journal *L'Egyptienne*, expressed her frustration with the IAW leadership's refusal to engage with the problems of Palestinian women under the British mandate:

What did we demand? A little sympathy for the unfortunates who suffer in the East from the wrongs of imperialist politics . . . [The IAW] should have given the Eastern world proof that women are sincere and disinterested when they speak of justice and liberty, that they know how to disavow their governments when they do not apply these principles. . . . [B]y their refusal to interest themselves in Eastern problems they have proven that their magnificent program addresses itself only to certain people of the West, alone deigned to enjoy liberty.[17]

The failure of the IAW to put the nationalist, anticolonial concerns of colonized and formerly colonized women on its agenda was thus a source of deep-seated frustration to Egyptians and women from other countries confronting European colonialism and imperialism.

After the Copenhagen conference, the IAW and other international women's organizations largely ceased their activities because of the Second World War. When the IAW reconvened in 1946, the terrain of transnational women's activism had been reordered. The 1945 creation of the leftist Women's International Democratic Federation, which wedded gender struggle and class struggle, signaled one major split in international feminism along the East-West axis of the cold war.[18] The creation of the Afro-Asian People's Solidarity Movement and the Non-Aligned Movement in the 1950s and 1960s, which divided the movement along North-South lines, was the other. The first Asian-African Conference on Women, held in Colombo in 1958, for example, was confined to women's organizations from the twenty-nine countries of the Asian and African region that were represented at Bandung. The first Afro-Asian Women's Conference, which was convened in Cairo in 1961 under UAR sponsorship, grew out of a resolution from the earlier Cairo-sponsored AAPSC general conference in 1957.[19]

The existence of a transnational women's movement encompassing the colonized and formerly colonized world, led and driven by the concerns of non-Western women in the 1950s and 1960s, challenges conventional historical narratives of international feminism. According to such narratives, international feminism, originating in the struggles for women's suffrage in Europe and America at the turn of the century, largely ended when international connections between women were "severed" by the Second World War, to reemerge only in the 1970s and 1980s after a "lull" of some two decades.[20] Writing the struggles for decolonization (and the transnational movements that emerged from them) out of histories of international feminism ignores the critical impact that the South-South exchanges and solidarities produced by the Bandung moment have had on feminist thought and praxis in the last two decades, most notably the emergence of postcolonial critiques of Western feminism by women in the global South. Moreover, the elision of such struggles tends to reproduce a historical trajectory of feminism that situates Europe and America as the origin and locus of feminist thought and practice and the global South as passive consumer. Looking at Bandung as a formative moment in the history of global feminisms challenges both assumptions.

For the first time, movements like Bandung provided colonized and formerly colonized women an alternative to the political and organizational space of the prewar, Western-dominated, and imperial international women's movement. The novelty of the movement's location—and the connections that enabled—was not lost on its participants. Bahiyya Karam, an Egyptian activist who was appointed secretary of the preparatory committee for the 1961 Cairo Women's Conference, wrote in her introduction to the proceedings:

> It is for the first time in modern history, feminine history that is, that such a gathering of Afro-Asian women has taken place ... represent[ing] over 37 peoples, some of them participating for the first time in an international meeting. It was indeed a great pleasure, an encouragement to meet delegates from countries in Africa which the imperialists had never allowed before to leave the boundaries of their land. Delegates from Basutoland, Gambia, for example, had the chance for the first time to meet their sisters from other countries in Africa and Asia.[21]

Lakshmi Menon, leader of the Indian delegation to the Colombo Asian-African Conference of Women, marveled that women from Mongolia and Ghana would finally be able to meet their "sisters" from the Mediterranean to the Pacific.[22]

It was not only location that separated transnational women's activism in the Non-Aligned Movement and Afro-Asian People's Solidarity Movement from the activism of the IAW and other organizations as it had been in the first part of the century. Despite the imperial assumptions and uneven power relationships that contradicted its founding premise, the IAW consistently asserted biology (and a common experience of exclusion based on that biology) as the basis for women's solidarity and a unified feminist program. While not denying the importance of ties based on the purportedly "natural" division between the sexes, the activism of colonized and formerly colonized women stressed solidarity based on a common experience of subjugation created and perpetuated by Western imperialism, what Chandra Mohanty has called "an imagined community of third world oppositional struggles . . . women with divergent histories and social locations woven together by the political threads of opposition to forms of domination that are not only pervasive but systematic."[23] African and Asian women "suffered from the same disabilities" and were thus "struggling for the same aims."[24] In her speech at the 1961 Cairo conference, Egyptian delegate Karima Sa'id evoked such a shared genealogy of suffering and resistance: "We, Afro-Asian women, meet today representing two-thirds of the world population, tied by the unity of the great past, the struggling present and the glorious future—a unity of pains and aims—a unity of struggle for the rights and for the sake of freedom, peace and humanism."[25] It was the explicit purpose of conferences like the Afro-Asian Women's Solidarity Conference to establish a framework for exchanges between women of the global South.

One of the many outcomes of these exchanges were the articles on foreign women that appeared during this period in the Egyptian women's press. The Egyptian delegates to the 1961 women's conference included Amina Sa'id, the editor in chief of *Hawwa'*; Fathiyya Bahij, a journalist for *Akhir Sa'a* who often covered women's issues; and Suhayr Qalamawi, head of the Egyptian Press Syndicate and occasional contributor to the women's pages of various publications. An article on Vietnamese women in *Hawwa'* was based on an interview with Nguyen Thi Binh, a leader of the Vietnamese Women's Union, who visited Cairo as a delegate to the Plenary Committee of the Conference of Afro-Asian Solidarity.[26] A series of articles on women in Tanganyika was based on Sa'id's attendance of the Third Afro-Asian Solidarity Conference there. These articles on "other women" often grew directly out of Egyptian women's presence at such conferences and the presence of foreign women in Cairo. Their content both reflected and reinforced the context of postwar women's activism.

THE EGYPTIAN WOMEN'S PRESS

Articles about foreign women that appeared in the 1950s and 1960s were not a new feature of the Egyptian press. Rather, profiles of women from various countries had been featured in Egyptian magazines and journals almost since the inception of the popular press itself in the beginning of the twentieth century. Often these took the form of what Marilyn Booth has termed "prescriptive biographies"—biographical sketches of notable women meant to impart lessons to female readers about proper gender roles.[27] Following the Second World War, however, the prevalence of prescriptive biography in women's magazines greatly declined. In the Egyptian press of the 1950s and 1960s, unlike in the earlier period, articles about foreign women increasingly took the form of interviews, multipage features with photos, or less frequently, editorials. Consistent with the more general trends toward social realism in the visual arts, cinema, and literature, such articles made truth-claims through the author's offer of accurate, eye-witness testimony of the condition of women in other countries. Interviews were frequently presented in a question-and-answer format with the interviewee's responses being printed ostensibly verbatim. Foreign datelines, the rhetoric of witness (I was there and I saw with my own eyes), and the author's assertion of having had expectations about a country that were changed through experience were all ways in which these texts purported to give a real, unmediated picture of other women's lives.

While such articles were found in a variety of publications, the majority of them appeared in the Egyptian women's press, a term that encompasses not only magazines aimed at women but the women's pages of various magazines aimed at a more general readership and written by both men and women.[28] Readers interested in perusing an interview with Indira Gandhi, learning about women's political organizations in Kenya, or finding out about how the efforts of the Cuban government to draw women into the workforce were affecting family life there could turn not only to *Hawwa'* but also to the weekly news magazine *Akhir Sa'a* (Up to the Hour), where articles about women's issues could be found in the section of the magazine entitled "Hiya" (She); and to "Al-Nisf al-Halwa" (The Charming Half), the women's page in *Akhir Sa'a*'s competitor *Al-Musawwar* (The Illustrated).[29]

SOLIDARITY AND IDENTITY

What kind of community did articles about non-Egyptian women "imagine" for Egyptian readers as they flipped through the pages of the women's press?[30] With titles like "The Girls of Iran," "I Saw the Yemeni Woman Without a Veil!" "What Do You Know About the Yugoslavian Woman?" and "Thank God You're an Egyptian Woman," the articles seemed to imply the nation-state as the primary locus of allegiance and identity.[31] The placement of the articles as well as their rhetorical strategies, however, suggested that the magazine's readers might envision themselves as belonging to other sorts of communities as well.

The organization of the women's press created a discursive space of solidarity whose boundaries were shifting and contingent. In the women's sections of *Akhir Sa'a* and *Al-Musawwar* reports on the international, national, and local contexts of women's activism intermingled and overlapped seemingly at random. The news roundup section of *Hawwa'*, entitled "With *Hawwa'*," the section of the magazine where many of the articles about foreign women could be found, also featured news on the activities of local women's groups, announcements of visiting women dignitaries, and briefs on the participation of Egyptian women in various national and international conferences.

This sense of the kinship of women across national boundaries was further reinforced by the text of the articles themselves, which relied frequently on the trope of sisterhood and unity between women of different nationalities. An article about a meeting of Egyptian and other African women, for example, extolled the unity displayed by the "children of one continent."[32] Another claimed to inform its readers all about the lives of their "Iraqi sisters."[33] An article in *Al-Musawwar* about Sudanese women asserted, "women are women everywhere."[34] In addition, the prevalence of articles on women in countries such as Vietnam, Algeria, and Mozambique, which were undergoing or had recently emerged from wars of national liberation against European powers, stressed the solidarity of Egyptian women with colonized and formerly colonized women as victims of a common history of oppression and Western domination.[35] Such gendered representations of solidarity were not confined to articles in the women's press; a photograph in *Al-Musawwar* depicted a mural that was painted to welcome delegates to the Afro-Asian Youth Conference in 1959, which showed a smiling female figure clothed in the flags of the nations represented at the conference (Figure 5.1).

It would be a mistake to view the various national and supranational communities invoked by articles on non-Egyptian women as contradictory or mutually exclusive. To do so would risk missing the fluid nature of subjectivity and self-definition at a time in Egyptian history when the primacy of the nation-state as the locus of identity was largely taken for granted. I argue instead that representations of foreign women articulated multiple nexuses of identity, which were contextually specific and whose boundaries were perpetually shifting and overlapping. An Egyptian woman could be an Arab woman vis-à-vis non-Arab women, an Eastern woman vis-à-vis European women, a

Figure 5.1. Mural welcoming delegates to the Afro-Asian Youth Conference to Cairo in 1959. *Al-Musawwar,* Jan. 30, 1959, 11.

socialist woman vis-à-vis nonsocialist women, an African woman vis-à-vis Asian women, or a woman vis-à-vis an Egyptian man.

It is important to note here that the universalizing rhetoric of "sisterhood," not surprisingly, was class-specific; feminist theorizations of sisterhood and community as they appeared in these articles elided the class identity of writers and subjects alike by making it into a norm for progressive politics and proper citizenship. Interviews with and representations of the largely middle- and upper middle-class women from other countries who were most often the focus of these articles depicted them as prototypical representatives of their respective national womanhoods. For unlike prescriptive biography, which purported to tell the life stories of *exemplary* women, articles about "other women" tended to portray the attitudes and experiences of middle-class women as those of the "normal" national female subject.

DEFINING BACKWARDNESS AND CIVILIZATION

If articles about "other women" can be seen as part of the Nasser regime's attempts to contribute to the forging of a new world political order and the opening of new political spaces, they should also be located within the more local project of national (self)definition. In an article about women in West Germany, Amina Sa'id wrote, "Whenever I visit a foreign country for the first time . . . I observe the status of women in it and the status of our women and then I work from this to extract a comparison . . . the place of the modern Egyptian woman in the pageant of world civilization." Compared to advanced societies like Britain, France, and America, Egyptian women were still "at the bottom of the ladder."[36] However, compared to the conditions of most Asian and African women, she argued, Egyptian women were the pinnacle of culture and advancement. The rhetoric of superiority that often reared its head when Egyptian women wrote about other women has a prehistory that raises some uncomfortable questions about feminism, solidarity, and anticolonial politics. In her work on imperial feminism, Antoinette Burton has demonstrated how British feminist self-images were constructed through reading images of Indian women in the women's press: "Representing these women and making them topics of debate about femininity, emancipation and progress," she writes, "[British] feminists objectified women of the East into types of their own making."[37] Depictions of non-Egyptian women both subverted and reinscribed this imperial paradigm.

Representations in the Egyptian women's press were simultaneously a project of identification and objectification. On the one hand, the authors of these articles and indeed the rhetorical strategies of the articles themselves, were the product of a postcolonial, explicitly anti-imperial context that stressed the kinship and common struggles of non-Western women against Western oppression and domination. On the other hand, depictions of other women acted as a foil against which Egyptian women could exhibit their role as agents of civilization and the modernity of Egyptian society, primarily in relation to other colonized or formerly colonized nations of Africa, Asia, and the Arab world. "Whenever I go to the region of our Arab brothers and sisters, I find afflicted women," wrote Sa'id. "They fervently desire to follow our example and would benefit greatly if we took them by the hand in their striving to achieve a better life. . . . If we want, truly, to preserve our leadership in our greater nation (the Arab world) it is not right to confine our efforts to ourselves."[38] Fumiyal Labib, a male journalist who regularly wrote for *Ruz al-Yusuf* and *Al-Musawwar* and was an occasional contributor to *Hawwa'*, wrote a piece for the magazine about women in Pakistan based on observations he made during a trip there in 1960: "My impression of the Pakistani woman, from first to last, is that she is a backward woman [*imra'a mutakhalifa*], [but] I excuse her. Because the Pakistani woman is governed by traditions [*taqalid*] passed down for generations and centuries."[39]

Among the social practices that marked Pakistani womanhood as backward were the prevalence of adolescent marriage, uncontrolled reproduction, and the persistence of *purdah*—norms and social institutions that confined women to the homosocial space of the household and strictly regulated contact between unrelated males and females. In other articles, practices such as veiling and sex segregation were almost universally juxtaposed with the "new" activities women were undertaking in the public sphere, such as waged professional work and the pursuit of higher education. The home as a locus of women's oppression and ossified traditions exemplified by polygamy, arranged marriages, and extended kinship networks was posed against the more enlightened model of the nuclear family, companionate marriage, and bourgeois domesticity. The extent to which a nation could be considered "advanced" depended on the extent to which it adhered to a particular constellation of social, political, and economic practices identified as "modern." The assumptions behind what constituted modernity (and liberation) were highly gendered. Based on the condition and level of "emancipation" of their women, nations could be located along a linear continuum delineating the stages of social development from "backward" to "modern" or civilized.

The discourse of underdevelopment or backwardness as it appeared in these articles frequently erased complicated histories and relations of power between Egyptian women and foreign women. An article entitled "Your Sudanese Sister in Her Path to Liberation" traced early girls' education as the beginning of women's emancipation in Sudan and lauded the role of Egyptians who were among the first to establish girls' schools there.[40] What it failed to mention was that the presence of Egyptian educators in Sudan was a direct result of Egypt's colonial policies there.[41] Other articles provided justification for Egyptian military involvement in a brutal civil war in Yemen on the side of Abdullah al-Sallal, an officer in the Yemeni army brought to power by the military coup that overthrew Yemen's quasi-monarchical leader Imam Ahmad in 1962.[42] An article that appeared in *Hawwa'* in 1964, at the height of Egyptian involvement in the conflict, praised the Sallal government for bringing progress and enlightenment to Yemen's women.[43] The Yemeni woman, the article asserted, was "living the sweetest days of her life. She has begun to see the light and ascend to a vast new awakening of development and progress." Whereas she had suffered mutely under the "iron hand" of the monarchy, the Yemeni woman was now removing her veil and taking her rightful place in the perpetuation of the revolution and the building of her nation.[44] Another article, which appeared in the women's pages of *Akhir Sa'a*, purported to present "the true picture of the life led by women in post-revolutionary Yemeni society." The article's first page featured the heading "The Grip of the Imam Has Been Lifted from Around Her Neck."[45] A photo essay, also in *Akhir Sa'a*, juxtaposed pictures of a Yemeni woman, her entire body including her face obscured by a black burka, with a picture of two unveiled young women in school uniforms (Figure 5.2). According to the photo's caption, the two were learning math from one of the Egyptian women teachers who provided much of the staff for Yemen's system of female education.[46] Differences between Egyptian women also came to be constituted through articles on foreign women. The same article by Fumayil Labib that accused Pakistani women of backwardness also pointed to the similarities, in culture and situation, to peasant women in the Egyptian Sa'id (the South). Another piece, describing the traditional nature of Yemeni rural society, where strict division between the sexes was enforced and

Figure 5.2. "The Yemeni Woman." *Akhir Sa'a*, Aug. 11, 1965.

girls' education was virtually nonexistent, declared that "the Yemeni peasant woman is a picture of the Egyptian peasant woman."[47]

Through narratives of progress and (under)development, representations of other women constituted difference as a product not of politics and power but of temporal disjuncture. Taken as part of a wider discourse of secular modernity, however, such narratives were neither static nor coherent. Far from being a fixed set of norms, attributes, and relationships, what is identified as modern in these texts is fluid, indeterminate, and subject to multiple reinterpretations, contestation, resistance, and negotiation. Depictions of other women were a site for such negotiations by Egyptian women. What the "new woman" of state feminism was supposed to look like, how to reconcile the demands of development and progress with the preservation of Egyptian cultural authenticity, and what constituted appropriate norms of masculinity and femininity were (and remain) contentious issues. Representations of non-Egyptian women revealed the tensions that the project of making Egypt "modern" was fraught with, and the anxieties about changing gender roles. They also, however, textually provided ways for readers to reconcile those tensions and imagine new possibilities for their lives even as they foreclosed other possibilities.

SOVIET WOMEN

In an article entitled "Equality: Does It Make Women Happy?" Amina Sa'id wrote about the life of women in the Soviet Union.[48] The Soviet woman, she pointed out, has equal status with men in all areas of life. She works in medicine, engineering, law, and industry, and the law guarantees her equal salary and equal opportunity. At the same time, labor legislation offers her protection as a wife and mother, giving her generous maternity leave and the right to socialized day care for her children. Asserting that Soviet women enjoy more rights than women in any other nation in the world, she wrote: "I believe that equality, in this depiction, expresses the hope of women among many peoples and I don't doubt that many deem the Soviet woman fortunate in what has come to her. [But] I say equality in this absolute meaning inflicts grave hardships on the Soviet woman and make[s] her lose more than she gains."[49] The picture of Soviet womanhood that Sa'id goes on to present is a grim one. Her duties to home and to nation diminish her socially and physically. She is denied the valorization that accrues to women as the pillar of home and family without being exempted from domestic duties. She works eight hours a day and, returning home in the evening, cooks, cleans, and cares for her husband and children for another five. She does nothing but work and sleep. She is too tired to care for her physical appearance, which in any case begins to deteriorate at a young age. "Hard work," wrote Sa'id, "crushes her femininity." In this depiction, "modern" life and women's emancipation result in a process of desexualization and the destruction of gender difference.[50]

Other articles Sa'id wrote on her 1958 trip to the Soviet Union, however, provided an alternative narrative of Soviet womanhood. Of particular interest to Sa'id was the condition of women in the republics, particularly those like Azerbaijan and Uzbekistan, which had largely Muslim populations. In an article subtitled "Eastern in Form and Content," she portrayed the Uzbek woman as "fiercely" nationalistic in her adherence to Uzbek cultural values. This strong sense of national identity is mirrored by her preference for traditional Uzbek clothing over Western fashion, and her modesty in both dress and demeanor. The young Uzbek woman, Sa'id wrote, is a picture of "innocent femininity . . . she is [of all people] most emphatic in defense of her honor and purity." The preservation of cultural values, however, did not mean that Uzbek women were "backward." On the contrary, argued Sa'id in a second article, Uzbek women were not only economically and politically liberated like other Soviet women; they were socially liberated as well. At the same time, the Uzbek woman remains distinguished by "her dignity, refinement and modesty." She considers these a matter of propriety (*adab*), just as she considers it a matter of propriety to serve her nation through working for national development.[51]

What is important about these varying depictions of the condition of Soviet women is not that they are contradictory. Rather, it is how those contradictions attempted to resolve the tensions within notions of modernity and authenticity in the women's press and within Egyptian society generally. In particular, they represent ways for writers to reconcile anxieties about the effect that changing gender roles would have on the boundaries between masculinity and femininity and the health of the social order, which was predicated on the strict regulation of such boundaries. Through adherence to ostensibly authentic *national* cultural practices of gendered propriety and bodily discipline, the potential dangers of modern life could be averted and women could take their place in the nation as fully enfranchised citizens and national subjects. Representations of other women in the Egyptian women's press during the 1950s and 1960s offered a (textual) resolution to those tensions and anxieties engendered by the Nasserist state-building project's assumption that the "emancipation" of Egyptian women was a precondition for the emancipation and development of Egypt itself.

This linking of the liberation of women with the liberation of the nation, from colonial control and from backwardness, and the equating of *adab* with both women's participation in nation-building and gendered norms of modesty and refinement, was emancipatory as well as disciplinary. It allowed women to make new claims for rights and to envision new sorts of freedoms and gender roles in the name of progress and modernity, but it placed such roles in the context of submission to the national project. New or "nontraditional" roles for women could be justified in terms of service to the nation but only, ultimately, if cultural authenticity was preserved through the policing of other sorts of gendered boundaries.

REVOLUTIONARY WOMEN

In 1966, *Hawwa'* featured a portrait of Hu Dum, an eighteen-year-old Vietnamese woman who left her village and family to fight with the Vietnamese National Liberation Front forces on the Ho Chi Minh Trail. The article, written by Sabri Abu al-Majid, describes her as "a symbol of bravery" in her nation's fight against colonialism.[52] She became so well known and respected as a fighter and patriot that Ho Chi Minh himself reportedly gave her a "fatherly kiss" when he met her for the first time. However, she was also a potentially ambiguous figure who blurred the boundaries between masculinity and femininity. She is pictured in men's clothing carrying a rifle and is described as fighting alongside men in the field of battle. The author writes that as a child, she played with toy guns and airplanes instead of dolls. The possible conflict between ungendered national duty and the norms of proper female gendered subjectivity is ultimately resolved. With her long, silky black hair, gentle smile, and soft-spoken manner, she is portrayed as the picture of modern Vietnamese womanhood—militant, determined, and self-sacrificing in the cause of national liberation, but demure, modest, and feminine—a dutiful daughter in the service of the Vietnamese national family.[53]

The "domestication" of revolution was a common trope in depictions of fighting women. One of the most chronicled individual women in these articles was the Algerian freedom fighter Jamila Buhayrid. Buhayrid's contribution to the armed resistance against French control waged in Algeria from 1954 to 1962 and her arrest by colonial authorities made her a heroine across the Arab world. She was featured on the cover of a number of Egyptian magazines, including *Al-Musawwar*, and her life story was made into a feature film by internationally known Egyptian director Youssef Chahine. An article about Buhayrid, which appeared in *Hawwa'*, portrays the Algerian revolution as a family affair. Jamila becomes politicized by hearing her female schoolmates talk about their fathers and brothers fighting in the mountains. She is pictured at home trying to answer her younger siblings' questions about the conflict. Her uncle, a *mujahid* (freedom fighter), provides her an example of the worthiness of struggle. A faithful husband and a good father, he never shirks his family duties towards the nation or the struggle.[54] In an article entitled "The Algerian Woman," Algerian women's participation in armed struggle is presented as a function of their role within the family as the guardian and embodiment of national culture and the boundary marker of communal identity: "The lovely half (of society) has carried half the burden in national struggle and the gentle sex has traveled side by side with the other sex . . . she knows how to kill and how to meet death." Yet at the same time, it is a "secret" that the same freedom fighter is also conservative in her home and family. The author attributes this to the fact that fathers and grandfathers handed down customs and traditions along with patriotism and love for the nation (*watan*). It was the gender-specific duty of Algerian women to retain and protect such customs from "corruption" by French colonialism.[55] Thus, even as she takes up arms at the side of her Algerian "brothers," she remains firmly located within the realm of cultural authenticity represented by ties of kinship.[56]

CHINESE WOMEN

In contrast to the women's press, articles in the mainstream press tended not to offer such resolutions to their readers. A comparison between two articles on women in China that appeared within several years of each other in different publications is instructive. An article in the more mainstream magazine *Ruz al-Yusuf* stressed the defeminizing aspects of China's drive to modernize.[57] The author begins the piece by declaring that although he had run across plenty of Chinese men who looked like women and carried women's names, he had not seen even one female, or one female that displayed any of the "distinguishing marks of femininity." In fact, with hair tightly braided or hidden under a cap, and in the harsh, navy blue pants and blouse that provided the ubiquitous national uniform in Maoist China, she is indistinguishable from a man, even to the point of possessing masculinity (*rajula*). The article marvels at the number of women in the workforce, but also blames production for the erasure of gender boundaries. After numerous descriptions of the backbreaking labor undertaken by Chinese women in factories and fields, the author goes on to present a picture of women in China that is barely human. Chinese women, he writes, have no notion of love, either for husbands or children. In fact, he asserts, they feel oppressed by their duties as wives and mothers. Despite the presence of child care facilities at factories and labor regulations that stipulate women's right to take a break during the day to visit their children, few women exercise this right. "The madness of production in China is a sickness spread among the ranks of women," the article concludes. Women are also, however, the source of China's development: "The Chinese Woman, not the Chinese man, is the sinew of the new renaissance and the pillar upon which the government is based. New China!"[58]

By contrast, an article in *Hawwa'* that appeared a few years after the *Ruz al-Yusuf* piece was entitled "The Chinese Woman Has Ended the Battle of Construction and Has Begun the Battle of Beauty and Elegance."[59] The article begins in a way reminiscent of the *Ruz al-Yusuf* article, with the author recalling a previous visit to China when he asked his female interpreter about the blurring of gender boundaries he observed there. Her reply is printed (ostensibly) verbatim: "Listen. The Chinese woman is like every woman in the world.

She is concerned about her clothes and elegance. But today we are building the nation. For the sake of this great goal we dedicate all the minutes of our lives." After the nation has been developed, she says, "the Chinese woman will turn your gaze with her charms." Five years later, the author writes, "Chinese women have returned to the world of femininity . . . [T]he fashion of Chinese girls will come to rival that of American and European girls." The photo spread that accompanies the article underscores this conclusion. One photo shows a woman shopping for fabric in a chic, Western-looking store. Another shows a mother with her fashionably dressed child, with the caption "Elegance extends to the small child in China. And this picture is evidence of the extent to which children here are given attention."[60] According to the *Hawwa'* article, the potentially destabilizing effects of development on gender boundaries were averted by the reinscription of those boundaries once the process of modernization was completed.

CONCLUSION

The nation-state was not the only site for the elaboration of secular modernity and its attendant state feminist project. The reiteration of international feminism in the context of decolonization provided the occasion for new actors to engage in the project of refashioning women in ways that were not so much a departure but a rearticulation, having its own contextual and historical specificities. Representations of foreign women in the Egyptian women's press were intimately tied up with wider discussions about liberation, progress, and national subjectivity and self-definition. They also suggest much about how the liberating, emancipatory possibilities of postcolonial, anti-imperialist projects limit their own possibility for realization. The vision of an anti-imperialist global sisterhood in these articles was undermined by Egyptian authors' recourse to a colonialist discourse of development and progress that objectified non-Egyptian women as a locus of debate about gender and modernity in Egypt.

Acknowledging the imperial genealogy of such discourses, however, should not prevent us from recognizing that they had complicated histories as well. The representations through which Egyptian women authors attempted to make sense of their identities as national subjects and to resolve the gender tensions that were part of that subjectivity do not conform to an East/West binary. As conversations about what it meant to be a modern citizen in a modern society, depictions of "other women" during the era of state feminism and decolonization in Egypt challenge arguments that debates over modernity in the postcolonial world have simplistically embraced Western knowledges and technologies. On the contrary, such depictions were products of a historical moment when "modernity" as a universal project could be claimed by colonized and formerly colonized people as a basis of national struggle and international solidarity. If defining what the meanings of that project would be entailed drawing distinctions between women, the process of imagining "other women" was also a means to imagining other possible futures.

CONCLUSION

The Legacies of State Feminism

IN AN INTERVIEW CONDUCTED a few years before her death in 1996, Latifa al-Zayyat told her interviewer that her landmark novel, *The Open Door,* hailed by critics as a poignant expression of the hopes and aspirations of a revolutionary generation, is now "an impossibility."[1] Over the last three decades, Nasserist narratives of modernity have been challenged by the failures of state socialism, the policy of *infitah* (open door policy) that began Egypt's transition to market capitalism and its incorporation into global markets in 1974, and the Islamization of Egyptian society and politics.

The devastating and humiliating defeat suffered by Arab armies in the 1967 war with Israel, referred to collectively as "the setback" (*al-naksa*), marked for many the end of an era. The corruption of the Nasser regime and the vacuousness of its political slogans and solutions, which had promised liberation and brought only destruction, were revealed in the cold and sordid light of the post-1967 defeat. Although Nasser himself remained in power after an outpouring of public support, it was a moment of profound disillusionment, exacerbated by Nasser's unexpected death in 1970. His successor, Anwar al-Sadat, sought to distance himself personally and politically from his predecessor. In 1974, Sadat announced that he would abandon the import substitution policies of the Nasser regime in favor of *infitah* (opening), which would open Egyptian markets to Western capitalist investment. Such policies, coupled with privatization and the scaling back of public sector services, have had a profound effect on Egyptian society. The widening gap between a wealthy, *infitah*-created elite and the rest of society; the eroding economic fortunes of the professional middle classes that had been created by state socialism; the social dislocations left by the retreat of the state in its commitment to providing social services to its citizens; and the increasing visibility of Islamist political groups (initially encouraged by Sadat as a counterweight to remaining pro-Nasserist forces)—all have combined to underscore popular disillusionment with the secular modernist solutions of the previous era and have given support to the fashioning of Islamist modernist futures.

Reflecting on Egypt's neoliberal present from the vantage point of its state socialist past, Zayyat told her interviewer, "roads to salvation are blocked; the common ground of shared values seem to break down into multiple different sets of values according to the varied social strata; the common sensibility and its language is no more; people lacking national unity are divided and subdivided until each is turned into an insular island." "Young Egyptian women," one Egyptian critic wrote several years ago, "don't see themselves in the heroine of *The Open Door*. They no longer believe that what Layla achieves by the end of the book is possible for them."[2]

This book has been an attempt to grapple with the promises and pitfalls of nation- and state-building during a pivotal and, today, very much contested period of Egyptian history; it has tried to attend to the ways that notions of feminism shaped (and were shaped by) the conditions of political possibility that were claimed by a revolutionary generation at a moment of great hope and optimism. To scholars of gender, nationalism, and feminism in twentieth-century Egypt, the Nasser regime's policies towards women appear as something of a paradox. The regime suppressed independent feminist activism and organization at the same time that it created institutions and structures giving Egyptian women new opportunities to work, to gain an education, and for some, to access positions of authority and prominence in their chosen professions. It promised emancipation to all Egyptian women, but its primary beneficiaries were women of the middle class. While the revolutionary regime spoke in the voice of secular modernization, it bowed to the forces of religious conservatism by failing to heed the calls for the reform of the personal status laws, thus perpetuating a vision of Egyptian womanhood that reaffirmed traditional cultural and religious visions of women as essentially dependent beings. Egyptian women were subordinated to a state that, while having an interest in mobilizing them in the service of its own development projects, left patriarchal family relations largely untouched, and proved itself to be hostile to dissenting voices and independent activism. In this sense, the 1952 revolution seems to mark yet another betrayal of Egyptian women, not unlike that of earlier male nationalists, who welcomed women's participation in anticolonial activism but excluded them from political participation after independence.

This study bears many of these assessments out. But it also questions the tendency to locate the problematic nature of Nasserist gender politics largely within its failures as a progressive nationalist project—its failure to reform patriarchal relations within the family, to allow independent feminists a measure of autonomy, and to live up to its promises of liberation and social justice for all Egyptian women. These failures are real enough. But foregrounding them has meant that scholars have missed some of the broader significances of state feminism, its novelties, and how its paradoxes speak to the wider contradictions of modernizing state projects. What does looking at the project of fashioning revolutionary womanhood tell us about feminism, modernity, and the state during this period?

Historians of the Nasser period have frequently pointed to the regime's lack of ideological consistency. And yet, its rendering of "the woman question" and its attempts to transform Egyptian women as historical individuals into the singular "revolutionary woman" as an exemplar of national progress were not as ad hoc as scholars have suggested. This is not to suggest that such measures were either seamless or uncontested but to argue that state feminism was bounded by the history of debates—about modernity, gender, national identity, and social progress—that had shaped the woman question since its emergence at the end of the nineteenth century and had made projects of remaking women central to fashioning a modern nation-state, populated by self-governing national subjects. It points to the stubborn persistence of such framings at a period in Egyptian history that witnessed significant social, political, and ideological transformations. Nasserist discourses on Egyptian womanhood reproduced earlier nationalist formulations that made effecting progress contingent on both a modern, reformed female presence in the domestic realm and a disciplined female presence within a heterosocial sphere of public participation and sociability.

What was novel was the revolutionary regime's success in linking a normative vision of liberation and Egyptian womanhood to the hegemonic visions and regulatory mechanisms of modern state-building, a process that had its roots in earlier colonial and nationalist projects aimed at remaking women but one that became fully operational only in the period following the revolution. The regime's appropriation of the woman question was significant, not only because it reconfigured women's citizenship and made the state the focus of claiming and contesting gendered boundaries and rights but also because citizenship—as many works on gender and citizenship have pointed out—is a process of subject-making, which in the name of progress, development, and social justice the regime claimed for itself, on a scope unprecedented in Egyptian history.[3] Attempts to reimagine and transform space, notions of the body, relations and sentiments of affectivity, religiosity, law, and moral virtue were central to defining the conditions of political and social possibility in the context of revolutionary change, and the complex meanings of citizenship and state-building for the women who were simultaneously its subjects and its objects.

Understanding some of what was at stake in that process means examining critically not only who the beneficiaries of this project were (and who was excluded from it, and in what ways) but the ways state feminism reconfigured the meanings of gender and liberation, making them central to new narratives of modernity as well as the "discrepant desires" such narratives produced.[4] During the Nasser period, those desires appeared more universal and yet also more authentically Egyptian than ever before. I am reminded here of a conversation I had with an Egyptian acquaintance of mine who had been a teenager in Cairo during the 1950s and 1960s and who had grown up in a middle-class milieu of miniskirts, the pulpy novels of author Ihsan Abdel Qaddus—featuring the trials and tribulations of the new revolutionary woman—and after-school pilgrimages with school friends to downtown Cairo cinemas, where movie stars like Suad Husni and Shadia lit up the screen. Over a cup of tea proffered to a nosy foreign guest, she reflected on those days, concluding, "Islamists today complain about how after the revolution women became so Westernized," she said. "But we never thought about it as being Westernized, we just thought of it as being modern." Her observation of the past, framed as it is by the preoccupations of the contemporary moment as well as her own class position, nevertheless speaks to the wider claims to universalism that postrevolutionary renderings of modernity invoked.

Shorn of its political and cultural associations with the domination by a Europeanized elite, its complicated colonial genealogies effaced, the Nasserist discourse on modernity provided "a new hegemonic interpretation of lived experience" (as Lisa Rofel has put it) in which the local project of building an Egyptian nation-state and the transglobal phenomena of decolonization, nonalignment, and postcolonial solidarity movements intersected to shape political and ideological practices as a means of envisioning, and creating, a world free of colonial domination and imperialist exploitation.[5] The promises of this discourse lay in its vision of an imagined future, a vision lent credence by its claims to universality. In her study of gender and narratives of modernity in China, Rofel has pointed out that modernity's insistent power as an imagined status (much in the same way that the nation functions as an imagined community) is what leads government leaders, agents of development, intellectual elites, culture producers, subaltern workers, peasants, and women—those who represent political power as well as those who are objects of its operations—to act in the name of the desires it engenders. That they do so, she has argued, is because of the techniques of normalization secured in modernity's name.[6] With this point in mind, it is not enough to say that state feminism benefited only middle-class women. Rather, we must attend to the ways in which normative definitions of revolutionary womanhood, which are foundational to Egyptian narratives of modernity during this period, set the terms of engagement that all Egyptians have had to grapple with—to embrace, to reject, resist, redefine, negotiate, and challenge.

This brings me to another point. Insofar as state feminism was a politically prescriptive project, it not only entailed authoritarian political repression but also demanded the refashioning of the sensibilities, commitments, and social worlds of women (and men) whose lives contrasted with its emancipatory vision. Universal rights coincided with the development of new forms of discipline, producing new regimes of gender and class difference. Discourses of inclusion, national unity, and social welfare acted to consign gendered notions of personhood, social practices, and forms of attachment that appeared stubbornly and persistently inimical to the task of national development to the realm of the atavistic, and made their transformation central to the realization of an inevitable unbounded future. Such disciplinary maneuvers intended to uplift women were not confined to the lower classes; but the figuration of subaltern women in national development projects points to how state feminism effaced gender and class differences and also reconfigured them through the construction of a singular notion of revolutionary womanhood to which all Egyptian women were expected to conform. Attributing the paradoxes of state feminism to an undifferentiated notion of "patriarchy," localized in the home and represented by religious conservatives, whose authority the state failed to sufficiently curb, obscures how hierarchies of gender and class were actively produced. Some forms of masculine authority, such as those presumed by forms that cohered to a vision of family consistent with heterosexual intimacy and rationalized reproduction, were normalized and reaffirmed; others—because of presumed notions of family and sociability that ran counter to hegemonic definitions of appropriate gender relations—were viewed as exceptionally problematic from the perspective of state feminism. Some manifestations, practices, and structures of religiosity (with their attendant notions of gender difference) were explicitly part of the engineered inclusion of religion that was characteristic of Egyptian definitions of secularism; others were repudiated as backwards. The inclusions, exclusions, occlusions, and erasures that state feminism as a project was predicated upon forged vertical and horizontal linkages, hierarchies of dependence, and affiliation based on structuring dichotomies of male/female, urban/rural, and backward/enlightened; this was a process that entailed a complex recognition of gendered agency as well as its foreclosure.

Given how notions of gender became so centrally entwined with the processes of the secular modernizing state, what are the legacies of state feminism at a moment when such secular visions of modernity are being increasingly questioned and challenged by Islamism, and when the state itself has retreated? A visitor to a government or corporate office in contemporary Egypt will see a space that looks somewhat different from its appearance in the 1960s. For one thing, that space contains more women. The policies adopted to encourage women's participation in the formal waged labor force during the period of state socialism—particularly the expansion of educational opportunities—have born fruit in succeeding generations. Since the 1960s, women's participation in the formal waged labor force has grown to 24 percent, much of that a reflection of the influx of women into middle- or lower-level professional positions. The majority of women in that space will also look different. The shorter skirts that provided the working uniform for the "new woman" of the 1960s have been replaced in many urban areas by longer skirts, longer sleeves, and a headscarf, which covers to various degrees the hair and neck—garments collectively referred to as *hijab* or *al-ziyy al-Islami* (Islamic dress).

The mid-1970s witnessed the beginning of what some have termed a "return" to the practice of veiling. In fact, this practice was something new. Beginning on college campuses and eventually spreading to other parts of the population, the "new veiling," as Arlene MacLeod has referred to it, was at least initially a primarily urban middle- and lower middle-class phenomenon. Its practitioners were precisely those women who, a generation later, were the beneficiaries of the educational and work opportunities created by state feminism and socialist nation-building.

For secularist liberals and progressives, the Islamization of Egyptian society, most visibly symbolized by the proliferation of veiling, is representative of wider and troubling attempts by Islamists to circumscribe women's rights and to return women to traditional roles in the home. In a 1984 issue of *Hawwa'* devoted to "the modern woman in Egypt," Amina Saʿid decried the veil as a form of women's enslavement. More recently, Minister of Culture Faruq Husni touched off a storm of protest when he referred to veiling as a manifestation of backwardness and social regress. Such critiques and narratives of loss, like those with which this conclusion began, evidence a considerable anxiety about the fate of secularism in Egypt, an anxiety heightened by the fact that the Islamists—whose pamphlets and recorded sermons proliferate on the pavement stands and kiosks of urban Egyptian streets, and whose television programs instruct Egyptian viewers how to be proper Muslims in their everyday lives—are addressing those messages to the very "masses" whose cause the secular nation-state has championed and whose condition secular modernizing projects have claimed to uplift.

Islamists, for their part, have viewed the effects of secular nationalism as particularly corrosive to Egyptian society and claim to offer a more "authentic approach," one not tainted by Westernization, crass borrowing, and the importation of foreign practices and their imposition on a Muslim society. Attempts to elaborate and disseminate visions of a new Muslim womanhood have been central to projects aimed at the creation of a more Islamic society. Although Islamist prescriptions for change are quite diverse, and visions of normative gender relations may differ in their particulars, they share some general commonalities. One of these is the advocacy of *hijab* as a religious duty. Other aspects of Islamist gender prescriptions include an emphasis on women's roles in the family, particularly as mothers, the inculcators of appropriate Muslim values to children, and as supportive spouses to husbands. The valorization of the domestic as the proper sphere of women's activities has led many prominent Islamist thinkers to voice concerns about the potentially corrosive and disruptive effects of women's waged labor outside the home. This, coupled with the advocacy for veiling, seems to signal a "return" to traditional family forms and a wholesale rejection of state feminism and the gendered tenets of secular modernity it was predicated on.

And yet, Islamist prescriptions, no less than other projects of remaking women, are projects of modernity, albeit a modernity framed in religious as opposed to secular terms. Questions about everyday life, which are the primary focus of those advocating for an Islamization of social relations—What is the proper gendered division of labor in the home? What should Muslim women do to maintain proper standards of propriety and modesty in co-ed workplaces? How should good Muslims go about choosing a spouse? What kind of education should women receive in order to become properly pious subjects?—are asked precisely because institutions like marriage, the family, education, labor, and social welfare have been incorporated into the regulatory structures of the modernizing state.[7]

Moreover, as various scholars who work on gender and Islamism have pointed out, the framing of such questions, as well as the various solutions posed, reveal significant overlaps between secular and religious prescriptions for appropriate gender relations, overlaps that are effaced by analyses that take dichotomies between religion and modernity as axiomatic.[8] Islamists reject some aspects of state feminism, such as family planning and the unveiled presence of women in public, as alien to Islamic societies, the useless aping of Western ways, at best, or at worst, projects that bolster Western imperialism. Other foundational tenets of Egyptian modernizing projects, however, are adopted largely without question as the means of investing modernity with Islamic values. These gendered practices and prescriptions of modernity have genealogies that predate the 1952 revolution, but it was during the Nasser period when such practices and prescriptions became truly nationalized.

Polemics on veiling, for example, share significant assumptions with Nasserist gender discourses in which the uncovered, unveiled presence of women marked the public sphere as modern and secular. For Islamists, part of what is at stake is the visibility of Islam within the public sphere, signaled by the visibility of the veiled body. Covering is what makes women legible as proper pious subjects or (to its opponents) backwards subjects whose presence is threatening to secular nationalism. *Hijab* is a complicated practice with various aesthetic, social, and religious meanings to the women who adopt it, and it resists being reduced to any one framing. However, in the most general sense, *hijab* is the means by which Muslim women are able to maintain obligatory standards of modesty and propriety in contexts where they are in constant contact with unrelated men. Veiling presumes the presence of women in public space, defined by its heterosociability, and not their seclusion from it. Islamist discourses on domesticity—which focus on delineating the material and affective contributions spouses owe to each other, and the critical contributions mothers make to raising the next generation of enlightened Muslims—are undergirded by assumptions about heterosexual intimacy as the basis of the nuclear family. Girls' education, up to and including university education, is largely presumed and often actively embraced as contributing to the advance and greater benefit of Islamic society. Zaynab al-Ghazali, who was perhaps the most influential female Islamist in Egypt until her death in 2005, enjoined the young Muslim woman at school or college "to be a good example for her colleagues so she makes sure she achieves the highest of grades in her lessons and thus becomes an example of positive achievements and practical achievements."[9] Even women working outside the home, if not recognized by all Islamists as an ideal to aspire to, is acknowledged as a socioeconomic reality.

Education as the means to civilizational uplift, companionate marriage, enlightened motherhood, veiling as a means of claiming public space, work as a social reality—all of these aspects of Islamist gender discourses signal that Islamist cultural projects aimed at fashioning a new Muslim woman are an engagement with the institutional, discursive, and epistemological frameworks of the secular nation-state. They are negotiations with modernity rooted in the state feminism and modernizing projects of postcolonial state-building.

NOTES

Introduction

1. See Mervat Hatem, "Economic and Political Liberation and the Demise of State Feminism," *International Journal of Middle East Studies* 24 (1992): 231–251; "Secularist and Islamist Discourses on Modernity in Egypt and the Evolution of the Postcolonial Nation-State," in *Islam, Gender and Social Change*, ed. Yvonne Haddad and John Esposito (Oxford, UK: Oxford University Press, 1998), 85–99; "The Pitfalls of Nationalist Discourse on Citizenship in Egypt," in *Gender and Citizenship in the Middle East*, ed. Suad Joseph (Syracuse, NY: Syracuse University Press, 2000), 33–57.

2. James Jankowski, "Arab Nationalism in 'Nasserism' and Egyptian State Policy, 1952–1958," in *Rethinking Nationalism in the Arab Middle East*, ed. James Jankowski and Israel Gershoni (New York: Columbia University Press, 1997), 150–167; *Nasser's Egypt, Arab Nationalism and The United Arab Republic* (Boulder, CO: Lynne Rienner, 2002); Kirk Beattie, *Egypt During the Nasser Years: Ideology, Politics and Civil Society* (Boulder, CO: Westview Press, 1994); Joel Gordon, *Nasser's Blessed Movement* (New York: Oxford University Press, 1992); Leonard Binder, *In a Moment of Enthusiasm: Political Power and the Second Stratum in Egypt* (Chicago: University of Chicago Press, 1978); Anouar Abdel-Malek, *Egypt, Military Society: The Army, The Left and Social Change Under Nasser*, trans. Charles Lam Markmann (New York: Random House, 1968); Hrair Dekmenjian, *Egypt Under Nassir: A Study in Political Dynamics* (Albany: State University of New York Press, 1971); Derek Hopwood, *Egypt Politics and Society, 1945–1990* (London: Routledge Press, 1993); Mahmoud Hussein, *Class Conflict in Egypt, 1940–1975* (New York: Monthly Review Press, 1973); Peter Mansfield, *Nasser's Egypt* (London: Methuen Educational, 1963); Nessim Rejwan, *Nasserist Ideology: Its Exponents and Critics* (New York: John Wiley, 1974); P. J. Vatikiotis, *Nasser and His Generation* (London: Croom Helm, 1978); John Waterbury, *The Egypt of Nasser and Sadat: The Political Economy of Two Regimes* (Princeton, NJ: Princeton University Press,

1983); Kenneth Wheelock, *Nasser's New Egypt* (Westport, CT: Greenwood Press, 1975); Ahmed Hamrush, *Qissat Thawrat Yulyu* (Beirut: Al-Mu'assasa al-'Arabiyya li-l-Tiba'a wa-l-Nashr, 1978); Rif'at al-Sa'id, *Ta'ammulat fi al-Nasiriyya* (Cairo: Al-Mada, 2000).

3. Joel Gordon, *Revolutionary Melodrama: Popular Film and Civic Identity in Nasser's Egypt* (Chicago: Middle East Documentation Center, 2002); Elie Podeh and Onn Winckler (eds.), *Rethinking Nasserism: Revolution and Historical Memory in Modern Egypt* (Gainesville: University Press of Florida, 2004); Amira Sonbol, *The New Mamluks: Egyptian Society and Modern Feudalism* (Syracuse, NY: Syracuse University Press, 2000), ch. 5.

4. Such an understanding of both gender and politics derives from the work of Joan Scott. Joan Scott, *Gender and the Politics of History* (New York: Columbia University Press, 1988).

5. Camron Amin, *The Making of the Modern Iranian Woman: Gender, State Policy, and Popular Culture, 1865–1946* (Gainesville: University Press of Florida, 2002); Selma Botman, *Engendering Citizenship in Egypt* (New York: Columbia University Press, 1999); Sondra Hale, *Gender Politics in Sudan: Islamism, Socialism, and the State* (Boulder, CO: Westview Press, 1996); Marnia Lazreg, *The Eloquence of Silence: Algerian Women in Question* (New York: Routledge Press, 1994); Afsaneh Najmabadi, *Women with Mustaches, Men Without Beards: Gender and Sexual Anxieties of Iranian Modernity* (Berkeley: University of California Press, 2005); Parvin Paidar, *Women and the Political Process in Twentieth-Century Iran* (Cambridge, UK: Cambridge University Press, 1995); Lisa Pollard, *Nurturing the Nation: The Family Politics of the 1919 Revolution* (Berkeley: University of California Press, 2004); Elizabeth Thompson, *Colonial Citizens: Republican Rights, Paternal Privilege and Gender in French Syria and Lebanon* (New York: Columbia University Press, 2000).

6. Deniz Kandiyoti, "Introduction," in *Women, Islam and the State*, ed. Deniz Kandiyoti (Philadelphia: Temple University Press, 1991), 1.

7. Mervat Hatem, "Toward a Critique of Modernization: Narrative in Middle East Studies," *Arab Studies Quarterly* 15 (Spring 1993): 9.

8. Peter Dodd, "Youth and Women's Emancipation in the United Arab Republic," *Middle East Journal* 22 (Summer 1968): 159–172; David Lerner, *The Passing of Traditional Society* (Glencoe, IL: Free Press, 1958).

9. Ijlal Khalifa, *al-Haraka al-Nisa'iyya* (Cairo: Al-Matba'a al-'Arabiyya al-Haditha, 1973).

10. Such a view is reproduced even in much more sophisticated treatments of Egyptian women. These works, which are quite careful to attend to the differences of class and location between women and are much more sanguine about the state as an agent of gender liberation, nonetheless reinscribe the assumption that women's access to the public sphere is necessarily emancipatory while the private remains the prima-

ry locus of gender inequality. See Soha Abdel Kader, *Egyptian Women in a Changing Society, 1899–1987* (New York: Lynne Rienner, 1987); Leila Ahmed, *Women and Gender in Islam: Historical Roots of a Modern Debate* (New Haven, CT: Yale University Press, 1992); Selma Botman, *Engendering Citizenship in Egypt* (New York: Columbia University Press, 1999); Nikkie Keddie, *Women in the Middle East: Past and Present* (Princeton, NJ: Princeton University Press, 2007), 122–123; Earl Sullivan, *Women in Egyptian Public Life* (Cairo: American University in Cairo Press, 1986).

11. Hatem, "Toward a Critique of Modernization," 9.

12. See, for example, Hibba Abugedieri, *Gender and the Making of Modern Medicine* (Aldershot, UK: Ashgate, 2010); Judith Tucker, *Women in 19th Century Egypt* (Cambridge, UK: Cambridge University Press, 1985).

13. Lila Abu-Lughod, "Introduction," in *Remaking Women: Feminism and Modernity in the Middle East*, ed. Lila Abu-Lughod (Cairo: American University in Cairo Press, 1998), 7.

14. Ibid., 6.

15. Margot Badran, *Feminism in Islam: Secular and Religious Convergences* (Oxford, UK: Oneworld, 2009), ch. 1; Selma Botman, "The Experience of Women in the Egyptian Communist Movement, 1939–1954," *Women's Studies International Forum* 11:2 (1988): 117–126; Amal al-Subky, *Al-Haraka al-Nisaʿiyya fi Misr* (Cairo: Al-Hayʾa al-Misriyya al-ʿAmma li-l-Kitab, 1984); Cynthia Nelson, *Doria Shafik, Egyptian Feminist* (Cairo: American University in Cairo Press, 1996).

16. See Nadje al-Ali's ethnography of the Egyptian women's movement for an account of how different generations of women activists have experienced and remembered the post-1952 period. Nadje al-Ali, *Secularism, Gender and the State in the Middle East: The Egyptian Women's Movement* (Cambridge, UK: Cambridge University Press, 2000).

17. Tani Barlow, *The Question of Women in Chinese Feminism* (Durham, NC: Duke University Press, 2006), 65.

18. Badran, *Women, Islam and Nation*, 20.

19. Ahmed, *Women and Gender in Islam*, ch. 8.

20. Barlow, *Question of Women in Chinese Feminism*, 4.

21. Roel Meijer, *The Quest for Modernity: Secular Liberal and Left-Wing Political Thought in Egypt, 1945–1958* (London: RutlegdeCurzon, 2002), 177.

22. See, for example, Chandra Mohanty, "Under Western Eyes: Feminist Scholarship and Colonial Discourses," in *Third World Women and the Politics of Feminism*, ed. Chandra Mohanty, Ann Russo, and Lourdes Torres (Bloomington: Indiana University Press, 1991), 51–80, and her later follow-up, "Under Western Eyes Revisited: Feminist Solidarity Through Anti-Capitalist Struggle," in her book, *Feminism Without Borders: Decolonizing Theory, Practicing Solidarity* (Durham, NC: Duke University Press, 2004), 221–251.

23. For a definition of colonial modernity, see Tani Barlow, "Introduction," in *Formations of Colonial Modernity in East Asia* (Durham, NC: Duke University Press, 1997), 1–21.

24. Partha Chatterjee, *The Nation and Its Fragments* (Princeton, NJ: Princeton University Press, 1993), 10.

25. Chatterjee, *Nation and Its Fragments*, 116–145; Dipesh Chakrabarty, "The Difference-Deferral of a Colonial Modernity: Public Debates on Domesticity in Bengal," in *The Tensions of Empire: Colonial Cultures in a Bourgeois World*, ed. Frederick Cooper and Ann Stoler (Berkeley: University of California Press, 1997), 373–406.

26. Baron, *Egypt as a Woman*; Marilyn Booth, *May Her Likes Be Multiplied* (Berkeley: University of California Press, 2001).

27. This is a point that Omnia Shakry has also made for an earlier period. Omnia Shakry, "Schooled Mothers, Structured Play: Child Rearing in Turn of the Century Egypt," in Abu-Lughod, *Remaking Women*, 130.

28. In addition to previously mentioned works on Egypt, see Ellen Fleischmann, *The Nation and Its "New" Women: The Palestinian Women's Movement, 1920–1948* (Berkeley: University of California Press, 2003); Elizabeth Thompson, *Colonial Citizens: Republican Rights, Paternal Privilege and Gender in French Syria and Lebanon* (New York: Columbia University Press, 2000); Marnia Lazreg, *The Eloquence of Silence: Algerian Women in Question* (New York: Routledge Press, 1994).

29. Saba Mahmood, *The Politics of Piety: The Islamic Revival and the Female Subject* (Princeton, NJ: Princeton University Press, 2005); Fadwa El Guindi, *Veil: Modesty, Privacy and Resistance* (London: Berg, 1999); Azza Karam, *Women, Islamisms and the State* (London: Macmillan, 1998); Ghada Talhami, *The Mobilization of Muslim Women in Egypt* (Gainesville: University Press of Florida, 1996); Sherifa Zuhur, *Revealing Reveiling: Islamist Gender Ideology in Contemporary Egypt* (Albany: State University of New York Press, 1992).

30. See Ami Ayalon, "Journalists and the Press: The Vicissitudes of Licensed Pluralism," in *Egypt from Monarchy to Republic: A Reassessment of Revolutionary Change*, ed. Shimon Shamir (Boulder, CO: Westview Press, 1995), 267–282.

31. Cynthia Nelson's biography of Duriyya Shafiq is a notable exception. See Nelson, *Doria Shafik*.

32. Booth hypothesizes that increases in female literacy and the spread of the novel displaced prescriptive biographies in magazines.

33. *Hawwa*"'s major competitor *Bint al-Nil* (Daughter of the Nile) was closed in 1957 when its founder and editor, Duriyya Shafiq, was placed under house arrest for her criticism of the regime's increasing authoritarianism.

34. When she graduated in 1935, Amina Sa'id was the first woman to receive a de-

gree in English from Cairo University's Faculty of Arts. Duriyya Shafiq was one of the first Egyptian women in Egypt to gain a French baccalaureate.

35. These supranational visions of identity included Islamic, pan-Arab, and communist. See Israel Gershoni and James Jankowski, *Redefining the Egyptian Nation* (Cambridge, UK: Cambridge University Press, 1995).

36. Abu-Lughod, "Introduction," 13.

Chapter 1

1. Gamal Abdel Nasser, *The Charter* (Cairo: Maslahat al-Isti'lamat, 1962), 49.

2. Latifa al-Zayyat, *The Open Door*, trans. Marilyn Booth (Cairo: American University in Cairo Press, 2000), 24.

3. Ibid., 79.

4. Ibid., 218–219.

5. Nasser, *Charter*, 92–93.

6. See Ahmed, *Women and Gender in Islam*, for a detailed discussion of Amin and the reception of his works.

7. For a particularly nuanced account of how such questions emerged around womanhood and family, see Lisa Pollard's groundbreaking study, *Nurturing the Nation: The Family Politics of Modernizing, Colonizing and Liberating Egypt* (Berkeley: University of California Press, 2005).

8. The complex discursive and material ways in which colonizing projects marked out indigenous domestic practices and family models as both symbol and source of native backwardness, in contrast to the enlightenment and modernity of middle-class European family norms, have been well documented, as have the ways in which such notions structured colonial states' claims to political authority. See, for example, Janice Boddy, *Civilizing Women: British Crusades in Colonial Sudan* (Oxford, UK: Oxford University Press, 2007); Dipesh Chakrabarty, "The Difference-Deferral of a Colonial Modernity: Public Debates on Domesticity in Bengal," in *The Tensions of Empire: Colonial Cultures in a Bourgeois World*, ed. Frederick Cooper and Ann Laura Stoler (Berkeley: University of California Press, 1997), 373–405; Julia Clancy-Smith and Frances Gouda, eds., *Domesticating the Empire: Race, Gender and Family Life in French and Dutch Colonialism* (Charlottesville: University Press of Virginia, 1998); Anna Davin, "Imperialism and Motherhood," *History Workshop Journal* 5 (Spring 1978): 9–66; Inderpal Grewel, *Home and Harem: Nation, Gender Empire and the Cultures of Travel* (Durham, NC: Duke University Press, 1996); Karen Hansen, ed., *African Encounters with Domesticity* (New Brunswick, NJ: Rutgers University Press, 1992).

9. See Omnia Shakry, "Schooled Mother and Structured Play: Child Rearing in Turn of the Century Egypt," in Abu-Lughod, *Remaking Women*, 126–170.

10. Beth Baron, "Mothers, Morality and Nationalism in pre-1919 Egypt," in *The*

Origins of Arab Nationalism, ed. Rashid Khalidi et al. (New York: Columbia University Press, 1991), 271–288; Afsaneh Najmabadi, "Crafting an Educated Housewife in Iran," in Abu-Lughod, *Remaking Women*, 91–125; Samita Sen, "Motherhood and Mother-craft: Gender and Nationalism in Bengal," *Gender and History* 5 (Summer 1993):s 231–243.

11. For a useful overview of the debates and struggles engendered by reformer Qa-sim Amin's call for "the liberation of women," see Juan Cole, "Feminism, Class and Islam in Turn-of-the-Century Egypt," *International Journal of Middle East Studies* 13 (Fall 1981): 387–407.

12. I take the term *effendiyya nationalism* from Israel Gershoni and James Jankowski. According to Gershoni and Jankowski, *effendi* was a term used in Egypt in the early twentieth century to refer to a new urban, educated, professional middle class of native Egyptians, which stood, on the one hand, below the existing Ottoman elite (mostly of Turco-Circassian background) and the European *haute bourgeoisie* and, on the other hand, above the urban working classes and the masses of the rural peasantry. Israel Gershoni and James Jankowski, *Redefining the Egyptian Nation, 1930–1945* (Cambridge, UK: Cambridge University Press, 1995), 11.

13. The Wafd Party developed out of an organization that was formed in 1918 by lawyer and former minister of justice Saʿd Zaghlul to take Egyptian demands for independence from British rule to the Paris Peace conference. The political and social unrest that culminated in a mass uprising of Egyptians against British colonial control was touched off by the British decision, in March of that year, to exile Zaghlul and his supporters to the island of Malta.

14. Pollard, *Nurturing the Nation*, 8.

15. On the symbolic importance of Safiyya Zaghlul and its wider connection to gendered visions of the nation, see chapter 6 in Beth Baron's book *Egypt as a Woman: Nationalism, Gender and Politics* (Berkeley: University of California Press, 2005).

16. R. W. Connell, "The State, Gender, and Sexual Politics: Theory and Appraisal," *Theory and Society* 19 (Oct. 1990): 507–544.

17. Elizabeth Thompson, *Colonial Citizens: Republican Rights, Paternal Privilege and Gender in French Syria and Lebanon* (New York: Columbia University Press, 2000), 67. Paternalism is distinguished from patriarchy by its fluidity. While patriarchy connotes the structural subordination of women to men, paternalism signifies a system of negotiated relations and hierarchies in which elite men continually reconstruct their authority over women as well as subaltern men.

18. Lynn Hunt, *The Family Romance of the French Revolution* (Berkeley: University of California Press, 1992), xiii. See also Geraldine Heng and Jenandas Devan, "State Fatherhood: The Politics of Nationalism, Sexuality and Race in Singapore," in *Nationalisms and Sexualities*, ed. Andrew Parker et al. (New York: Routledge, 1992), 343–364;

Anne McClintock, "Family Feuds: Gender, Nationalism and the Family," *Feminist Review* 44 (Summer 1993): 61–80.

19. As quoted in Margot Badran, *Feminism in Islam: Secular and Religious Convergences* (Oxford, UK: Oneworld, 2009), 24. The 1929 electoral law, passed six years later, further restricted voting and holding of office to male property holders, disenfranchising male subalterns.

20. These included requiring a sizeable fee to run in elections, thus identifying the right to hold office with those of financial means and the extraordinary powers given to the king, including the right to dissolve parliament and to appoint one third of the members of the senate, enshrining the privilege of a Turco-Circassian elite that had ruled Egypt since the nineteenth century. Mervat Hatem, "The Pitfalls of Nationalist Discourses on Citizenship in Egypt," in *Gender and Citizenship in the Middle East*, ed. Suad Joseph (Syracuse, NY: University of Syracuse Press, 2000), 35–37.

21. Thus, Selma Botman argues that "The decision to proscribe women from performing duties of citizenship was consistent with the power men possessed: Men assigned social roles and women accepted their designated lot. . . . The patriarchal family survived because the state circumscribed the temporal rights of women." Botman, *Engendering Citizenship in Egypt*, 40. For accounts of women's participation in the events of 1919, see Badran, *Feminists, Islam and Nation*, ch. 4; Baron, *Egypt as a Woman* ch. 5; Thomas Phillipp, "Feminism and Nationalist Politics in Egypt," in *Women in the Muslim World*, ed. Lois Beck and Nikki Keddie (Cambridge, MA: Harvard University Press, 1978), 277–294.

22. The 1929 electoral law restricted voting and holding of office to male property holders, disenfranchising male subalterns.

23. Pollard, *Nurturing the Nation*, 209.

24. Lisa Pollard has suggested that the relative lack of state interest in the provision of social services was consistent with the attempt of liberal-nationalist elites to give paternalism a more masculine cast. The imagery of Egyptian nationalism, because of its emphasis on the nurturing roles that male nationalist elites had played in "birthing" a new political system, had forced elites to take gendered feminine stances in response to the British occupation. After independence, images of "Egypt-as-woman" and depictions of nationalist leaders in nurturing paternal (and sometimes maternal) roles were gradually replaced by depictions of leaders in hypermasculine activities, like bricklaying, which symbolized the process of state-building (as opposed to nation-building). See Lisa Pollard, "Manly Men or Colonized Effeminates? Gender in Egypt's Colonial and Post-Colonial Political Experience," paper presented at conference "Gendering the Middle East," Middle East and Middle Eastern American Center, City University of New York, Dec. 12, 2003.

25. As quoted in Hatem, "Pitfalls of Nationalist Discourses," 72.

26. Cathlyn Mariscotti makes this point in a much more sustained way in *Gender*

and Class in the Egyptian Women's Movement, 1929–1935 (Syracuse, NY: Syracuse University Press, 2008).

27. My point here is not that male laborers were imagined as autonomous political subjects and women were not. The paternalism of liberal-nationalist rule translated into a concept of the worker as a dutiful subject of elite nationalist leadership. The point is that working-class women were not "imagined" to be laboring subjects at all. See Zachary Lockman and Joel Beinin, *Workers on the Nile: Nationalism, Communism, Islam, and the Egyptian Working Class, 1882–1954* (Princeton, NJ: Princeton University Press, 1987); Zachary Lockman, "Imagining the Working Class: Culture, Nationalism and Class Formation in Egypt, 1899–1914," *Poetics Today* 15 (Summer 1994): 157–190.

28. Hatem, "Pitfalls of Nationalist Discourses," 43.

29. Enrollment in general at secondary schools tripled in the ten years between 1925 and 1935, while enrollment in higher education doubled. By 1945, there were more than four times the number of secondary and university students than there had been twenty years earlier. The expansion of education, particularly at the secondary and university levels, contributed to the growth of a professional class. A degree from a secondary school or university was a passport into one of the professions of the then prestigious civil service. From 1937 to 1947 the number of government clerks, teachers, medical and legal specialists, engineers, writers, and journalists is estimated to have increased by almost 40 percent. Nonetheless, demand for civil servants seemed unable to keep pace with the supply of graduates.

30. Gershoni and Jankowski, *Redefining the Egyptian Nation*.

31. As quoted in Samia Kholoussi, "Fallahin: The 'Mud Bearers' of Egypt's 'Liberal Age,'" in *Re-Envisioning Egypt: 1919–1952*, ed. Arthur Goldschmidt, Amy Johnson, and Barak Salmoni (Cairo: American University in Cairo Press, 2005), 284.

32. Amy Johnson attributes the popularization of this phrase, which would become a catchphrase to describe social conditions in Egypt throughout reformist discourses, to Wendall Cleland, an American social researcher who was a professor at the American University in Cairo. See Amy Johnson, *Reconstructing Rural Egypt: Ahmed Hussein and the History of Egyptian Development* (Syracuse, NY: Syracuse University Press, 2004).

33. For more in-depth discussion of *The Policy of Tomorrow*, which situates it within wider currents of reform and political developments, see Meijer, *Quest for Modernity*, ch. 1. For an account of how Ghali's depictions intersected with other cultural and political representations of the peasantry, see Kholoussi, *Fallahin*.

34. Related measures pertaining specifically to state extension of control to the countryside included the creation of the Fallah department of the Ministry of Social Affairs and the establishment of a rural health section within the Ministry of Public Health.

35. As quoted in Johnson, *Reconstructing Rural Egypt*, 52.

36. Omnia El Shakry, *The Great Social Laboratory: Subjects of Knowledge in Colonial and Postcolonial Egypt* (Stanford, CA: Stanford University Press, 2007), 166.

37. The Rural Social Centers project, a pilot project for rural reconstruction launched by Hussein under the auspices of the Ministry of Social Affair's Fallah department in 1942, was typical of such projects. Posted at each Rural Social Center was a female "health visitor" whose duties included visiting each home regularly to instruct village women in proper housekeeping methods, hygiene, and child care. This included such novel approaches as holding a "cleanest home" contest, as well as the more traditional approach of holding lectures and classes for village women. Health visitors, who were graduates of a technical training program in nursing run by Cairo's Qasr el-Aini Hospital, were also charged with training a few promising young village women in nursing and midwifery in order to help raise the health standard of pregnant women and newborns. For a more detailed account of the Rural Social Centers project, see Johnson, *Reconstructing Rural Egypt*, ch. 3; Amy Johnson and Scott David McIntosh, "Empowering Women, Engendering Change: Aziza Hussein and Social Reform in Egypt," in Goldschmidt, Johnson, and Salmoni, *Re-Envisioning Egypt*, 249–277.

38. The best and most theoretically nuanced account of this shift is El Shakry, *Great Social Laboratory*, particularly chs. 4 and 5.

39. Wendell Cleland, *The Population Problem in Egypt* (Lancaster, PA: Science Press, 1936). Cleland, an American sociologist who was a professor at the American University, was responsible for drawing up a plan for the creation of "model villages" in Egypt that became a blueprint for rural reconstruction. A pilot project based on his work was eventually implemented by the Ministry of Social Affairs in the Delta villages of Manyal and Shatanuf.

40. Wendell Cleland, "Egypt's Population Problem," *L'Egypte Contemporaine* 167 (1937): 82.

41. Cleland, "Egypt's Population Problem," 85.

42. El Shakry, *Great Social Laboratory*, ch. 5.

43. A. M. Annous, "The Dangers of Frequent Childbearing and Necessity of Birth Control," *Journal of the Egyptian Medical Association* 20 (July 1937): 273.

44. El Shakry, *Great Social Laboratory*, 191. See also Rayna Rapp and Faye Ginsberg, "Introduction," in *Conceiving the New World Order: The Global Politics of Reproduction*, ed. Rayna Rapp and Faye Ginsburg (Berkeley: University of California Press, 1995), 1–18.

45. Amy Johnson and Scott David McIntosh, "Empowering Women, Engendering Change: Aziza Hussein and Social Reform in Egypt," in Goldschmidt, Johnson, and Salmoni, *Re-Envisioning Egypt*, 257.

46. I take the term "social housekeeping" from Mary Ryan. Mary Ryan, *Mysteries*

of Sex: Tracing Women and Men Through American History (Chapel Hill: University of North Carolina Press, 2006), 165.

47. Mervat Hatem, "Bayn Ru'ya Qadima wa Jadida," in *Min Ra'idat al-Qarn al-'Ashrin: Shakhsiyyat wa Qadaya*, ed. Huda Sada (Cairo: Multaqa al-Mar'a wa-l-Dhakira, 2001), 15–35.

48. Afsaneh Najmabadi, "(Un) Veiling Feminism," *Social Text* 64 (Fall 2000): 29–45.

49. See Hasan Banna, *Al-Mar'a Al-Muslima* (Cairo: Dar al-Kutub al-Salafiyya, 1983).

50. Walter Armbrust, *Mass Culture and Modernism in Egypt* (Cambridge, UK: Cambridge University Press, 1996), 83. Lucy Ryzova makes a similar point in her chapter "Egyptianizing Modernity Through 'The New Effendiyya': Social and Cultural Constructions of the Middle Class in Egypt Under the Monarchy," in Goldschmidt, Johnson, and Salmoni, *Re-Envisioning Egypt*, 124–163.

51. Baron, *Egypt as a Woman*, 199–200.

52. The fact that Ahmad herself veiled did not seem to preclude her use of this symbol in the first decade of the journal's publication.

53. Duriyya Shafiq's mother was from an old and eminent landowning family, but her father was a government-employed engineer, as was Latifa al-Zayyat's. Sa'id's father was a physician who had been jailed for his anti-British activities in 1919, and Suhayr Qalamawi's father was also a doctor. There were important exceptions to this: Zaynab al-Ghazali's father was an al-Azhar–educated cotton merchant. Inji Aflatun was from a wealthy Turco-Circassian family but, unusual for a woman of her background, attended a national university.

54. Suhayr Qalamawi, a writer and literary scholar, graduated in the first class of matriculated women from the faculty of arts before going on to earn her PhD in 1941. Sa'id, who would become the editor of the magazine *Hawwa'* and the most public advocate of state feminism in the post-1956 period, received a degree in English in 1935. Aflatun and al-Zayyat, who would become known both for their cultural achievements (Aflatun was a painter and al-Zayyat became a writer) and for their activism in leftist politics, were members of the faculty of arts in the 1940s.

55. Ahmed, *Women and Gender in Islam*, 189.

56. As quoted in Selma Botman, "The Experience of Women in the Egyptian Communist Movement," *Women's Studies International Forum* 2 (1988): 124.

57. Ibid., 125.

58. As quoted in Valerie Hoffman, "An Islamic Activist: Zaynab al-Ghazali," in *Women and Family in the Middle East*, ed. Elizabeth Fernea (Austin: University of Texas Press, 1985), 234.

59. Ibid., 235–236.

60. I take this term from Lila Abu-Lughod, "The Marriage of Feminism and Is-

lamism in Egypt: Selective Repudiation as a Dynamic of Postcolonial Cultural Politics," in Abu-Lughod, *Remaking Women*, 243–269.

61. Among these were the Union of Higher Institutes and University Women, which was founded in 1945. Although it was closed down a year later in a general government crackdown against leftist organizations, over the subsequent years the general membership of the group reorganized itself under different names with the same twenty or thirty core members. General membership fluctuated between 100 and 250. For a more detailed history of these organizations, see Akram Khater and Cynthia Nelson, "Al-Harakah Al-Nissa'iyah: The Woman's Movement and Political Participation in Modern Egypt," *Women's Studies International Forum* 11 (1988): 465–483; Selma Botman, *The Rise of Egyptian Communism: 1939–1970* (Syracuse, NY: Syracuse University Press, 1991); Amal al-Subki, *Al-Haraka Al-Nisa'iyya fi Misr Bayn al-Thawratayn 1919–1952* (Cairo: al-Hay'a al-Misriyya al-'Amma li-l-Kitab, 1984).

62. Botman, "Experience of Women in the Egyptian Communist Movement," 121.

63. As quoted in ibid., 123.

64. According to Margot Badran, it was an exclusively Cairo organization, which ultimately had a limited influence. It lasted only a few years.

65. In 1953 Bint al-Nil organized as a political party, which was dissolved a year later along with all other parties.

66. Fatima Ni'mat Rashid, "Hizbuna Laysa Hizbiyyan," *Fatat al-Ghad*, July 5, 1945.

67. See, for example, 'Atiya Fahmi, "Hal Han al-Waqt li-l-Mutaliba bi Huqquqina al-Siyasiyya?" *Fatat al-Ghad*, Oct. 6, 1945.

68. "Barlamanuna al-Awwal," *Bint al-Nil*, Jan. 14, 1954.

69. Nasser's father was a postman, and Sadat's was a clerk at a military hospital.

70. Anouar Abdel-Malek, *Egypt: Military Society; The Army, The Left and Social Change Under Nasser*, trans. Charles Lam Markmann (New York: Random House, 1968); Hamied Ansari, *Egypt: The Stalled Society* (London: Oxford University Press, 1963); Kirk Beattie, *Egypt During the Nasser Years: Ideology, Politics and Civil Society* (Boulder, CO: Westview Press, 1994); Leonard Binder, *In a Moment of Enthusiasm: Political Power and the Second Stratum* (Chicago: University of Chicago Press, 1978); Hrair Dekmejian, *Egypt Under Nasir: A Study in Political Development* (Albany: State University of New York Press, 1971); Joel Gordon, *Nasser's Blessed Movement: Egypt's Free Officers and the July Revolution* (New York: Oxford University Press, 1992); Ahmad Hamrush, *Qissat Thawrat Yulyu* (Beirut: Al-Mu'asasa al-'Arabiyya li-l-Tiba'a wa al-Nashr, 1978); James Jankowski, *Nasser's Egypt, Arab Nationalism and The United Arab Republic* (Boulder, CO: Lynne Rienner, 2002); Mahmoud Hussein, *Class Conflict in Egypt, 1945–1970* (New York: Monthly Review Press, 1973); Elie Podeh and Onn Winckler, eds., *Rethinking Nasserism* (Gainesville: University Press of Florida,

2004); Shimon Shamir, ed., *From Monarchy to Republic: A Reassessment of Revolution and Change* (Boulder, CO: Westview Press, 1995); John Waterbury, *The Egypt of Nasser and Sadat: The Political Economy of Two Regimes* (Princeton, NJ: Princeton University Press, 1983).

71. First of these was the Liberation Rally created in 1953, which was responsible for little more than holding lavish demonstrations and commemorative events in support of the regime. It was followed by the National Union in 1956 and, finally, in 1961 by the Arab Socialist Union, the most highly organized of the three. Membership in the ASU reached the five million mark in the last half of the 1960s, but only a small percentage of these were likely active members.

72. Waterbury, *Egypt of Nasser and Sadat*, 221.

73. Hekmat Abou-Zeid et al., *The Education of Women in the U.A.R. During the 19th and 20th Centuries* (Cairo: U.A.R., National Commission of UNESCO, 1970).

74. Joel Gordon's book *Nasser's Blessed Movement* remains the best chronicle of the years following the revolution and the evolving ideological and political orientations of the regime.

75. Land redistribution in Egypt, for example, was less radical in form and content than contemporaneous projects of land reform in Taiwan and South Korea, which were decidedly antirevolutionary in intention. I want to thank the series editor for alerting me to this point.

76. Meijer, *Quest for Modernity*, 13–14.

77. A recent, noteworthy exception is Christopher Lee's edited volume. Christopher Lee, ed., *Making a World After Empire: The Bandung Moment and Its Political Afterlives* (Athens: University of Ohio Press, 2010).

78. Meijer, *Quest for Modernity*, 230–232.

79. Gamal Abdel Nasser, *Falsafat al-thawra* (Cairo: Dar al-Ma'arif, 1960).

80. Nelson, *Doria Shafik*, 185.

81. As Earl Sullivan argues, this was largely the case until Anwar Sadat's wife, Jihan, redefined the role of Egyptian presidential wives to one more closely approximating that of an American "first lady." See Earl Sullivan, *Women in Egyptian Public Life* (Cairo: American University in Cairo Press, 1986), ch. 3.

82. The regime banned the Muslim Brotherhood after an attempt on Nasser's life that occurred in October 1954. Despite the regime's leftist orientation, Egyptian communists were alternatively repressed and tolerated throughout the years 1958–1964. In 1965 the Communist Party disbanded in order to join the Arab Socialist Union.

83. The National Congress of Popular Forces was made up of representatives from peasant, laborer, professional, and occupational associations chosen as delegates by the regime.

84. Amira Sonbol makes a similar point when she analyzes Nasser era socialism as

a kind of feudalism. Amira Sonbol, *The New Mamluks: Egyptian Society and Modern Feudalism* (Syracuse, NY: Syracuse University Press, 2000), ch. 5.

85. As quoted in United Arab Republic, Al-Lajna al-tahdiriyya li-l-Mu'tamar al-Watani li-l-Quwa al-Sha'biyya, *Al-Tariq ila al-Dimuqratiyya* (Cairo: Maslahat al-isti'lamat, 1961), 45–46.

86. Katherine Verdery, "From Parent-State to Family Patriarchs: Gender and Nation in Contemporary Eastern Europe," *East European Politics and Societies* 8 (Spring 1994): 226.

Chapter 2

1. "Banatuna fi Sahaf al-Almaniyya," *Ruz al-Yusuf*, Nov. 2, 1962.

2. Sa'id Na'matullah, "Hikayat Khams banat," *Akhir Sa'a*, Nov. 13, 1963, 19–21; Ibrahim al-Ba'thi, "Banat al-Sa'id ya'malna li-Awal Marra fi Masna' al-Ghazl," *Hawwa'*, July 21, 1962; "Nisa' Qina yunaqishna al-Mithaq," *Al-Ahram*, June 21, 1962, 1.

3. Na'matullah, "Hikayat Khams banat," 20.

4. Ibid.

5. Ibid., 21.

6. al-Ba'thi, "Banat al-Sa'id ya'malna li-Awal Marra fi Masna' al-Ghazl."

7. One of the reasons the factory girls of Qina became such a focus of interest and propaganda was the factory's location. In Egyptian nationalist imaginings, Upper Egypt, the eternal "Sa'id" was the land that time forgot—simultaneously a site of backwardness and trenchant resistance to the civilizing impulses emanating from Cairo, and a space where Egyptian cultural authenticity was preserved. The Upper Egyptian (Sa'idi) woman—ignorant, shrouded in black, locked away behind the walls of her home, literally and figuratively invisible—was a foundational marker of Upper Egypt's essential temporal otherness. For more about this ambivalence, see Jessica Winegar, *Creative Reckonings: The Politics of Art and Culture in Contemporary Egypt* (Stanford, CA: Stanford University Press, 2006), 81–87; Lila Abu-Lughod, *Dramas of Nationhood: The Politics of Television in Egypt* (Chicago: University of Chicago Press, 2004); Elliot Colla, "Shadi 'Abd al-Salam's *Al-Mummiya*: Ambivalence in the Egyptian Nation-State," in *Beyond Colonialism and Nationalism in the Maghrib: History Culture, Politics,* ed. Ali Abdullatif Ahmida (New York: Palgrave, 2000), 109–143.

8. United Arab Republic, Ministry of National Guidance, *The Role of Women in the UAR* (Cairo: State Information Service, 1967). The pamphlet appeared in Arabic, French, and English editions. See also United Arab Republic, Ministry of National Guidance, *Al-Mar'a fi-l-Jumhuriyya al-'Arabiyya al-Muttahida* (Cairo: State Information Service, 1966); The Arab Republic of Egypt, *Egyptian Women: A Long March from the Veil to Oct. 6, 1973* (Cairo: State Information Service, 1974).

9. *Ahlam al-banat*, dir. Berlanti 'Abd al-Hamid, 1960; *Li-l-Rijal Faqat*, dir. Mahmud Zul-Fiqar, 1964; *Mrati Mudir 'Amm*, dir. Fatin 'Abd al-Wahhab, 1966.

10. Nor were such images confined to an Egyptian audience. The Kuwaiti magazine *Al-'Arabi*, which was not distributed throughout the Arab world, often featured on its cover photos of Egyptian working women, whom it portrayed as representative of "the new Arab Woman."

11. On this issue, see Heba Aziz El-Kholy, *Defiance and Compliance: Negotiating Gender in Low-Income Cairo* (New York: Berghahn Books, 2002); Nadia Hijab, *Womanpower: The Arab Debate on Women at Work* (Cambridge, UK: Cambridge University Press, 1988).

12. I take the term "ideological work" from Mary Poovey, who uses it to describe gender relations in mid-Victorian England. Poovey argues that representations of gender constituted one of the sites on which ideological systems were simultaneously constructed and contested. . . . a locus of assumptions used to underwrite the very authority that authorized these struggles. Mary Poovey, *Uneven Developments: The Ideological Work of Gender in Mid-Victorian England* (Chicago: University of Chicago Press, 1988), 2.

13. Nilufer Gole and Alev Cinar have made a similar point about the ways in which the Kemalist program in Turkey represented women's unveiled presence in public as a symbol of the replacement of an Ottoman imperial system with that of a secular nation-state. See Nilufer Gole, *The Forbidden Modern: Civilization and Veiling* (Ann Arbor: University of Michigan Press, 1996), 71–74; Alev Cinar, *Modernity, Islam and Secularism* (Minneapolis: University of Minnesota Press, 2005).

14. For a more detailed discussion of Egyptian women in the labor force prior to 1947, see Soha Abdel Kader, *A Report on the Status of Egyptian Women, 1900–1973* (Cairo: American University in Cairo, Social Science Research Center, 1973); Margot Badran, *Feminism, Islam and Nation* (Princeton, NJ: Princeton University Press, 1995); Ijlal Khalifa, *Al-Haraka al-Nisa'iyya al-Haditha* (Cairo: Al-Matba' al-'Arabiyya al-Haditha, 1973); Latifa Salim, *Al-Mar'a al-Misriyya wa-l-Taghyir al-Ijtima'i* (Cairo: Al-Hai'a al-Misriyya al-'Amma li-l-Kitab, 1984); Taha Ahmad Taha, *Al-Mar'a: Kifahuha wa 'Amluha* (Cairo: Dar al-Jamahir, 1964); Judith Tucker, "Egyptian Women in the Workforce: An Historical Survey," *MERIP* 50 (Aug. 1976): 3–9, 26. Khalifa and Salim focus predominately on middle-class professional women.

15. Cathlyn Mariscotti has argued that protective legislation may have actually harmed working-class women by circumscribing the sorts of labor they could perform. Cathlyn Marriscotti, *Gender and Class in the Egyptian Women's Movement, 1929–1935: Changing Perspectives* (Syracuse, NY: Syracuse University Press, 2008).

16. Examples include mine work, work in foundries, or work that entailed the

operation of machinery, the manufacture of alcoholic beverages, and slaughtering animals.

17. For an account of trade union activity during this period, see Joel Beinin and Zachary Lockman, *Workers on the Nile: Nationalism, Communism, Islam, and the Egyptian Working Class, 1882–1954* (Princeton, NJ: Princeton University Press, 1987), ch. 13.

18. See Selma Botman, "The Experience of Women in the Egyptian Communist Movement, 1939–1954," *Women's Studies International Forum* 11 (1988): 121.

19. Laura Bier, "The Family Romance of Egyptian Labor: Gender and the Making of the Egyptian Working Class," unpublished manuscript.

20. This program was partially laid out in two five-year plans drawn up for the years 1960–65 and 1965–70, although the second was never implemented.

21. As a result of these measures, the workforce grew by nearly 22 percent, with the largest proportional growth occurring in civil service jobs.

22. Republic of Egypt, *Al-Dustur* (Cairo: Al-Matba' al-Amiriyya, 1956).

23. United Arab Republic, *Al-Mar'a fi al-Jumhuriyya al-'Arabiyya al-Muttahida*, 35.

24. Amira Sonbol, *The New Mamluks: Egyptian Society and Modern Feudalism* (Syracuse, NY: Syracuse University Press, 2000), 66–67.

25. By 1973, one quarter of all professional positions in Egypt were held by women. By 1976, educated women (those who had completed intermediate education and above) made up nearly half of the formal female labor force, despite composing just over 5 percent of the entire female population over the age of ten. Kader, *Report on the Status of Egyptian Women*, 44; Barbara Ibrahim, "Women in the Workforce," in *At the Crossroads: Education in the Middle East*, ed. Adnan Badran (New York: Paragon House, 1989), 282–302.

26. On the spread of education, see Ibrahim Hafez, *Education in the UAR, an Outline* (Cairo: Ministry of Education, 1964). In 1950, 24 percent of elementary teachers were women; by 1956, this number had risen to 34.6 percent. See United Arab Republic, Ministry of Education, Lajnat Bahth Shu'un al-Mudarrisat wa-l-Muwaziffat, *Bahth wa 'Alaj Mushkilat al-Mar'a al-Muwazzifa* (Cairo: Wizarat al-Tarbiyya wa-l- Ta'lim, 1959), 146.

27. In 1950, female students composed approximately 5.4 percent of the university student population. By 1964, that number had grown to 24 percent.

28. For a more detailed overview of the expansion of the public sector, see John Waterbury, *The Egypt of Nasser and Sadat*. According to Ijlal Khalifa, nationalization created work opportunities for Egyptian women who were brought in to take positions formerly held by foreign women. Khalifa, *Al-Haraka al-Nisa'iyya*.

29. See Kamal Sa'd, "Al-Waza'if al-'Aliyya Mahruma 'ala al- Nisa'," *Al-Musawwar,* June 16, 1964, 9–11. The barring of women from judgeships was a particular concern of

women activists. See "Limadha La Tusbihu al-Mar'a Qadiyya," *Akhir Sa'a*, July 1, 1964; "Hal Tusbihu Qadiyya?" *Akhir Sa'a*, June 13, 1962, 17.

30. Mervat Hatem, "The Paradoxes of State Feminism in Egypt," in *Women and Politics Worldwide*, ed. Barbara Nelson and Najwa Chadhury (New Haven, CT: Yale University Press, 1994).

31. See Mona Abaza, "The Changing Image of Women in Rural Egypt," *Cairo Papers in Social Science* 10 (Fall 1987): 60; Tucker, "Egyptian Women in the Workforce," 5.

32. According to Waterbury, the number of women working in agriculture declined from 244,000 women in 1961 to 206,000 in 1969.

33. Wage structures established the minimum wage for traditionally female tasks, such as cotton picking and the removal of cotton worms during cultivation, at two-thirds that of masculine tasks, such as plowing. Such wage structures were a significant cause of the seasonal demand for female labor, although demand for cotton pickers during the month of September (when cotton is picked) outweighed the available supply of women and children available to work. James Toth found that men preferred to engage in migrant labor, which was carried out almost exclusively by men and was better paid. James Toth, *Rural Labor Movements in Egypt and Their Impact on the State, 1961–1992* (Gainesville: University Press of Florida, 1999).

34. By comparison, women composed 45 percent of the Soviet labor force in 1954. Wendy Goldman, *Women at the Gates: Gender and Industry in Stalin's Russia* (Cambridge, UK: Cambridge University Press, 2002); Natasha Kolchevska, "Angels in the Home and at Work: Russian Women in the Khrushchev Years," *Women's Studies Quarterly* 33 (Fall 2005): 114–147. On women and labor mobilization in China, see Delia Davin, *Woman-Work: Women and the Party in Revolutionary China* (Oxford, UK: Oxford University Press, 1979); Kimberley Manning, "Making a Great Leap Forward? The Politics of Women's Liberation in Maoist China," *Gender and History* 18 (Nov. 2006): 574–593; Jin Yihong, "Rethinking the 'Iron Girls': Gender and Labour During the Chinese Cultural Revolution," *Gender and History* 18 (Nov. 2006): 613–634.

For comparisons with Eastern Europe, see Malgorzata Fidelis, "Equality Through Protection: The Politics of Women's Employment in Postwar Poland, 1945–1956," *Slavic Review* 63 (Summer 2004): 301–324; Eva Fodor, *Working Difference: Women's Working Lives in Hungary and Austria, 1945–1995* (Durham, NC: Duke University Press, 2003); Joanna Goven, "The Gendered Politics of Hungarian Socialism: State, Society and the Anti-Politics of Anti-Feminism, 1948–1990," PhD diss., University of California, Berkeley, 1993.

35. Hatem, "Paradoxes of State Feminism."

36. Muhammad Farghali Faraj and 'Abd al-Halim Mahmud al-Sayyid, *Taghyir al-Wad' al-Ijtima'i li-l-Mar'a fi Misr al-Mu'asira* (Cairo: al-Markaz al-Qawmi li-l-Buhuth al-Ijtima'iyya wa al-Jina'iyya, 1974).

37. See, for example, Joan Landes, *Women and the Public Sphere in the Age of the*

French Revolution (Ithaca, NY: Cornell University Press, 1988); Carol Pateman, *The Sexual Contract* (Stanford, CA: Stanford University Press, 1988).

38. Botman, "Engendering Citizenship," ch. 3; Hatem, "Paradoxes of State Feminism."

39. In her discussion of Moroccan women's entrance into the workforce, Fatima Mernissi argues that a woman's public presence is always an instance of trespassing in male space and as such is always counted as an aggressive and threatening act. Fatima Mernissi, *Beyond the Veil* (Bloomington: Indiana University Press, 1987), 144.

40. The *harim* was an institution associated with the Turco-Circassian political elite. The domestic arrangements that characterized elite Turco-Circassian households included polygamy, slavery, gender segregation, and bonds based on fictive (as opposed to biological) kinship ties. Unlike "the home" of Egyptian bourgeois imagination, the household was not defined as a discrete physical space but as a network of patronage in which all those who owed allegiance were supported by the master of the household and/or were counted as its members even when they lived in separate dwellings.

41. Timothy Mitchell, *Colonizing Egypt* (Berkeley: University of California Press, 1991), 112–113.

42. United Arab Republic, *Long March from the Veil,* n.p.

43. Partha Chatterjee, *The Nation and Its Fragments: Colonial and Post-Colonial History* (Princeton, NJ: Princeton University Press, 1993), 116–145. For a similar assessment of how gender served as a temporal marker in Chinese nationalist discourses, see Prasenjit Duara, "The Regime of Authenticity: Timelessness, Gender and National History in Modern China," *History and Theory* 37 (1988): 287–308.

44. "Is'aluni," *Al-Musawwar,* Jan. 22, 1965, 68.

45. "Is'aluni," *Al-Musawwar,* July 2, 1964, 54.

46. Amina Sa'id, "Hawl Tahrir al-Mar'a bi-l-'Aml," *Hawwa',* June 11, 1966, 13–14.

47. Evelyn Riyad, "Ta'attul al-Mar'a Akthar Khatiran 'ala al-Mujtama' min Bitalat al-Rajul," *Akhir Sa'a,* Jan. 10, 1962.

48. Amina Sa'id, "La Tabaqiyya fi al-Mabadi'," *Hawwa',* June 18, 1966, 16–17.

49. Amina Sa'id, "Limadha Nashtaghilu," *Hawwa',* Mar. 31, 1963, 14–15.

50. Yusuf Jabara, "Sa'adatuki fi al-Bayt wa Najahuki fi al-'Aml: Ittikayt al-Mar'a al-'Amila," *Hawwa',* July 15, 1961.

51. *Mrati Mudir 'Amm,* dir. Fatin 'Abd al-Wahhab, 1966.

52. Among them, the short story "Work," by Ihsan 'Abd al-Qaddus; and the film *Ustadha Fatima,* dir. Fatin 'Abd al-Wahhab, 1952. For works that locate films on working women within wider trends in the depiction of women during the Nasser period, see Viola Shafik, *Popular Egyptian Cinema: Gender, Class and Nation* (Cairo: American University in Cairo Press, 2007), part 2; Joel Gordon, *Revolutionary Melodrama:*

Popular Film and Civic Identity in Nasser's Egypt (Chicago: University of Chicago Middle East Center, 2002), ch. 4.

53. Nasser, *Charter*, 92–93.

54. See Nancy Reynolds, "Sharikat al-Bayt al-Misri: Domesticating Commerce in Egypt: 1931–1956," *Arab Studies Journal* 7 (Fall 1999/Spring 2000): 75–99.

55. See Ministry of Education, Lajna Bahth Shu'un al-Mudarissat wa-l-Muwazzifat, *Bahth wa 'Alaj Mushkillat al-Mar'a al-Muwazzifa* (Cairo: Wizarat al-Tarbiyya wa-l-Ta'lim, 1959); Ministry of Social Affairs, Al-Lajna al-Da'ima li-Shu'un al-Mar'a, *Mu'tamar Shu'un al-Mar'a al-'Amila*, Nov. 23–27, 1963; Hamid Sulayman, "Mata'ib al-mar'a Kharij al-Bayt," *Akhir Sa'a*, Oct. 7, 1963, 17–21.

56. Ministry of Education, Lajna Bahth Shu'un al-Mudarissat wa-l-Muwazzifat, *Bahth wa 'Alaj Mushkilat al-Mar'a al-Muwazzifa*, 6.

57. Wadi' Farid, "Thalathat Anwa' min al-Mar'a al-'Amila," *Hawwa'*, May 5, 1962, 36–37. The problem of teachers knitting during class time was perceived as so widespread in the public school system that the Ministry of Education eventually issued a decree that explicitly prohibited teachers from knitting at work.

58. Amina Sa'id, "Dur al-Hadana Khayr Hadiyya Nuqaddimuha li-l-Ummahat al-'Amilat," *Hawwa'*, Mar. 17, 1962.

59. "Insafu al-Mar'a al-'Amila," *Hawwa'*, Oct. 11, 1958, 40–41; Sabri Abu al-Majid, "al-Mudarissat bayn Mata'ib al-Mihna wa Qaswa al-Hayyat," *Hawwa'*, May 31, 1958, 40–41; Amina Sa'id, "Mushkilat al-Muwazzafat al-Mutazawwijat," *Hawwa'*, Apr. 11, 1958, 12–13; Su'ad Zuhayr, "Hal Taslah al-Mar'a Mudirat Masna'?" *Hawwa'*, Dec. 29, 1958.

60. This may be in part due to the routine provision of day care and other forms of child care services in rural social units.

61. Amina Sa'id, "Dur al-Hadana Khayr Hadiyya." For more detailed statistics, see Husayn 'Abd al-Qadar Ali, "al-Takhtit li-Dur al-Hadana," in *Proceedings of the Conference on the Family, Dec. 19–26, 1964 Cairo, Egypt* (Cairo: Ministry of Social Affairs, 1965), 301–365; United Arab Republic, *Mu'tamar Shu'un al-Mar'a al-'Amila*, 200–201.

62. "Azma Ismuha Dur al-Hadana," *Akhir Sa'a*, Sept. 15, 1965, 15–17.

63. United Arab Republic, *Mu'tamar Shu'un al-Mar'a al-'Amila*, 199.

64. See Omnia Shakry, "Schooled Mothers, Structured Play: Childrearing in Turn of the Century Egypt," in Abu-Lughod, *Remaking Women*, 126–170; Rebecca Joubin, "Creating the Modern Professional Housewife: Scientifically Based Advice Extended to Middle and Upper Class Egyptian Women, 1920s–1930s," *Arab Studies Journal* 4 (July 1996): 32–35; Hibba Abugedieri, *Gender and the Making of Modern Medicine* (Aldershot, UK: Ashgate Press, forthcoming).

65. Fathiyya Bahij, "Mushkila Khatira Tuwajihu Atfal 800 Alf Muwazzifa wa 'Amila," *Akhir Sa'a*, Dec. 11, 1957; Sa'id, "Dur al-Hadana Khayr" and "Azma Ismuha Dur al-hadana."

66. Sa'id, "Dur al-Hadana Khayr."

67. Bahij, "Mushkila Khatira."

68. Ministry of Education, Lajna Bahth Shu'un al-Mudarissat wa-l-Muwazzifat, *Bahth wa 'Alaj Mushkilat al-Mar'a al-Muwazzifa*, 137–138.

69. "Dur al-Hadana fi Kull Hay," *Akhir Sa'a*, Apr. 18, 1962.

70. Ibid.

71. For a similar description of an ideal day care, see "Suq al-Intaj: Madina Mustaqilla fi Qalb al-'Asima," *Al-Musawwar*, Dec. 19, 1958.

72. United Arab Republic, *Mu'tamar Shu'un al-Mar'a al-'Amila*, 58–59.

73. United Arab Republic, Ministry of Education, *Minhaj al-Marhala al-Ibtida'iyya al-Mutawwira* (Cairo: Wizarat Al-Tarbiyya wa-l-Ta'lim, 1965).

74. Amina Sa'id, "Al-Mar'a al-'Amila alaysat Imra'a?" *Hawwa'*, May 5, 1962, 14–15.

75. The Ideal Company started producing refrigerators in 1956—probably the first refrigerators ever produced in the Middle East. Air conditioners followed in 1956. By then, the company had expanded into three large factories with a capital of 1,000,600 Egyptian pounds. Mona Abaza, *Changing Consumer Cultures of Modern Egypt: Cairo's Urban Reshaping* (Leiden: Brill, 2006), 90–93.

76. Ibid., 93. See also Hendrick Smith, "Come to the Cairo Fair," *New York Times*, Mar. 26, 1966, 10; Harry Hopkins, *Egypt: The Crucible* (London: Secker and Warburg, 1969), 249.

77. This is a point that Katherine French-Fuller has also made for domestic appliances in Chile during the same period. See Katherine French-Fuller, "Gendered Invisibility, Respectable Cleanliness: The Impact of the Washing Machine on Daily Living in Post-1950 Santiago, Chile," *Journal of Women's History* 18 (Winter 2006): 79–100.

78. *Ruz al-Yusuf*, May 25, 1959, 25.

79. Smith, "Come to the Cairo Fair."

80. "Fi Manzilik Kull al-Was'il al-Hadith," *Ruz al-Yusuf*, Mar. 22, 1963.

81. The Ministry of Social Affairs carried out a study of employees and supervisors in the provincial governorates of Qalyubiyya, Sharqiyya, Fayum, and Bani Suwayf in September 1963. Of approximately 3,000 women workers surveyed, the study found that 2,299 had no household appliances. However, a study conducted under the auspices of the preparatory committee for the 1964 Conference of the Affairs of the Working Woman showed higher levels of appliance ownership among the 4,275 working women who were sampled, reflecting both the inclusion of urban centers like Cairo and Alexandria as well as the prevalence of midlevel public service workers (such as teachers) within the sample. That survey showed that of the 4,275 women surveyed, 1,348 had at least one appliance (the most prevalent was a butagaz stove), and 744 lived in households with multiple appliances.

Ministry of Social Affairs, Al-Lajna al-Da'ima li-Shu'un al-Mar'a, *Mu'tamar Shu'un al-Mar'a al-'Amila*, 225. In 1966, social researcher Ruqiya Barakat conducted a study of household technology among five hundred Cairo families of varying socioeconomic status. The study charted use of ten appliances, including sewing machines, refrigerators, water heaters, washing machines, butagaz stoves, electric irons, and vacuum cleaners. Barakat rated families that had all of these appliances at 100 percent. According to her results, the average family had between 25 and 50 percent (or between two and five appliances). Ruqiya Barakat, "'Alaqat al-Taghayyur al-Tiknulujiyya bi-Dawr al-Mar'a fi-l-Usra," *Al-Majalla al-Ijtima'iyya al-Qawmiyya,* 305/306 (1972): 20–28. The study was based on Barakat's 1968 MA thesis done in the Faculty of Literature, 'Ain Shams University.

82. John Waterbury, *The Egypt of Nasser and Sadat: The Political Economy of Two Regimes* (Princeton, NJ: Princeton University Press, 1983), 189–190.

83. "Musabiqa Kubra Tuqaddimuha Al-Ahram: Irif Muntajat Baladik fi Hadha al-Rasm," *Al-Ahram,* Aug. 6, 1962, 104–105.

84. See Reynolds, "Sharikat al-Bayt al-Misri," for a brief history of how transformations of domestic space linked to discourses of national progress.

85. *Al-Musawwar,* June 21, 1957, 17.

86. *Al-Musawwar,* Dec. 4, 1958, 20.

87. *Ruz al-Yusuf,* Jan. 11, 1960, 23.

88. "General Electric Advertisement," *Hawwa',* Oct. 24, 1960, 32.

89. *Ruz al-Yusuf,* Dec. 6, 1965, 39.

90. Iftitan Mumtaz, "al-Mar'a al-'Amila wa Rabbat al-Bayt," *Hawwa',* Aug. 10, 1963, 42–43.

91. Waterbury, *Egypt of Nasser and Sadat,* 209.

92. The classic study in this vein remains Ruth Schwartz Cowan, *More Work for Mother: The Ironies of Household Technology from the Open Hearth to the Microwave* (New York: Basic Books, 1983).

93. Mumtaz, "al-Mar'a al-'Amila wa Rabbat al-Bayt."

94. Ibid.

95. Ahmad Zaki 'Abd al-Halim, "Rihla fi Hayyat Umm 'Amila," *Hawwa',* Nov. 16, 1963, 16–19.

96. Mumtaz, "al-Mar'a al-'Amila wa Rabbat al-Bayt."

97. Inji Rushdi, "Hisab al-Arbah wa-l-Khasa'ir fi al-Hayat: Al-zawajat al-Mushtagilat," *Hawwa',* Jan. 4, 1958.

98. *Li-l-Rijal Faqat,* dir. Mahmud Zul-Fiqar, 1964.

99. Garay Menicucci, "Unlocking the Arab Celluloid Closet: Homosexuality in Egyptian Film," *MERIP* 206 (Spring 1998): 33.

100. Layla Marmush, "Wara' Kull 'Azim Sikritira," *Ruz al-Yusuf,* June 15, 1959, 26. See also Sami al-Laythi, "Wara' Kull Mudir Najih Sikritira Najiha," *Al-Musawwar,* Apr. 18, 1966, 62.

101. Ruz al-Yusuf, 12 May, 1959, 28.

102. As quoted in Meijer, *Quest for Modernity,* 221.

103. For the post-1952 debate around Egyptian national culture, see Meijer, *Quest for Modernity*, ch. 6.

104. *Al-badla al-sh'abiyya* was the term used to refer to the standard work outfit of both professional male civil servants and lower-level public sector workers. In the case of the former, the *badla sh'abiyya* consisted of a button-down shirt, suit jacket, pants, and tie. In the case of the latter, it referred to a safari-style suit, consisting of a thigh-length jacket buttoned up the front, and a matching pair of flared pants, usually in khaki or earth tones.

105. Appropriation of Sha'rawi's gesture by nationalist historians occludes the complicated meanings of *hijab* to Egyptian women. Different types of veils existed according to class, generation, and educational status. In the early twentieth century, urban women wore the *tarha*, a thin piece of fabric in black or white, to cover their hair. Upper-class women wore a *yashmak*, which was drawn across the face under the eyes as a marker of aristocracy. It was the *yashmak* that Sha'rawi removed at the train station. She continued to cover her hair for the remainder of her life. The *bisha* could be casually thrown over the whole face and had fewer class connotations. The *burqu'* was a mesh covering that was hung from under the eyes with a decorative gold or brass cylinder at its center, placed over the nose. In the 1960s, according to Ahdaf Soueif, the *tarha* continued to be worn generally by women of the working class and by some women over fifty. By the late 1940s, the *burqu'* could occasionally be spotted in some of the popular quarters of Cairo, while the *bisha* and the *yashmak* had largely disappeared.

106. Abaza, *Changing Consumer Cultures*; Ahdaf Soueif, "The Language of the Veil," *The Guardian*, Dec. 8, 2001, http://www.guardian.co.uk/weekend/story/0,3605,614360,00.html.

107. Abaza, *Changing Consumer Cultures*.

108. Soueif, "Language of the Veil."

109. Afsaneh Najmabadi, "Veiled Discourses-Unveiled Bodies," *Feminist Studies* (Fall 1993): 489.

110. "Mudhakkirat Sariha li-Fata 'Amila," *Akhir Sa'a*, Aug. 23, 1961.

111. "Fitna fi al-Islam," *Ruz al-Yusuf*, July 22, 1957.

112. Mernissi, *Beyond the Veil*, 31.

113. Harb pointed out that ancient Greek women, for example, covered their faces when they left the house and that Christian women in the Middle Ages wore the *khimar* when in public or performing prayers. The *khimar* was a piece of fabric that covered the head, shoulders, and chest, similar to a nun's wimple.

114. Latifa al-Zayyat, "Al-Mar'a al-'Amila wa Silahat al-Unutha," *Hawwa'*, Jan. 8, 1966, 15.

115. Ibid.

116. "Al-Sikritara," *Hawwa'*, Jan. 11, 1958.

117. Salama Musa, *Al-Mar'a Lysat Lu'bat al-Rajul* (Cairo: Al-Sharika al-'Arabiyya li-l-Tiba'a wa-l-Nashr wa-l-Tawzi', 1956).

118. Ibid., 72–73.

119. "Hal Tufaddilina al-'Amal ma' al-Rajul am al-Ma'ra?" *Hawwa'*, Mar. 19, 1960.

120. Ibid.

121. Ibid.

122. "Mut'ab al-Mar'a Kharij al-Bayt," *Akhir Sa'a*, July 10, 1963.

123. "Al-Mushtaghalat Ha'irat bayn al-Mujtama' wa Hukm al-Taqalid," *Hawwa'*, Feb. 7, 1959.

Chapter 3

1. Marnia Lazreg, "Citizenship and Gender in Algeria," in *Gender and Citizenship in the Middle East*, ed. Suad Joseph (Syracuse, NY: Syracuse University Press, 2000), 58–69. The term "dual legal system" has been used to refer not only to the mixture of secular and religious laws that typifies the legal systems of many Middle Eastern countries but also to countries in Africa that possess legal systems that are a mixture of civil and customary law.

2. Islamic *shari'a* and its principles are based on the Qur'an and the *sunna* (traditions derived from the sayings of the Prophet Muhammad) as interpreted, in the case of Sunni Islam, by the four officially recognized schools of legal interpretation, or *madhhab* (*madhahib* pl.): *Hanafi, Shafi'i, Malaki,* and *Hanbali.* Confessional courts were presided over by jurists chosen and appointed by individual sectarian communities.

3. Each courthouse had separate rooms for the various schools of law.

4. According to Amira Sonbol, the preference for particular *madhhab* in different parts of Egypt was indicative of the forms of patriarchy and male domination prevalent in local society. The choice of the *Shafi'i* school in the Delta suggests the prevalence of the extended family with the father as head of household, whereas in Upper Egypt the preference for the *Maliki* school reflected the male patriarchal order headed by male members of the wider clan, from father to clan head. Amira Sonbol, "Adults and Minors in Ottoman *Shari'a* Courts," in *Women, the Family and Divorce Laws in Islamic History*, ed. Amira Sonbol (Syracuse, NY: Syracuse University Press, 1996), 236–258.

5. Leslie Pierce, *Morality Tales: Law and Gender in the Court of Aintab* (Berkeley: University of California Press, 2003); Sonbol, "Adults and Minors in Ottoman *Shari'a* Courts"; Amira Sonbol, "Law and Gender Violence in Ottoman and Modern Egypt," in Sonbol, *Women, the Family and Divorce Laws*, 277–290; Judith Tucker, *In the House of the Law: Gender and Islamic Law in Ottoman Syria and Palestine* (Berkeley: University of California Press, 1998).

6. Tucker, *In the House of the Law*, 181–182.

7. Among the differences between Coptic and Islamic family law are different understandings of marriage and divorce. Within Coptic Christianity, marriage is legally viewed as a holy sacrament that can be dissolved only in limited circumstances with

the approval of religious authorities, while marriage and divorce within *shari'a* law are formally treated as a binding contract between two parties. Thus, while the church recognized *tatliq*, which is an indirect divorce concluded under the auspices of the church, *talaq*, the primary form of divorce under Islamic law, happens in accordance with the direct wishes of one or both of the married couple. See Mohammed Afifi, "Reflections on the Personal Status Laws of Copts," in Sonbol, *Women, the Family and Divorce Laws*, 202–219.

8. Saba Mahmood, *The Politics of Piety: The Islamic Revival and the Feminist Subject* (Princeton, NJ: Princeton University Press, 2005), 76–77. This is a point that Alev Cinar also makes for Turkish secularism. See Alev Cinar, *Modernity, Islam and Secularism in Turkey* (Minneapolis: University of Minnesota Press, 2005), 16. Rajeswari Sunder Rajan notes in the case of India that in the name of secularism, the state grants considerable recognition to religion by retaining personal status laws but also by actively regulating religious institutions: having the court administer personal status laws, managing religious trusts, opening entry to temples for lower-caste Hindus, and other similar interventions. Rajeswari Sunder Rajan, *The Scandal of the State: Women, Law and Citizenship in Postcolonial India* (Durham, NC: Duke University Press, 2003).

9. According to Talal Asad, the term *al-ahwal al-shakhsiyya* appeared nowhere in the codes of the *shari'a* courts prior to the restriction of *shari'a* to the adjudication of family matters. The term itself was apparently introduced from Europe, with the laws administered by the new National Courts and derived from the Napoleonic Code, which distinguished between "real status" and "personal status." "Personal status" referred to the "ensemble of juridical institutions that define the human person independent of his wealth, obligations and transactions." Talal Asad, *Formations of the Secular: Christianity, Islam, Modernity* (Stanford, CA: Stanford University Press, 2003), 231.

10. In a report on the *shari'a* courts, Muhammad 'Abdu, the noted jurist and a major figure in Islamic reform, wrote that the courts "intervene between husband and wife, father and sons, between brothers and between a guardian and his ward. There is no right relating to near or distant kin over which these courts do not have jurisdiction." This meant, he continued, "that *shari'a* judges look into matters which are very private and listen to what others are not allowed to hear. For even as they provide the framework of justice, they are also a repository for every family secret." It was the purpose of the court, he concluded, to both safeguard the privacy of the family and regulate its sentiments and relationships in order to further the welfare of society and the moral order which depend on it. As quoted in Talal Asad, "Thinking About Law and Secularism," *ISIM Papers* (2001): 9, http://www.isim.nl/files/paper_asad.pdf.

11. See Hanan Kholoussy, *For Better, For Worse: The Marriage Crisis Which Made Modern Egypt* (Stanford, CA: Stanford University Press, 2010), for an account of these campaigns and the debates surrounding them.

12. Amendments to the law of 1920, passed in 1929, expanded and rationalized the

provisions of divorce. Divorce pronouncements (*talaq*) uttered while the husband was intoxicated or under compulsion were invalid, as were those in fulfillment of an oath or when uttered as a threat to the wife. In addition, each iteration of *talaq* was considered as single and revocable. In order for repudiation of a wife to be finalized, *talaq* had to be pronounced three times on three separate occasions. See Ron Shaham, *The Family and the Courts in Modern Egypt* (Leiden: Brill, 1997).

13. What this meant, in effect, is that judges adjudicating claims of women claiming insult or physical violence based their decisions on normative ideas about what constituted acceptable behavior for various social classes. Beating was frequently upheld by judges as the only way a lower-class man had of disciplining his wife, while for upper-class women beatings and even insults were unacceptable and seen as an infringement of her honor. Ibid., 131–132. For the actual text of the provision, see J.N.D. Anderson, "Recent Developments in Shari'a Law V (The Dissolution of Marriage)," *The Muslim World* 41 (1951): 271–288.

14. For a succinct discussion of the issue of companionate marriage and its linkages to discourses of women's emancipation, see Lila Abu-Lughod, "The Marriage of Feminism and Islamism: Selective Repudiation as a Dynamic of Postcolonial Cultural Politics," in Abu-Lughod, *Remaking Women*, 255–261.

15. The explanatory memorandum written by jurists that accompanied the law stated:

> The wife's obedience is a husband's right while the maintenance is a wife's right. The fact that a husband no longer demands obedience from his wife does not prevent her from asking what is due her. This is agreed upon through *'urf* [custom]. Accordingly, a wife is not considered *nushuz* [rebellious] except if her husband demands that she move to his legal house and she refuses to do so.

As quoted in Sonbol, "Law and Gender Violence in Ottoman and Modern Egypt," 282.

16. The role of the police in enforcing obedience verdicts was established by a court decision in 1910 and upheld by subsequent laws.

17. See Nadav Safran, "The Abolition of the Shari'a Courts in Egypt," *The Muslim World* 48 (1958): 20–28, for an in-depth examination of terms of the unification of the court system.

18. The reorganization of Azhar gave the state jurisdiction over Azhar's administrative appointments and placed members of various government ministries on its councils. In addition, the measures introduced new bodies of knowledge into the curriculum (such as math, geography, medicine, and the natural sciences) alongside the existing religious subjects (Islamic law, Arabic language, and Qur'anic exegesis) and established a girls' college. Members of the Azhar faculty who opposed such measures were removed or demoted. See Michael Winter, "Islam and the State: Pragmatism and Growing Commitment," in *Egypt from Monarchy to Republic*, ed. Shimon Shamir

(Boulder, CO: Westview Press, 1995), 44–58; Tamir Moustafa, "Conflict and Cooperation Between the State and Religious Institutions in Contemporary Egypt," *International Journal of Middle Eastern Studies* 32 (Jan. 2000): 3–22; Malika Zeghal, "Religion and Politics in Egypt: The Ulama of al-Azhar, Radical Islam and the State: 1952–94," *International Journal of Middle East Studies* 31 (Aug. 1999): 371–399.

19. Although the law did not stipulate the religion of the presiding judges, what this in effect meant was that Muslim judges were now by and large presiding over the personal status cases of non-Muslims. According to Maurits Berger, the religion of judges presiding in the Family Section of the National Courts is not relevant to the assignment of cases. In theory, a Muslim judge may preside over a Christian divorce case and vice versa. However, in practice, his research indicated that a Christian judge "never" presided in a case that involved a Muslim and, as a rule, only Muslims preside in the National Courts. Maurits Berger, "Public Policy and Islamic Law: The Modern Dhimmi in Contemporary Egyptian Family Law," *Islamic Law and Society* 8 (2001): 114.

20. For a more in-depth discussion of the memorandum, see Safran, "Abolition of the Court System."

21. Ibid.

22. As quoted in Ibid., 21–22. The memorandum went on to enumerate the difficulties experienced by parties seeking to use the confessional courts. Some of the courts met only occasionally in areas that were far from the homes of the parties. The juridical rules, for the most part, were not codified and were dispersed in holy books and commentaries by jurists and clergy and written in languages (Greek, Latin, Syriac, Hebrew, Armenian, Coptic) that most parties to the disputes didn't understand.

23. Ibid.

24. The unification of Egypt and Syria (the UAR) in 1958 and the promulgation of the National Charter in 1961 resulted in the formation of committees charged by executive order with drafting a new family code consistent with new political realities, suggesting official support for legal change. A proposal was presented by a coalition of women activists in 1960 to the committee formed to discuss the unification of Syrian and Egyptian family law. The work of that committee ceased when the UAR was dissolved.

25. The 1979 law, popularly known as "Jihan's Law" after President Anwar Sadat's wife, raised the legal age of marriage for women from sixteen to eighteen, raised the period of *hadana* (child custody), abolished the principle of female obedience as a legal foundation for marriage, and granted women the right to a judicial divorce if their husband took a second wife. The law, established by executive decree, prompted an outcry, not only among the religious establishment but among secular activists, many of them women, who decried the law as an abuse of presidential power and political authoritarianism. In 1985, it was struck down by the Supreme Constitutional Court on procedural grounds.

26. Suad Joseph, "Gender and Citizenship in Middle Eastern States," *MERIP* 198 (Jan.–Mar. 1996): 4–10.

27. Suad Joseph, "Gender and Citizenship in Middle Eastern States," in Joseph, *Gender and Citizenship in the Middle East*, 3–32.

28. Republic of Egypt, Ministry of Justice, *Al-Dustur* (Cairo: Al-Matbʿat al-Amiriyya, 1956), 11.

29. Ibid.

30. United Arab Republic, *Charter*, 93.

31. In a rare statement on the issue of regulating divorce and polygamy, Gamal Abdel Nasser responded to a letter from an antireform group calling itself the Union of Women of the Republic, urging him not to support Amina Shukri's reform proposal (which was under consideration in the National Assembly at the time). Nasser wrote, "We are well acquainted with this subject which is one that the state is greatly concerned with, taking into consideration how to achieve the public good [*al-salah al-ʿamm*] without infringing on the basic organization of society." As quoted in Munira Husni, *Al-Zawaj wa-l-Talaq* (Cairo: Dar al-Fikr wa-l-Hadith, n.d.), 122.

32. Malika Zeghal defines the official *ulama* as Islamic jurists and scholars who had held official positions within al-Azhar University and within the religious bureaucracy. She sees this official *ulama* as distinct from a "peripheral" *ulama* that emerged in the 1970s and 1980s, whose religious careers (and authority) developed largely outside the official al-Azhar hierarchy, in private mosques and Islamic associations. Zeghal, "Religion and Politics in Egypt."

33. This is an argument that Louise Halper makes for women's activism in Iran during the same period. Louise Halper, "Law and Women's Agency in Post-Revolutionary Iran," *Harvard Journal of Law and Gender* 28 (Winter 2005): 85–138.

34. In fact, the practice of *bayt al-taʾa* was not confined to Muslims. In a 1953 case, a Coptic woman was ordered to be forcibly returned to the home of her husband by a judge. The *Majlis al-Milli* court quoted the biblical injunction to wives, "Be obedient to your husband as Sarah was to Abraham," stating: "The obedience of a wife to her husband is a duty according to the traditions of the *Majlis al-Milli*. [This is because obedience] is the cornerstone of the family no matter the severity involved in the interference of executive authorities to assure execution by forcible compulsion. Without this, the family would be under threat of tremendous dangers." As quoted in Amira Sonbol, "Taʾa and Modern Legal Reform," *Islam and Christian-Muslim Relations* 9 (1998): 285–294.

35. Amina Shafiq, "Matalib al-Usra al-Misriyya ... min Qanun al-Ahwal al-Shakhsiyya fi ʿAm 1965," *Al-Ahram*, Feb. 4, 1965, 8.

36. Amina Saʿid, "Ma Nuriduhu fi-l-Tashriyyʿat," *Hawwaʾ*, Dec. 4, 1959. See also Amina Saʿid, "ʿAdilu hadhhi al-Qanun," *Hawwaʾ*, Dec. 7, 1957.

37. 'Ali Hamdi al-Jamal, "Hadith al-Nass: al-Mar'a al-Misriyya wa Qanun al-Ah-wal al-Shakhsiyya," *Al-Ahram*, Mar. 7, 1967, 7.

38. Suhayr Qalamawi, "La Uridu an Usaddiqu," *Al-Ahram*, Nov. 25, 1959, 6.

39. Qalamawi, "La Uridu an Usaddiqu."

40. Husni, *Al-Zawaj wa-l-Talaq*.

41. Ibid.

42. Jamal al-Atayfi, "Nahnu fi Haja ila Thawra fi Tashri' al-Talaq," *Al-Ahram*, Mar. 29, 1960, 8. It should be pointed out that al-Atayfi's solution to this problem was not to limit divorce but to limit the court's role to certifying the legality of a divorce—whether the petition was brought by a man or a woman—and determining fault. This was, in many ways, a far more radical solution than the one proposed by reformers themselves, since it would have granted women rights to divorce on an equal footing with men.

43. "Awwal Ra'i al-Azhar fi Mushkilat al-Talaq," *Al-Ahram*, Oct. 25, 1959, 5.

44. The column, entitled "Give My Regards to Your Dear Husband," appeared weekly in *Ruz al-Yusuf* throughout the 1950s and 1960s. While "Mediha" did on occasion use her fashion column as a platform to make passing observations about contemporary political and social issues, the amount of space she devoted to the debate over personal status laws was exceptional. "Tahiyati 'ala Zawjik al-'Aziz," *Ruz al-Yusuf*, May 15, 1967, 50.

45. 'Aisha 'Abd al-Rahman, "Fi-l-Ahwal al-Shakhsiyya," *Al-Ahram*, Dec. 3, 1959, 6.

46. "Istifta' *Al-Ahram* fi Qanun al-Ahwal al-Shakhsiyya," *Al-Ahram*, Aug. 22, 1959.

47. "Hadith al-Nass: Nazra 'ala Qanun al-Ahwal al-Shakhsiyya," *Al-Ahram*, Feb. 13, 1967, 7.

48. "Bayt al-Ta'a," *Hawwa'*, Dec. 14, 1957.

49. 'Ali 'Abd al-Wahid, "Bayt al-Ta'a," *Al-Ahram*, Dec. 24, 1959, 6.

50. Ibid.

51. "Bayt al-Ta'a," *Hawwa'*, Dec. 14, 1957.

52. "al-Mufti Yaqul: Bayt al-Ta'a Baqa bi Shurut," *Al-Ahram*, May 15, 1960, 7.

53. "Al-Thamaniya aladhina Dakhalu al-Ahwal al-Shakhsiyya," *Al-Ahram*, Apr. 9, 1967.

Chapter 4

Portions of this chapter were adapted from Laura Bier, "The Family Is a Factory: Gender, Citizenship and the Regulation of Reproduction in Postwar Egypt," originally published in *Feminist Studies* 36:2 (Summer 2010): 404–432. Permission courtesy of Feminist Studies, Inc.

1. Yusuf Idris, *The Cheapest Nights and Other Stories*, trans. Wadida Wassef (Boulder, CO: Lynne Rienner, 1997), 1.

2. As quoted in Haifa Shanawany, "Stages in the Development of a Population Policy," in *Egypt: Population Problems and Prospects*, ed. Abdel R. Omran (Chapel Hill, NC: Carolina Population Center, 1973), 196.

3. 'Abbas 'Ammar, "The Population Situation in Egypt and the Necessity of Planning a Population Policy for the Country," in *The Egyptian Association for Population Studies* (Cairo: Imprimerie Misr S.A.E., 1960), 5–17.

4. India, for example, although it announced its plans to institute a national family planning program as early as 1951, placed most of its emphasis on industrialization and rural development as a precondition for the reduction of fertility rates, until the drafting of its second five-year plan in 1956. Matthew Connelly, "Population Control in India: Prologue to the Emergency Period," *Population and Development Review* 32 (Dec. 2006): 629–667.

5. For a complete discussion of transition theory in the context of the history of demography in the United States, see Susan Greenhalgh, "The Social Construction of Population Science: An Intellectual, Institutional and Political History of Twentieth Century Demography," *Comparative Studies in Society and History* 38 (Jan. 1996): 26–66.

6. Other possible contributing factors were a number of highly public political planning failures in the late 1950s and early 1960s, among them the 1961 dissolution of the short-lived United Arab Republic—the experiment in political union between Egypt and Syria begun in 1958—and the state of Tahrir (Liberation) Province, a desert reclamation project that was intended to showcase the regime's development scheme.

7. Abdel Omran, "The Population of Egypt, Past and Present," in Omran, *Egypt: Population Problems and Prospects*, 13.

8. Dennis Hodgson, "Demography as Social Science and Policy Science," *Population and Development Review* 9 (Winter 1983): 10–20.

9. The fall of China to the communists in 1949, which altered the map of the postwar world, created a crisis in American foreign policy, and engendered deep fears that communism would continue to spread, was an object lesson for Notestein and others about what could happen without active intervention in individual reproductive behavior. Greenhalgh, "Social Construction of Population Science," 39–40.

10. John Sharpless, "Population Science, Private Foundations, and Development Aid: The Transformation of Demographic Knowledge in the United States, 1945–65," in *International Development and the Social Sciences: Essays on the History and Politics of Knowledge*, ed. Frederick Cooper and Randall Packard (Berkeley: University of California Press, 1997), 176–202.

11. As quoted in John Caldwell and Pat Caldwell, *Limiting Population Growth and the Ford Foundation Contribution* (London: Frances Pinter, 1986), 14.

12. Hana Rizk, "Population Policies in Egypt," in *Report of the Proceedings: The*

Fifth International Conference on Planned Parenthood, 24–28 October 1955, Tokyo, Japan (London: International Planned Parenthood, 1955).

13. "Hal Nuhadid al-Nasl?" *Hawwa'*, Jan. 24, 1960.

14. The Egyptian Association for Population Studies, *The Egyptian Association for Population Studies* (Cairo: Jam'iyya al-Misriyya lil-buhuth al-sukkaniyya, 1960), 1.

15. Ibid., 3.

16. As quoted in Shanawany, "Stages in the Development of a Population Policy," 207.

17. Ibid.

18. Gamal Abdel Nasser, *The Charter* (Cairo: Maslahat al-isti'alamat, 1962).

19. Between 1962 and 1965, the state approved the establishment of seventy new family planning clinics, most of them run by private voluntary organizations that had played an important role in field-testing contraceptive services in the late 1950s. The government bureaucracy also began to take a more direct role in family planning administration; in 1964 the Ministry of Social Affairs established the Population and Family Planning Division to promote contraceptive services in combined health units, social centers, and government housing projects. The Ministry of Public Health, in 1965, followed suit and began including family planning services in their mother and child health centers. At the end of the same year, a presidential decree signed by President Nasser established the Supreme Council for Family Planning, which was charged with drawing up a total plan for the nationalization of family planning services.

20. In urban areas 575 clinics were opened, and in the countryside, 1,416.

21. Abdel Omran and Malek el-Nomrossey, "The Family Planning Effort in Egypt: A Descriptive Sketch," in Omran, *Egypt: Population Problems and Prospects*, 219–257.

22. In order to expand the range of its services, the state enlisted the help of various women's voluntary organizations that had a long history of providing health and social services to women and of providing contraceptive services. See Beth Baron, "The Origins of Family Planning: Aziza Hussein, American Experts and the Egyptian State," *Journal of Middle East Women's Studies* 4 (Fall 2008): 31–57.

23. Of these, 372 were run by voluntary organizations and the rest by the Ministry of Public Health. H. K. Toppozada, "Progress and Problems of Family Planning in the United Arab Republic," in *Demography* 5:2 (1968): 592.

24. John Waterbury, *Manpower and Population Planning in the Arab Republic of Egypt, Part IV: Egypt's Governmental Program for Family Planning* (Cairo: American University Field Staff, 1972), 8.

25. As quoted in "Bada'at Tajarib Tanzim al-Usra," *Akhir Sa'a*, June 6, 1962.

26. Ann Anagnost, "A Surfeit of Bodies: Population and the Rationality of the State in Post-Mao China," in *Conceiving the New World Order*, ed. Faye Ginsburg and Rayna Rapp (Berkeley: University of California Press, 1995), 31.

27. In this, Egypt was certainly not unique: historians have demonstrated how "the family," starting in the nineteenth century, was an increasing target of state in-

tervention and reform as notions of modernity, politics, and the emergence of "the social" as a category produced new sorts of linkages between domestic relations and the health of the body politic. See, for example, David Horn, *Social Bodies: Science, Reproduction and Italian Modernity* (Princeton, NJ: Princeton University Press, 1994); and Jacques Donzelot, *The Policing of Families*, trans. Robert Hurley (New York: Pantheon Books, 1979).

28. Hikmat Abu Zayd, "Al-Dawla wa al-Usra bayn 'Ahadayn," in *Proceedings of the Conference on the Family, Dec. 19–26, 1964 Cairo, Egypt* (Cairo: Ministry of Social Affairs, 1964), 23.

29. In a 1954 press conference, Husayn al-Shafi'i, the minister of social affairs, came out in favor of a national birth control policy on the grounds that overpopulation constituted a form of "overproduction," which resulted in "human waste." The biological impetus to reproduction, left unregulated, threatened to create a population of "weaklings, vagrants and beggars" who would be incapable of acting as productive citizens. As quoted in Rizk, "Population Policies in Egypt," 39.

30. United Arab Republic, Ministry of Education, *Al-Tilmiz fi Bi'atihi al-Mahalliyya* (Cairo: Wizarat al-Tarbiyya wa-l-Ta'lim, 1967), 11. By contrast, textbooks from as late as 1959 made no mention of overpopulation as a problem.

31. "Al-Da'wa li-Tanzim al-Nasl wa Takrim al-Usra," *Al-Ahram*, Mar. 15, 1965, 8. The contest continues to be run today with the same eligibility stipulations.

32. On the importance of play for conceptions of modern childhood, see Shakry, "Schooled Mothers, Structured Play," in Abu-Lughod, *Remaking Women*, 126–170.

33. As quoted in Ahmed Sharabassy, *Islam and Family Planning*, trans. Sayed Ismail (Cairo: Egyptian Family Planning Association, 1969), 143.

34. Ibid.

35. Muhammad Abu Zahra, *Tanzim al-Usra wa Tanzim al-Nasl* (Cairo: Dar al-Fikr al-'Arabi, 1976).

36. Amina Sa'id, "Tanzim al-Usra Wajib Watani," *Hawwa'*, Oct. 20, 1962.

37. As quoted in Sharabassy, *Islam and Family Planning*, 135.

38. Sa'id, "Tanzim al-Usra Wajib Watani." See also Amina Sa'id, "Tanzim Naslik Asbaha Wajiban Wataniyyan," *Hawwa'*, Feb. 8, 1964.

39. As quoted in Sharabassy, *Islam and Family Planning*, 135.

40. As quoted in ibid., 136.

41. Ibid., 42.

42. See Ahmad Khalifa, *Ra'i Muwatin fi Tanzim al-Usra* (Cairo: Ministry of Social Affairs, 1966).

43. "Al-Rifiyya al-Misriyya Akhsab Imra'a fi-l-'Alam," *Al-Musawwar*, Jan. 22, 1965, 29–30.

44. See, for example, Louis Kamal Malika and Salah al-Din Fa'iq, *Ittijahat al-*

Qarawiyin wa-l-'Ummal Nahwa Tanzim al-Usra (Sirs al Layaan, Egypt: Markaz Tan-miyya al-Mujtam'a fil 'Alam al 'Arabi, 1968).

45. See "Kayf Yumkin Tanzim al-Nasl bayn al-Fallahat," *Al-Ahram*, Apr. 6, 1966, 12; Fahmy Huwaidi, "Taqrir 'an Tajribat Tanzim al-Usra," *Al-Ahram*, Mar. 26, 1966, 7; "Afkar Qadima ma tazalu Tahakkum Tafkir," *Al-Ahram*, July 3, 1966, 1 (supplement); Khalifa, *Ra'i Muwatin.*

46. For a profile of Marzuq, see Perdita Huston, *Motherhood by Choice: Pioneers in Women's Health and Family Planning* (New York: Feminist Press of the City of New York, 1992). For an in-depth account of Aziza Hussein's life, see Amy Johnson's biography of her husband, social reformer and diplomat Ahmed Hussein. Amy Johnson, *Reconstructing Rural Egypt: Ahmed Hussein and the History of Egyptian Development* (Cairo: American University in Cairo Press, 2004).

47. As quoted in Suhayr al-Kayyal, "Kayf Nataghallibu 'ala Mashakil Ziyadat al-Nasl?" *Hawwa'*, July 13, 1963, 18.

48. Aziza Hussein, "Status of Women and Family Planning in a Developing Country—Egypt," in Omran, *Egypt: Population and Prospects*, 186.

49. "Muwajihat al-Waqqi'a fi Mushkilat Tanzim al-Usra," *Al-Ahram*, Feb. 20, 1965, 1 (insert).

50. Majid 'Atiya, "Ayna Takhtafi 'Aqras Man' al-Haml," *Al-Musawwar*, Jan. 15, 1965, 34–35.

51. Al-Kayyal, "Kayf Nataghallibu 'ala Mashakil Ziyadat al-Nasl?" 18.

52. Qalamawi never clearly specified how or by what means such limitations would be enforced.

53. According to Beth Baron, female reformers paid a price for their differences with state policy makers. Many of them who had been the foremost advocates of family planning and pioneers in its provision found themselves and their organizations marginalized within the national family planning bureaucracy, dominated as it was by male doctors and policy makers. See Baron, "Origins of Family Planning." See also Laura Bier, "From Mothers of the Nation and Daughters of the State," PhD diss., New York University, 2006, ch. 4.

54. Amina Sa'id, "Al-Ijhad Mubah Ahyanan," *Hawwa'*, Mar. 26, 1966, 13–14; Iftatan Mumtaz, "Al-Ijhad: Mushkila Tabhath 'an Hal," *Hawwa'*, Feb. 10, 1962, 24–25.

55. Wendy Brown, *States of Injury: Power and Freedom in Late Modernity* (Princeton, NJ: Princeton University Press, 1995).

56. As quoted in Waterbury, *Manpower and Population in the Arab Republic of Egypt: Part III*, 8.

57. Faye Ginsburg and Rayna Rapp, "The Politics of Reproduction," *Annual Review of Anthropology* 20 (1991): 322–323.

58. For a history of various nineteenth- and early twentieth-century attempts to incorporate women into the Egyptian health bureaucracy, see Hibba Abugedeiri,

"Egyptian Women and the Science Question: Gender in the Making of Colonized Medicine, 1893–1929," PhD diss., Georgetown University, 2001; Khalid Fahmy, "Women, Medicine and Power in Nineteenth Century Egypt," in Abu-Lughod, *Remaking Women*, 35–72; Laverne Kuhnke, *Lives at Risk: Public Health in Nineteenth-Century Egypt* (Berkeley: University of California Press, 1990).

59. Abugedeiri, "Egyptian Women and the Science Question."

60. *Daya*s undergoing training in the late 1950s and early 1960s received from six months to one year of practical training in obstetrics.

61. Laila el-Hamamsy, *The Daya of Egypt: Survival in a Modernizing Society* (Pasadena: California Institute of Technology, 1973), 8.

62. Ibid., 18.

63. Ibid.

64. Through providing prenatal care, aiding delivery, officiating at the *subu'* (customary festivities held on the seventh day following the birth of a child), and performing circumcisions in the case of infant girls, a *daya* could earn over a pound for the birth of a single child.

65. Criminal penalties for performing an abortion became part of the Egyptian legal code in 1936.

66. El-Hamamsy, *Daya of Egypt*, 19.

67. Ibid.

68. "Tajarib Jadida li-Tanzim al-Usra Bada'at fi Mastrad wa Assiyut," *Al-Ahram*, Apr. 2, 1967.

69. "Al-Daya Khatr Jadid fi Mashru' Tanzim al-Usra," *Akhir Sa'a*, Nov. 16, 1966.

70. "Bayn al-Daya wa Jihaz Jadid li-Tahdid al-Nasl," *Akhir Sa'a*, Jan. 12, 1965.

71. See, for example, "Bada'at Tajarib Tanzim al-Usra," *Akhir Sa'a*, June 6, 1962; "Al-Daya wa-l-Ma'zun Islahat Jadida li-Tahdid al-Nasl," *Akhir Sa'a*, Dec. 25, 1963; "Ma' al-Mar'a: al-Dayat Yada'un al-Ummhat ila al-Tardad 'ala Marakiz Tanzim al-Usra," *Al-Ahram*, Nov. 8, 1964.

72. "Ma' al-Mar'a: al-Dayat Yada'un al-Ummhat ila al-Tardad 'ala Marakiz Tanzim al-Usra," *Al-Ahram*, Nov. 8, 1964.

73. In practice, however, according to el-Hamamsy, collaboration continued between doctors and nurses and the local midwives operating in their districts.

74. Saad Gadalla, *Is There Hope? Fertility and Family Planning in a Rural Egyptian Community* (Cairo: American University in Cairo Press, 1978); Saad Eddin Ibrahim, "State, Women and Civil Society: An Evaluation of Egypt's Population Policy," in *Family, Gender and Population in the Middle East*, ed. Carla Makhlouf Obermeyer (Cairo: American University in Cairo Press, 1995), 59–79.

75. Laura Briggs, *Reproducing Empire: Race, Sex, Science and U.S. Imperialism in Puerto Rico* (Berkeley: University of California Press, 2003), 145.

76. 'Ayub al-Akhirin Tamna' Tanzim al-Nasl," *Ruz al-Yusuf*, Dec. 6, 1965.

77. Ibid.

78. 'Abdulla Imam, "Tanzim al-Usra fi Haja ila Tanzim!" *Ruz al-Yusuf,* Jan. 8, 1968, 24–25.

79. Imam, "Tanzim al-Usra fi Haja ila Tanzim!" 24.

80. Kamran Ali, "Faulty Deployments: Persuading Women and Constructing Choice in Egypt," *Comparative Studies in Society and History* 44 (Spring 2002): 382.

81. Marcia Inhorn, *The Quest for Conception: Gender, Infertility and Egyptian Medical Traditions* (Philadelphia: University of Pennsylvania Press, 1994).

82. Zahya Marzuq, *Al-Darasat al-Maydania fi Majal Tanzim al-Usra fi Iskandari-yya* (Alexandria: Supreme Council for Social Services in Alexandria and Sabra Printing Co., 1965).

83. "Tajarib Ladida li-Tanzim al-Usra Bada'at fi Mastrad wa Assiyut," *Al-Ahram,* Mar. 2, 1967, 1; Soheir Morsy, "Deadly Reproduction Among Egyptian Women: Maternal Mortality and the Medicalization of Population Control," in Ginsburg and Rapp, *Conceiving the New World Order,* 162–176.

84. This belief is referred to as *kabsa.*

85. See Ali, *Planning the Family in Egypt: New Bodies, New Selves* (Austin: University of Texas Press, 2002), ch. 4; Inhorn, *Quest for Conception,* ch. 5. For an examination of the ways in which medicalized regimes of contraception in India presumed an individualized conception of the body, see Kathryn Robinson, "Government Agency, Women's Agency: Feminism, Fertility and Population Control," in *Borders of Being: Citizenship, Fertility, and Sexuality in Asia and the Pacific,* ed. Margaret Jolly and Kalpana Ram (Ann Arbor: University of Michigan Press, 2001), 36–57.

86. The term *baladi* is an adjective, which literally translated means "native or indigenous" as opposed to foreign. It is also used, however, to signify practices or ideas that are "traditional" as opposed to "modern." For discussions that trace the varied social meanings and connotations of the term, see Evelyn Early, *Baladi Women of Cairo: Playing with an Egg and a Stone* (Boulder, CO: Lynne Rienner, 1993); Sawsan al-Messiri, "Self Images of Traditional Urban Women in Cairo," in *Women in the Muslim World,* ed. Lois Beck and Nikki Keddie (Cambridge, MA: Harvard University Press, 1978), 522–540.

87. Zahya Marzuq, "Social Studies on Fertility and Conception in Alexandria," in Omran, *Egypt: Population Problems and Prospects,* 386.

88. Marzuq, "Social Studies on Fertility." See also "Tajribat Ra'ida bi-l-Iskandari-yya," *Al-Ahram,* Feb. 28, 1967, 4.

89. Baron, "Origins of Family Planning," 36.

90. Marzuq, "Social Studies on Fertility," 386.

91. Ibid.

92. "Jama'iyya Zira'iyya li-Tahdid al-Nasl," *Ruz al-Yusuf,* Feb. 17, 1965, 48–49.

93. "Al-Sa'id wa Mushkilat Tanzim al-Usra," *Al-Ahram,* Jan. 10, 1965.

94. "Al-Daya wa al-Ma'zun Islaha Jadida li-Tanzim al-Usra," *Akhir Sa'a*, Dec. 25, 1963.

95. Ibid.

96. "Jama'iyya Zira'iyya li-Tahdid al-Nasl."

97. Ibid.

98. "Fallahat Qura al-Manufiyya Yuqbilna 'ala Marakiz Tanzim al-Usra," *Al-Ahram*, Dec. 12, 1965, 9.

99. Ibid.

Chapter 5

A version of this chapter appears in the book "Making a World After Empire: The Bandung Moment and Its Political Afterlives," ed. Christopher J. Lee. I thank Ohio University Press, in Athens, Ohio, for granting me permission to reproduce it here.

1. "Al-Zawaj, Tanzim al-Usra wa-l-Salam," *Hawwa'*, Feb. 21, 1959, 30–31.

2. Vijay Prashad, *The Darker Nations: A People's History of the Third World* (New York: New Press, 2007). I take the term "political imaginary" from Susan Buck-Morss, *Dreamworld and Catastrophe: The Passing of Utopia in East and West* (Cambridge, MA: MIT Press, 2000), 12.

3. These included India, Pakistan, North and South Vietnam, the Philippines, Burma, Sri Lanka, Malaysia, Ethiopia, Libya, Egypt, Sudan, and Ghana as well as countries like Turkey, China, Iran, Thailand, and Japan, which had never been formally colonized but had been subjected at various times to European "semicolonial" control and influence. A few countries, like Algeria, which were in the midst of struggles for decolonization, also participated.

4. Odd Arne Westad, *The Global Cold War: Third World Interventions and the Making of Our Times* (Cambridge, UK: Cambridge University Press, 2007), 98.

5. As quoted in Westad, *Global Cold War*, 100.

6. Anwar Sadat, "Opening Address," in *Proceedings of the Afro-Asian People's Solidarity Conference, Cairo, Dec. 26, 1957 to Jan. 1, 1958* (Moscow: Foreign Languages Publishing House, 1958). As quoted in A. W. Singham and Shirley Hume, *Non-Alignment in an Age of Alignments* (London: Zed Press, 1986), 90.

7. James Jankowski, *Nasser's Egypt, Arab Nationalism and The United Arab Republic* (Boulder, CO: Lynne Rienner, 2002).

8. Prashad, *Darker Nations*, 45.

9. For a complete history of the EFU, see Margot Badran, *Women, Islam and Nation* (Princeton, NJ: Princeton University Press, 1995).

10. This program dovetailed nicely with the newly expanded agenda of the EFU, which after Egyptian independence in 1922 broke away from the Wafd Party for failing to meet its demands for women's rights under the new constitution.

11. See Leila Rupp, *Worlds of Women* (Princeton, NJ: Princeton University Press, 1991), for an overview of the history of the IAW and other international feminist groups prior to 1945. For discussion of European women's relations with non-Western women within these groups, see Antoinette Burton's excellent work *Burdens of History: British Feminist, Indian Women and Imperial Culture, 1865–1915* (Chapel Hill: University of North Carolina Press, 1994).

12. Burton, *Burdens of History*, 173.

13. Ibid., 191.

14. Ibid., 171.

15. Badran, *Women, Islam and Nation*, 108.

16. As quoted in ibid., 232.

17. As quoted in ibid., 235.

18. The IAW continued to espouse a Western liberal feminist program.

19. A second Afro-Asian Women's Conference was held in Ulan Bator, Mongolia, in 1972.

20. Rupp, *Worlds of Women*, 3–4.

21. Bahiyya Karam, "Introduction," in *Proceedings of the First Afro-Asian Women's Conference, Cairo Jan. 14–23, 1961* (Cairo: Amalgamated Press of Egypt, 1961), 9.

22. Lakshmi Menon, "Closing Remarks," in *Report of the Proceedings of the First Asian-African Conference of Women, Held in Colombo, Ceylon 15–24 of February, 1958* (Bombay: Mouj Printing Bureau, 1958), 293.

23. Chandra Mohanty, "Introduction: Cartographies of Struggle," in *Third World Women and the Politics of Feminism*, ed. Chandra Mohanty (Bloomington: Indiana University Press, 1991), 4.

24. Daw Khin Hla, "Leader of the Burmese Delegation's Remarks at the Plenary Session," in *Proceedings of the First Asian-African Conference of Women*, 15.

25. Karima Sa'id, "Opening Remarks," in *Proceedings of the First Afro-Asian Women's Conference*, 9. Karima Sa'id was the sister of *Hawwa'* editor Amina Sa'id and was the Egyptian undersecretary of education.

26. Suhayr al-Kayyal, "Fi Viyitnam al-Janubiyya: Tuqadim al-'Arus Nisf al-Mahr li-Hamatha!" *Hawwa'*, Mar. 13, 1963, 43.

27. Marilyn Booth, *May Her Likes Be Multiplied: Biography and Gender Politics in Egypt* (Berkeley: University of California Press, 2001).

28. What provides the coherence to the term "women's press" is a common politics of address, a common historical genealogy, which was part of, yet also distinct from, the development of the press in Egypt as a whole, as well as shared tropes, points of reference, and genres of writing, rather than an underlying biological or essential cultural distinction that separates "women's writing" from other sorts of writing. For a basic account of the women's press in Egypt, see Badran, *Women, Islam and Nation*; Beth Baron, *The Woman's Awakening in Egypt* (New Haven, CT: Yale University Press,

1994); Ijlal Khalifa, "Al-Sihafa al-Nisa'iyya fi Misr, 1919–1939," MA thesis, Cairo University, 1966; "Al-Sihafa al-Nisa'iyya fi Misr 1940–1965," PhD diss., Cairo University, 1969.

29. The largest weekly news magazine and most serious rival to *Akhir Sa'a* and *Al-Musawwar*, *Ruz al-Yusuf* did not have a women's page after the early 1950s.

30. Benedict Anderson, *Imagined Communities: Reflections on the Origins and Spread of Nationalism* (London: Verso, 1983).

31. Muhammad Rif'at, "Banat Iran," *Hawwa'*, Feb. 12, 1960; "Ra'itu al-Mar'a al-Yamaniyya bila Hijab," *Al-Musawwar*, Mar. 18, 1958, 14–15; "Madha Ta'rifina 'an al-Mar'a fi Yughuslavia?" *Hawwa'*, Dec. 12, 1958, 18–19; Mahmud Najib al-Layl, "Ihmdi Rabbana innaki Misriyya," *Hawwa'*, Aug. 27, 1966, 38–39.

32. Suhayr al-Kayyal, "Za'imat Ifriqiyyat fi al-Mu'tamar al-Kabir," *Hawwa'*, Mar. 1, 1961, 20–21.

33. Muhammad Rif'at, "Ukhtik al-'Iraqiyya," *Hawwa'*, Oct. 25, 1958, 10–11. See also Sabri Abu al-Majid, "Ukhtik al-'Iraqiyya fi Maydan al-Khidma al-Ijtima'iyya," *Hawwa'*, Dec. 23, 1961, 22–23.

34. Aifun Bishara, "Al-Ma'ra al-Sudaniyya Tuharibu al-Hijab," *Hawwa'*, Mar. 8, 1957, 22–25.

35. Sabri Abu al-Majid, "Intisar Bint Ifriqiyya 'ala Mu'amarat al-Isti'mar," *Hawwa'*, Aug. 20, 1960, 42–43; Suhayr al-Kayyal, "al-Hakima illati tuqadir Kifah al-Mar'a fi Batsulanda," *Hawwa'*, June 9, 1962, 24–25; Amina Sa'id, "Al-Istiqlal Yuharrir al-Mar'a fi Tanjaniqa," *Hawwa'*, Sept. 9, 1963, 14–15; Habib Jamati, "Al-Ma'ra al-Jaza'iriyya: Qissa Kifah Ra'i' wa Intisar Majid," *Hawwa'*, July 14, 1960, 32–33; Sabri Abu al-Majid, "6 Milayyin Imra'a fi Ma'arkat al-Jaza'ir," *Hawwa'*, Mar. 10, 1962, 32–33; "Jamila min Balad al-Abtal," *Akhir Sa'a*, May 29, 1963, 16; Muhammad Rif'at, "4 Haribat min Jahim al-Kamirun," *Al-Musawwar*, Feb. 13, 1959, 46; Salah Jawdat, "Jamila taqud Tabur al-Mujahidat," *Al-Musawwar*, Mar. 30, 1962.

36. Amina Sa'id, "al-Zawj al-Almani Hakim bi Amrihi," *Hawwa'* Oct. 4, 1958, 14–15.

37. Burton, *Burdens of History*, 101. See also Billie Melman, *Women's Orients—English Women and the Middle East, 1718–1918: Sexuality, Religion, and Work* (Ann Arbor: University of Michigan Press, 1992).

38. Amina Sa'id, "Nahnu Muqassirat fi Haqq Akhwatina al-'Arabiyyat," *Hawwa'*, Feb. 12, 1961, 14–15.

39. Fumiyal Labib, "Al-Mar'a fi Pakistan," *Hawwa'*, July 9, 1960, 26–27.

40. Fumiyal Labib, "Shaqiqatuki al-Sudaniyya fi Tariqha ila al-Tahrir," *Hawwa'*, Dec. 12, 1959, 38–39.

41. Eve Troutt Powell, *A Different Shade of Colonialism: Egypt, Great Britain, and the Mastery of the Sudan* (Berkeley: University of California Press, 2003); Heather

Sharkey, Living with *Colonialism: Nationalism and Culture in the Anglo-Egyptian Sudan* (Berkeley: University of California Press, 2003).

42. Yemen has been described as Egypt's Vietnam. In 1962, Yemen was ruled by Imam Ahmed in the north, and the British, who retained their colonial control of Aden, in the south. In September, a military coup brought Abdullah al-Sallal to power. Imam Ahmed's heir, Mohammed Badr, fled to the north where with the support of affiliated tribesmen and the financial and material backing of Saudi Arabia, he mounted armed resistance to the Sallal government. Sallal requested aid from Egypt, which Nasser granted. Over the course of the next two years, Egypt's troop commitment grew from eight thousand to seventy thousand. Fighting became increasingly brutal as the conflict dragged on. Repeated negotiations between Saudi Arabia and Egypt failed to end the conflict until 1967.

43. Sabri Abu al-Majid, "Ta'aysh al-Mar'a al-Yamaniyya ahla' Ayyam Hayatiha," *Hawwa'*, Mar. 11, 1964, 36–37.

44. Ibid.

45. Halim Muwafi, "Hakadha Ta'aish al-Mar'a fi-l-Yemen," *Akhir Sa'a*, June 7, 1965, 22–24.

46. Ibid.

47. "Ra'itu al-Mar'a al-Yamaniyya bila Hijab!" *Al-Musawwar*, Mar. 18, 1958, 14–15.

48. Amina Sa'id, "al-Musawa: Hal Tus'idu al-Mar'a?" *Hawwa'*, Nov. 29, 1958, 12–14.

49. Ibid.

50. Amina Sa'id, "Al-Sufiyatiyya al-Muslima ta'khudu al-Mahr," *Hawwa'*, Nov. 8, 1958, 12–13.

51. Ibid.

52. Sabri Abu al-Majid, "Al-Mar'a fi Viyitnam," *Hawwa'*, Aug. 27, 1966, 40–41. Interestingly, feminist antiwar activists in the United States during the 1970s invoked similar images of Vietnamese women as the archetype of the revolutionary woman. See Elizabeth Armstrong and Vijay Prashad, "Solidarity: War Rites and Women's Rites," *CR: The New Centennial Review* 5 (Spring 2005): 222.

53. Abu al-Majid, "Al-Ma'ra fi Viyitnam."

54. Qadri Qil'aji, "Batulat Fata Jamila Buhayrid," *Hawwa'*, Mar. 15, 1958, 16–17.

55. Jamati, "Al-Mar'a al-Jaza'iriyya."

56. As Deniz Kandiyoti has argued, the identification of the (gendered) private with the inner sanctum of group identity has had serious implications for women's citizenship within the context of secular nationalist projects. Deniz Kandiyoti, "Identity and Its Discontents: Women and the Nation," *Millennium* 20 (1991): 435. See Marnia Lazreg, *The Eloquence of Silence: Algerian Women in Question* (New York: Routledge Press, 1994), for the legacy that the dynamics and outcome of national struggle and the association of women with the inner sanctum of communal identity have left in Algeria.

57. Isma'il al-Habruk, "Al-Mar'a fi al-Sin," *Ruz al-Yusuf*, Feb. 6, 1956, 24–25.

58. Ibid.

59. Sabri Abu al-Majid, "Intahat al-Ma'ra al-Siniyya min Ma'rakat al-Bina' wa Bada'at Ma'rakat al-Jamal wa-l-Anaqa," *Hawwa'*, Feb. 3, 1962, 28–29.

60. Ibid.

Conclusion

1. Amal Amireh, "Remembering Latifa al-Zayyat," *al-Jadid* 2 (Oct. 1996), www .aljadid.com/features/RememberingLatifaal-Zayyat.html.

2. Ibid.

3. See, for example, Kathleen Canning and Sonya Rose, "Introduction," in *Gender, Citizenship and Subjectivities*, ed. Kathleen Canning and Sonya Rose (London: Blackwell, 2002), 5.

4. Lisa Rofel, *Other Modernities: Gendered Yearnings in China After Socialism* (Berkeley: University of California Press, 1999), 9.

5. Ibid., 26.

6. Ibid., 17–18.

7. Charles Hirschkind, "What Is Political Islam?" *MERIP* 205 (Oct.–Dec. 1997), http://www.merip.org/mer/mer205/hirschk.htm.

8. Lila Abu-Lughod, "The Marriage of Feminism and Islamism in Egypt: Selective Repudiation as a Dynamic of Postcolonial Cultural Politics," in Abu-Lughod, *Remaking Women*, 243–270; Suzanne Brenner, "Reconstructing Self and Society; Javanese Women and 'the Veil,'" *American Ethnologist* 23 (Nov. 1996): 673–697; Mervat Hatem, "Secularist and Islamist Discourses on Modernity in Egypt and the Evolution of the Postcolonial Nation-State," in *Islam, Gender and Social Change*, ed. Yvonne Yazbeck and John Esposito (Oxford, UK: Oxford University Press, 1998), 85–99; Valerie Hoffman-Ladd, "Polemics on the Modesty and Segregation of Women in Contemporary Egypt," *International Journal of Middle East Studies* 19 (Feb. 1987): 23–50.

9. As quoted in Azza Karam, *Woman, Islamisms and the State: Contemporary Feminisms in Egypt* (New York: St. Martin's Press, 1998), 209.

BIBLIOGRAPHY

Arabic-Language Periodicals

Al-Ahram
Akhbar al-Yawm
Akhir Sa'a
Bint al-Nil
Fatat al-Ghad
Fatiyat Misr
Hawwa'
Al-Musawwar
Ruz al-Yusuf

Films

Li-l-Rijal Faqat. Dir. Mahmud Zul-Fiqar, 1964.
Mrati Mudir 'Amm. Dir. Fatin Abdel Wahab, 1966.

Dissertations and Theses

Abugedeiri, Hibba. "Egyptian Women and the Science Question: Gender in the Making of Colonized Medicine, 1893–1929." PhD diss., Georgetown University, 2001.
Bier, Laura. "From Mothers of the Nation and Daughters of the State: Gender and the Politics of Inclusion in Egypt, 1922–1967." PhD diss., New York University, 2006.
Goven, Joanna. "The Gendered Politics of Hungarian Socialism: State, Society and the Anti-Politics of Anti-Feminism, 1948–1990." PhD diss., University of California, Berkeley, 1993.
Khalifa, Ijlal. "Al-Sihafa al-Nisa'iyya fi Misr 1940–1965." PhD diss., Cairo University, 1969.

———. "Al-Sihafa al-Nisa'iyya fi Misr, 1919–1939." MA thesis, Cairo University, 1966.

State Publications

Abou-Zeid, Hekmat, et al. *The Education of Women in the U.A.R. During the 19th and 20th Centuries.* Cairo: National Commission of UNESCO, 1970.

Abu Zayd, Hikmat. "Al-Dawla wa al-Usra bayn 'Ahadayn." In *Proceedings of the Conference on the Family, Dec. 19–26, 1964, Cairo, Egypt.* Cairo: Ministry of Social Affairs, 1965.

'Ammar, 'Abbas. "The Population Situation in Egypt and the Necessity of Planning a Population Policy for the Country." In *The Egyptian Association for Population Studies,* 5–17. Cairo: Imprimerie Misr S.A.E., 1960.

Arab Republic of Egypt. *Egyptian Women: A Long March from the Veil to Oct. 6, 1973.* Cairo: State Information Service, 1974.

Faraj, Mohammad Farghuli, and 'Abd al-Halim Mahmud al-Sayyid. *Taghyir al-Wad' al-Ijtima'i li-l-Mar'a fi Misr al-Mu'asira.* Cairo: al-Markaz al-Qawmi li-l-Buhuth al-Ijtima'iyya wa-l-Jina'iyya, 1974.

Hafez, Ibrahim. *Education in the UAR, an Outline.* Cairo: Ministry of Education, 1964.

Hafiz, Yusuf. *Al-'Amal al-Maydani fi Tanzim al-Usra.* Alexandria, Egypt: Alexandria Family Planning Association, 1969.

Khalifa, Ahmad. *Ra'y muwatin fi tanzim al-usra.* Cairo: Ministry of Social Affairs, 1966.

Marzuk, Zahya. *al-Dirasat al-Maydania fi Majal Tanzim al-Usra fi Iskandariyya.* Alexandria, Egypt: Supreme Council for Social Services in Alexandria and Sabra Printing Co., 1965.

Nasser, Gamal Abdel. *The Charter.* Cairo: Maslahat al-Isti'alamat, 1962.

———. *Falsafat al-thawrah.* Cairo: Dar al-Ma'arif, 1960.

Republic of Egypt. Ministry of Justice. *Al-Dustur.* Cairo: Al-Matba'at al-Amiriyya, 1956.

El-Sharabassy, Ahmad. *Islam and Family Planning.* Translated by Sayed Ismael. Cairo: Al-Ahram Printing House, 1969.

United Arab Republic. *al-Dustur.* Cairo: Maslahat al-'Isti'lamat, 1964.

———. Al-Lajna al-Tahdiriyya li-l-Mu'tamar al-Watani li-l-Quwa al-Sha'biyya. *Al-Tariq ila al-Dimuqratiyya.* Cairo: Maslahat al-Isti'alamat, 1961.

———. Ministry of Education. *Al-Tilmiz fi bi'atihi al-Mahalliyya.* Cairo: Wizarat al-Tarbiyya wa-l-Ta'lim, 1967.

———. Ministry of Education. *Minhaj al-Marhala al-Ibtida'iyya al-Mutawwira.* Cairo: Wizarat al-Tarbiyya wa-l-Ta'lim, 1965.

———. Ministry of Education. Lajna Bahth Shu'un al-Mudarissat wa-l-Muwazzifat. *Bahth wa 'Alaj Mushkillat al-Mar'a al-Muwazzifa.* Cairo: Wizarat al-Tarbiyya wa-l-Ta'lim, 1959.

———. Ministry of National Guidance. *The Role of Women in the UAR*. Cairo: State Information Service, 1967.

———. Ministry of National Guidance. *Al-Mar'a fi al-Jumhuriyya al-'Arabiyya al-Muttahida*. Cairo: State Information Service, 1966.

———. Ministry of Social Affairs. Al-Lajna al-Da'ima li-Shu'un al-Mar'a. *Mu'tamar Shu'un al-Mar'a al-'Amila*, Nov. 23–27, 1963.

Works in Arabic

Abu Zahra, Muhammad. *Tanzim al-Usra wa Tanzim al-Nasl*. Cairo: Dar al-Fikr al-'Arabi, 1976.

Aflatun, Inji. *Mudhakirat Inji Aflatun*. Kuwait: Dar Su'ad al-Sabah, 1993.

Banna, Ḥasan. *Al-Mar'a Al-Muslima*. Cairo: Dar al-Kutub al-Salafi yya, 1983.

Barakat, Ruqiya. "'Alaqat al-Taghayyur al-Tiknulujiyya bi-Dur al-Mar'a fi-l-Usra." *Al-Majalla al-Ijtima'iyya al-Qawmiyya* 305/306 (1972): 20–28.

al-Ghazali, Zaynab. *Ayyam min Hayati*. Kuwait: Al-Ittihad al-Islami al-'Alamili-l-Munazzamat al-tullabiyya, 1980.

Hamrush, Ahmad. *Qisat Thawra Yulyu*. Beirut: Al-Mu'asasa Al-'Arabiyya li-l-Tiba' wa-l-Nashr, 1978.

Hatem, Mervat. "Bayn Ru'ya Qadima wa Jadida." In *Min Ra'idat al-Qarn al-'Ashrin: Shakhsiyyat wa Qadaya*, edited by Hoda Sada, 15–35. Cairo: Maltaqa al-Mar'a wa-l-Dhakira, 2001.

Husni, Munira. *Al-Zawaj wa-l-Talaq*. Cairo: Dar al-Fikr wa-l-Hadith, n.d.

Khalifa, Ijlal. *Al-Haraka al-Nisa'iyya al-Haditha*. Cairo: Al-Matba' al-'Arabiyya al-Haditha, 1973.

Malika, Liwis Kamal, and Salah al-Din Fa'iq. *Ittijahat al-Qarawiyun wa-l-'Ummal Nahwa Tanzim al-Usra*. Sirs al Layaan, Egypt: Markaz Tanmiyya al-Mujtam'a fi al-'Alam al- 'Arabi, 1968.

al-Sa'id, Rif'at. *Ta'ammulat fi-l-Nasiriyya*. Cairo: al-Mada, 2000.

Salim, Latifa. *Al-Mar'a al-Misriyya* wa-l-*Taghyir al-Ijtima'i*. Cairo: al-Hai'a al-Misriyya al-'Amma li-l-Kitab, 1984.

al-Subky, Amal. *al-Haraka al-Nisa'iyya fi Misr Bayn al-Thawratayn 1919–1952*. Cairo: al-Ha'ia al-Misriyya al-'Amma lil-Kitab, 1984.

Taha, Ahmad Taha. *Al-Mar'a: Kifahuha wa 'Amalha*. Cairo: Dar al-Jamahir, 1964.

Works in English

Abaza, Mona. *Changing Consumer Cultures of Modern Egypt: Cairo's Urban Reshaping*. Leiden: Brill, 2006.

———. "The Changing Image of Women in Rural Egypt." *Cairo Papers in Social Science* 10 (Fall 1987).

Abdel Kader, Soha. *Egyptian Women in a Changing Society, 1899–1987.* New York: Lynne Reiner, 1987.

———. *A Report on the Status of Egyptian Women, 1900–1973.* Cairo: American University in Cairo, Social Science Research Center, 1973.

Abdel-Malek, Anouar. *Egypt: Military Society; The Army, the Left, and Social Change Under Nasser.* Translated by Charles Lam Markmann. New York: Random House, 1968.

Abugedieri, Hibba. *Gender and the Making of Modern Medicine.* Aldershot, UK: Ashgate, *forthcoming.*

Abu-Lughod, Lila. *Dramas of Nationhood: The Politics of Television in Egypt.* Chicago: University of Chicago Press, 2004.

———. "Introduction." In *Remaking Women: Feminism and Modernity in the Middle East*, edited by Lila Abu-Lughod, 3–32. Cairo: American University in Cairo Press, 1998.

———. "The Marriage of Feminism and Islamism: Selective Repudiation as a Dynamic of Postcolonial Cultural Politics." In *Remaking Women: Feminism and Modernity in the Middle East*, edited by Lila Abu-Lughod, 255–261. Cairo: American University in Cairo Press, 1998.

Afifi, Mohammed. "Reflections on the Personal Status Laws of Copts." In *Women, the Family and Divorce Laws*, edited by Amira Sonbol, 202–219. Syracuse, NY: Syracuse University Press, 1996.

Ahmed, Leila. *Women and Gender in Islam: Historical Roots of a Modern Debate.* New Haven, CT: Yale University Press, 1992.

Ali, Kamran. *Planning the Family in Egypt: New Bodies, New Selves.* Austin: University of Texas Press, 2002.

———. "Faulty Deployments: Persuading Women and Constructing Choice in Egypt." *Comparative Studies in Society and History* 44 (Spring 2002): 370–394.

al-Ali, Nadje. *Secularism, Gender and the State in the Middle East: The Egyptian Women's Movement.* Cambridge, UK: Cambridge University Press, 2000.

Amin, Camron. *The Making of the Modern Iranian Woman: Gender, State Policy and Popular Culture, 1865–1946.* Gainesville: University Press of Florida, 2002.

Amireh, Amal. "Remembering Latifa al-Zayyat." *al-Jadid* 2 (Oct. 1996), www.aljadid.com/features/RememberingLatifaal-Zayyat.html.

Anagnost, Ann. "A Surfeit of Bodies: Population and the Rationality of the State in Post-Mao China." In *Conceiving the New World Order*, edited by Faye Ginsburg and Rayna Rapp, 22–44. Berkeley: University of California Press, 1995.

Anandhi, S. "Reproductive Bodies and Regulated Sexuality: Birth Control Debates in Early 20th Century Tamil Nadu." In *A Question of Silence: The Sexual Economies of Modern India*, edited by Janaki Nair and Mary Johns, 139–166. London: Zed Books, 2000.

Anderson, Benedict. *Imagined Communities: Reflections on the Origins and Spread of Nationalism.* London: Verso, 1983.

Anderson, J.N.D. "Recent Developments in Shariʻa Law V (The Dissolution of Marriage)." *Muslim World* 41 (1951): 271–288.

Annous, A. M. "The Dangers of Frequent Childbearing and Necessity of Birth Control." *Journal of the Egyptian Medical Association* 20 (July 1937): 270–275.

Ansari, Hamied. *Egypt: The Stalled Society.* London: Oxford University Press, 1963.

Armbrust, Walter. *Mass Culture and Modernism in Egypt.* Cambridge, UK: Cambridge University Press, 1996.

Armstrong, Elisabeth, and Vijay Prashad. "Solidarity: War Rites and Women's Rites." *CR: The New Centennial Review* 5 (Spring 2005): 213–255.

Asad, Talal. *Formations of the Secular: Christianity, Islam, Modernity.* Stanford, CA: Stanford University Press, 2003.

———. "Thinking About Law and Secularism." *ISIM Papers* (2001): 9, http://www.isim.nl/files/paper_asad.pdf.

Ayalon, Ami. "Journalists and the Press: The Vicissitudes of Licensed Pluralism." In *Egypt from Monarchy to Republic: A Reassessment of Revolutionary Change*, edited by Shimon Shamir, 267–282. Boulder, CO: Westview Press, 1995.

Badran, Margot. *Feminism in Islam: Secular and Religious Convergences.* Oxford, UK: Oneworld, 2009.

———. *Women, Islam and Nation.* Princeton, NJ: Princeton University Press, 1995.

Barlow, Tani. *The Question of Women in Chinese Feminism.* Durham, NC: Duke University Press, 2006.

———. "Introduction." In *Formations of Colonial Modernity in East Asia*, edited by Tani Barlow, 1–21. Durham, NC: Duke University Press, 1997.

Baron, Beth. "The Origins of Family Planning: Aziza Hussein, American Experts and the Egyptian State." *Journal of Middle East Women's Studies* 4 (Fall 2008): 31–57.

———. *Egypt as a Woman: Nationalism, Gender and Politics.* Berkeley: University of California Press, 2005.

———. *The Woman's Awakening in Egypt.* New Haven, CT: Yale University Press, 1994.

———. "Mothers, Morality and Nationalism in pre-1919 Egypt." In *The Origins of Arab Nationalism*, edited by Rashid Khalidi et al., 271–288. New York: Columbia University Press, 1991.

Beattie, Kirk. *Egypt During the Nasser Years: Ideology, Politics and Civil Society.* Boulder, CO: Westview Press, 1994.

Beinin, Joel, and Zachary Lockman. *Workers on the Nile: Nationalism, Communism, Islam, and the Egyptian Working Class, 1882–1954.* Princeton, NJ: Princeton University Press, 1987.

Berger, Maurits. "Public Policy and Islamic Law: The Modern Dhimmi in Contemporary Egyptian Family Law." *Islamic Law and Society* 8 (2001): 88–136.

Bier, Laura. "The Family Romance of Egyptian Labor: Gender and the Making of the Egyptian Working Class." Unpublished manuscript, n.d.

Binder, Leonard. *In a Moment of Enthusiasm: Political Power and the Second Stratum.* Chicago: University of Chicago Press, 1978.

Boddy, Janice. *Civilizing Women: British Crusades in Colonial Sudan.* Oxford, UK: Oxford University Press, 2007.

Booth, Marilyn. *May Her Likes Be Multiplied: Biography and Gender Politics in Egypt.* Berkeley: University of California Press, 2001.

Botman, Selma. *Engendering Citizenship in Egypt.* New York: Columbia University Press, 1999.

———. *The Rise of Egyptian Communism: 1939–1970.* Syracuse, NY: Syracuse University Press, 1991.

———. "The Experience of Women in the Egyptian Communist Movement." *Women's Studies International Forum* 11 (1988): 117–126.

Brenner, Suzanne. "Reconstructing Self and Society; Javanese Women and 'the Veil,'" *American Ethnologist* 23 (Nov. 1996): 673–697.

Briggs, Laura. *Reproducing Empire: Race, Sex, Science and U.S. Imperialism in Puerto Rico.* Berkeley: University of California Press, 2003.

Brown, Wendy. *States of Injury: Power and Freedom in Late Modernity.* Princeton, NJ: Princeton University Press, 1995.

Buck-Morss, Susan. *Dreamworld and Catastrophe: The Passing of Utopia in East and West.* Cambridge, MA: MIT Press, 2000.

Burton, Antoinette. *Burdens of History: British Feminist, Indian Women and Imperial Culture, 1865–1915.* Chapel Hill: University of North Carolina Press, 1994.

Caldwell, John, and Pat Caldwell. *Limiting Population Growth and the Ford Foundation Contribution.* London: Frances Pinter, 1986.

Canning, Kathleen, and Sonya Rose. "Introduction." In *Gender, Citizenship and Subjectivities,* edited by Kathleen Canning and Sonya Rose. London: Blackwell, 2002.

Chakrabarty, Dipesh. *Provincializing Europe: Postcolonial Thought and Historical Difference.* Princeton, NJ: Princeton University Press, 2000.

———. "The Difference-Deferral of a Colonial Modernity: Public Debates on Domesticity in Bengal." In *The Tensions of Empire: Colonial Cultures in a Bourgeois World,* edited by Frederick Cooper and Ann Laura Stoler, 373–405. Berkeley: University of California Press, 1997.

Chatterjee, Partha. *The Nation and Its Fragments.* Princeton, NJ: Princeton University Press, 1993.

Cinar, Alev. *Modernity, Islam and Secularism in Turkey.* Minneapolis: University of Minnesota Press, 2005.

Clancy-Smith, Julia, and Frances Gouda, eds. *Domesticating the Empire: Race, Gender and Family Life in French and Dutch Colonialism.* Charlottesville: University Press of Virginia, 1998.

Cleland, Wendell. "Egypt's Population Problem." *L'Egypte Contemporaine* 167 (1937): 67–87.

———. *The Population Problem in Egypt*. Lancaster, PA: Science Press, 1936.

Cole, Juan. "Feminism, Class and Islam in Turn-of-the-Century Egypt." *International Journal of Middle East Studies* 13 (Fall 1981): 387–407.

Colla, Elliot. "Shadi Abd-al Salam's *al-Mumiya*: Ambivalence and the Egyptian Nation-State." In *Beyond Colonialism and Nationalism in the Maghrib: History, Culture, Politics,* edited by Ali Abdullatif Ahmida, 109–143. New York: Palgrave, 2000.

Connell, R. W. "The State, Gender, and Sexual Politics: Theory and Appraisal." *Theory and Society* 19 (Oct. 1990): 507–544.

Connelly, Matthew. "Population Control in India: Prologue to the Emergency Period." *Population and Development Review* 32 (Dec. 2006): 629–667.

Cowan, Ruth Schwartz. *More Work for Mother: The Ironies of Household Technology from the Open Hearth to the Microwave*. New York: Basic Books, 1983.

Davin, Anna. "Imperialism and Motherhood." *History Workshop Journal* 5 (Spring 1978): 9–66.

Davin, Delia. *Woman-work: Women and the Party in Revolutionary China*. Oxford, UK: Oxford University Press, 1979.

Dekmejian, Hrair. *Egypt Under Nasir: A Study in Political Development*. Albany: State University of New York Press, 1971.

Dodd, Peter. "Youth and Women's Emancipation in the United Arab Republic." *Middle East Journal* 22 (Summer 1968): 159–172.

Donzelot, Jacques. *The Policing of Families*. Translated by Robert Hurley. New York: Pantheon Books, 1979.

Duara, Prasenjit. "The Regime of Authenticity: Timelessness, Gender and National History in Modern China." *History and Theory* 37 (1988): 287–308.

Early, Evelyn. *Baladi Women of Cairo: Playing with an Egg and a Stone*. Boulder, CO: Lynne Rienner, 1993.

Fahmy, Khalid. "Women, Medicine and Power in Nineteenth Century Egypt." In *Remaking Women: Feminism and Modernity in the Middle East*, edited by Lila Abu-Lughod, 35–72. Cairo: American University in Cairo Press, 1998.

Fay, Mary Ann. "From Warrior Grandees to Domesticated Bourgeoisie: The Transformation of the Elite Egyptian Household into a Western-Style Nuclear Family." In *Family History in the Middle East*, edited by Bishara Doumani, 77–97. Albany: State University of New York Press, 2003.

Fidelis, Malgorzata. "Equality Through Protection: The Politics of Women's Employment in Postwar Poland, 1945–1956." *Slavic Review* 63 (Summer 2004): 301–324.

Fodor, Eva. *Working Difference: Women's Working Lives in Hungary and Austria, 1945–1995*. Durham, NC: Duke University Press, 2003.

French-Fuller, Katherine. "Gendered Invisibility, Respectable Cleanliness: The Impact of the Washing Machine on Daily Living in post-1950 Santiago, Chile." *Journal of Women's History* 18 (Winter 2006): 79–100.

Gershoni, Israel, and James Jankowski. *Redefining the Egyptian Nation.* Cambridge, UK: Cambridge University Press, 1995.

———. *Egypt, Islam and the Arabs: The Search for Egyptian Nationhood, 1900–1930.* New York: Oxford University Press, 1986.

Ginsburg, Faye, and Rayna Rapp. "The Politics of Reproduction." *Annual Review of Anthropology* 20 (1991): 311–343.

Goldman, Wendy. *Women at the Gates: Gender and Industry in Stalin's Russia.* Cambridge, UK: Cambridge University Press, 2002.

Gole, Nilufer. *The Forbidden Modern: Civilization and Veiling.* Ann Arbor: University of Michigan Press, 1996.

Gordon, Joel. *Revolutionary Melodrama: Popular Film and Civic Identity in Nasser's Egypt.* Chicago: Middle East Documentation Center, 2002.

———. *Nasser's Blessed Movement: Egypt's Free Officers and the July Revolution.* New York: Oxford University Press, 1992.

Greenhalgh, Susan. "The Social Construction of Population Science: An Intellectual, Institutional and Political History of Twentieth Century Demography." *Comparative Studies in Society and History* 38 (Jan. 1996): 26–66.

Grewel, Inderpal. *Home and Harem: Nation, Gender Empire and the Cultures of Travel.* Durham, NC: Duke University Press, 1996.

Hale, Sondra. *Gender Politics in Sudan: Islamism, Socialism, and the State.* Boulder, CO: Westview Press, 1996.

Halper, Louise. "Law and Women's Agency in Post-Revolutionary Iran." *Harvard Journal of Law and Gender* 28 (Winter 2005): 85–138.

el-Hamamsy, Laila. *The Daya of Egypt: Survival in a Modernizing Society.* Pasadena: California Institute of Technology, 1973.

Hansen, Karen, ed. *African Encounters with Domesticity.* New Brunswick, NJ: Rutgers University Press, 1992.

Hatem, Mervat. "The Pitfalls of Nationalist Discourses on Citizenship in Egypt." In *Gender and Citizenship in the Middle East*, edited by Suad Joseph, 33–57. Syracuse, NY: University of Syracuse Press, 2000.

———. "Secularist and Islamist Discourses on Modernity in Egypt and the Evolution of the Postcolonial Nation-State." In *Islam, Gender and Social Change*, edited by Yvonne Haddad and John Esposito, 85–99. Oxford, UK: Oxford University Press, 1998.

———. "The Paradoxes of State Feminism in Egypt." In *Women and Politics Worldwide*, edited by Barbara Nelson and Najwa Chadhury, 226–242. New Haven, CT: Yale University Press, 1994.

———. "Toward a Critique of Modernization: Narrative in Middle East Studies." *Arab Studies Quarterly* 15 (Spring 1993): 117–122.

———. "Economic and Political Liberation and the Demise of State Feminism." *International Journal of Middle East Studies* 24 (1992): 231–251.

Heng, Geraldine, and Jenandas Devan. "State Fatherhood: The Politics of Nationalism, Sexuality and Race in Singapore." In *Nationalisms and Sexualities*, edited by Andrew Parker et al., 343–364. New York: Routledge, 1992.

Hijab, Nadia. *Womanpower: The Arab Debate on Women at Work*. Cambridge, UK: Cambridge University Press, 1988.

Hirschkind, Charles. "What Is Political Islam?" *MERIP* 205 (Oct.–Dec. 1997), http://www.merip.org/mer/mer205/hirschk.htm.

Hla, Daw Khin. "Leader of the Burmese Delegation's Remarks at the Plenary Session." In *Proceedings of The First Asian-African Conference of Women Cairo Jan. 14–23, 1961*. Cairo: Amalgamated Press of Egypt, 1961.

Hodgson, Dennis. "Demography as Social Science and Policy Science." *Population and Development Review* 9 (Winter 1983): 10–20.

Hoffman, Valerie. "An Islamic Activist: Zaynab al-Ghazali." In *Women and Family in the Middle East*, edited by Elizabeth Fernea, 233–254. Austin: University of Texas Press, 1985.

Hoffman-Ladd, Valerie. "Polemics on the Modesty and Segregation of Women in Contemporary Egypt." *International Journal of Middle East Studies* 19 (Feb. 1987): 23–50.

Hopkins, Harry. *Egypt: The Crucible*. London: Secker and Warburg, 1969.

Hopwood, Derek. *Egypt Politics and Society, 1945–1990*. London: Routledge Press, 1993.

Horn, David. *Social Bodies: Science, Reproduction and Italian Modernity*. Princeton, NJ: Princeton University Press, 1994.

Hunt, Lynn. *The Family Romance of the French Revolution*. Berkeley: University of California Press, 1992.

Hussein, Aziza. "The Status of Women and Family Planning in a Developing Country—Egypt." In *Egypt: Population and Prospects*, edited by Abdel R. Omran, 181–188. Chapel Hill, NC: Carolina Population Center, 1973.

Hussein, Mahmoud. *Class Conflict in Egypt, 1945–1970*. New York: Monthly Review Press, 1973.

Huston, Perdita. *Motherhood by Choice: Pioneers in Women's Health and Family Planning*. New York: Feminist Press of the City of New York, 1992.

Ibrahim, Barbara. "Women in the Workforce." In *At the Crossroads: Education in the Middle East*, edited by Adnan Badran, 282–302. New York: Paragon House, 1989.

Ibrahim, Saad Eddin. "State, Women and Civil Society: An Evaluation of Egypt's Population Policy." In *Family, Gender and Population in the Middle East*, edited by Carla Makhlouf Obermeyer, 59–79. Cairo: American University in Cairo Press, 1995.

Idris, Yusuf. *The Cheapest Nights and Other Stories.* Translated by Wadida Wassef. Boulder, CO: Lynne Rienner, 1997.

Inhorn, Marcia. *The Quest for Conception: Gender, Infertility and Egyptian Medical Traditions.* Philadelphia: University of Pennsylvania Press, 1994.

Jankowski, James. *Nasser's Egypt, Arab Nationalism and the United Arab Republic.* Boulder, CO: Lynne Rienner, 2002.

———. "Arab Nationalism in 'Nasserism' and Egyptian State Policy, 1952–1958." In *Rethinking Nationalism in the Arab Middle East*, edited by James Jankowski and Israel Gershoni, 150–167. New York: Columbia University Press, 1997.

Jayawardana, Kumari. *Feminism and Nationalism in the Third World.* London: Zed Press, 1986.

Johnson, Amy. *Reconstructing Rural Egypt: Ahmed Hussein and the History of Egyptian Development.* Cairo: American University in Cairo Press, 2004.

Johnson, Amy, and Scott David McIntosh. "Empowering Women, Engendering Change: Aziza Hussein and Social Reform in Egypt." In *Envisioning Egypt: 1919–1952*, edited by Arthur Goldschmidt et al., 249–276. Cairo: American University in Cairo Press, 2005.

Jolly, Margaret, and Kalpana Ram, eds. *Borders of Being: Citizenship, Fertility, and Sexuality in Asia and the Pacific.* Ann Arbor: University of Michigan Press, 2001.

Joseph, Suad. "Gender and Citizenship in Middle Eastern States." In *Gender and Citizenship in the Middle East*, edited by Suad Joseph, 3–32. Syracuse, NY: Syracuse University Press, 2000.

———. "Gender and Citizenship in Middle Eastern States." *MERIP* 198 (Jan.–Mar. 1996): 4–10.

Joubin, Rebecca. "Creating the Modern Professional Housewife: Scientifically Based Advice Extended to Middle and Upper Class Egyptian Women, 1920s–1930s." *Arab Studies Journal* 4 (July 1996): 19–45.

Kandiyoti, Deniz. "Introduction." In *Women, Islam and the State*, edited by Deniz Kandiyoti, 1–21. Philadelphia: Temple University Press, 1991.

———. "Identity and Its Discontents: Women and the Nation." *Millennium* 20 (1991): 429–444.

Karam, Azza. *Woman, Islamisms and the State: Contemporary Feminisms in Egypt.* New York: St. Martin's Press, 1998.

Karam, Bahiyya. "Introduction." In *Proceedings of the First Afro-Asian Women's Conference, Cairo, Jan. 14–23, 1961.* Cairo: Amalgamated Press of Egypt, 1961.

Keddie, Nikkie. *Women in the Middle East: Past and Present.* Princeton, NJ: Princeton University Press, 2007.

Khater, Akram, and Cynthia Nelson. "Al-Harakah al-Nissa'iyah: The Woman's Movement and Political Participation in Modern Egypt." *Women's Studies International Forum* 11 (1988): 465–483.

Kholoussi, Samia. "Fallahin: The 'Mud Bearers' of Egypt's 'Liberal Age'." In *Re-En-*

visioning Egypt: 1919–1952, edited by Arthur Goldschmidt et al., 277–316. Cairo: American University in Cairo Press, 2005.

Kholoussy, Hanan. *For Better, For Worse: The Marriage Crisis Which Made Modern Egypt.* Stanford, CA: Stanford University Press, 2010.

El-Kholy, Heba Aziz. *Defiance and Compliance: Negotiating Gender in Low-Income Cairo.* New York: Berghahn Books, 2002.

Kolchevska, Natasha. "Angels in the Home and at Work: Russian Women in the Khrushchev Years." *Women's Studies Quarterly* 33 (Fall 2005): 114–147.

Kuhnke, Laverne. *Lives at Risk: Public Health in Nineteenth-Century Egypt.* Berkeley: University of California Press, 1990.

Landes, Joan. *Women and the Public Sphere in the Age of the French Revolution.* Cornell, NY: Cornell University Press, 1988.

Lazreg, Marnia. "Citizenship and Gender in Algeria." In *Gender and Citizenship in the Middle East*, edited by Suad Joseph, 58–69. Syracuse, NY: Syracuse University Press, 2000.

———. *The Eloquence of Silence: Algerian Women in Question.* New York: Routledge Press, 1994.

Lerner, David. *The Passing of Traditional Society.* Glencoe, IL: Free Press, 1958.

Lockman, Zachary. "Imagining the Working Class: Culture, Nationalism and Class Formation in Egypt, 1899–1914." *Poetics Today* 15 (Summer 1994): 157–190.

Mahmood, Saba. *The Politics of Piety: The Islamic Revival and the Feminist Subject.* Princeton, NJ: Princeton University Press, 2005.

Manning, Kimberley. "Making a Great Leap Forward? The Politics of Women's Liberation in Maoist China." *Gender and History* 18 (Nov. 2006): 574–593.

Mansfield, Peter. *Nasser's Egypt.* London: Methuen Educational, 1963.

Mariscotti, Cathlyn. *Gender and Class in the Egyptian Women's Movement, 1929–1935.* Syracuse, NY: Syracuse University Press, 2008.

Marzuq, Zahya. "Social Studies on Fertility and Conception in Alexandria." In *Egypt: Population Problems and Prospects*, edited by Abdel R. Omran, 371–386. Chapel Hill, NC: Carolina Population Center, 1973.

McClintock, Anne. "Family Feuds: Gender, Nationalism and the Family." *Feminist Review* 44 (Summer 1993): 61–80.

Meijer, Roel. *The Quest for Modernity: Secular, Liberal and Left-Wing Thought in Egypt, 1945–1958.* London: Routledge Curzon, 2002.

Melman, Billie. *Women's Orients—English Women and the Middle East, 1718–1918: Sexuality, Religion, and Work.* Ann Arbor: University of Michigan Press, 1992.

Menicucci, Garay. "Unlocking the Arab Celluloid Closet: Homosexuality in Egyptian Film." *MERIP* 206 (Spring 1998): 32–36.

Menon, Lakshmi. "Closing Remarks." In *Report of the Proceedings of the First Asian-*

African Conference of Women, Held in Colombo, Ceylon, 15–24 of February, 1958. Bombay: Mouj Printing Bureau, 1958.

Mernissi, Fatima. *Beyond the Veil.* Bloomington: Indiana University Press, 1987.

al-Messiri, Sawsan. "Self Images of Traditional Urban Women in Cairo." In *Women in the Muslim World*, edited by Lois Beck and Nikki Keddie, 522–540. Cambridge, MA: Harvard University Press, 1978.

Mitchell, Timothy. *Colonizing Egypt.* Berkeley: University of California Press, 1991.

———. "The Invention and Reinvention of the Egyptian Peasant." *International Journal of Middle East Studies* 22 (May 1990): 129–150.

Mohanty, Chandra. *Feminism Without Borders: Decolonizing Theory, Practicing Solidarity.* Durham, NC: Duke University Press, 2004.

———. "Introduction: Cartographies of Struggle." In *Third World Women and the Politics of Feminism*, edited by Chandra Mohanty et al., 1–51. Bloomington: Indiana University Press, 1991.

———. "Under Western Eyes: Feminist Scholarship and Colonial Discourses." In *Third World Women and the Politics of Feminism*, edited by Chandra Mohanty et al., 51–80. Bloomington: Indiana University Press, 1991.

Morsy, Soheir. "Deadly Reproduction Among Egyptian Women: Maternal Mortality and the Medicalization of Population Control." In *Conceiving the New World Order: The Global Politics of Reproduction*, edited by Rayna Rapp and Faye Ginsburg, 162–176. Berkeley: University of California Press, 1996.

Moustafa, Tamir. "Conflict and Cooperation Between the State and Religious Institutions in Contemporary Egypt." *International Journal of Middle Eastern Studies* 32 (Jan. 2000): 3–22.

Najmabadi, Afsaneh. *Women with Mustaches, Men Without Beards: Gender and Sexual Anxieties of Iranian Modernity.* Berkeley: University of California Press, 2005.

———. "(Un) Veiling Feminism." *Social Text* 64 (Fall 2000): 29–45.

———. "Crafting an Educated Housewife in Iran." In *Remaking Women: Feminism and Modernity in the Middle East*, edited by Lila Abu-Lughod, 91–125. Cairo: American University in Cairo Press, 1998.

———. "Veiled Discourses—Unveiled Bodies." *Feminist Studies* (Fall 1993): 487–518.

Nelson, Cynthia. *Doria Shafik, Egyptian Feminist.* Cairo: American University in Cairo Press, 1996.

Newland, Linda. "The Deployment of the Prosperous Family: Family Planning in West Java." *National Women's Studies Association Journal* 13 (2002): 22–49.

Omran, Abdel. "The Population of Egypt, Past and Present." In *Egypt: Population Problems and Prospects*, edited by Abdel R. Omran, 3–38. Chapel Hill, NC: Carolina Population Center, 1973.

———, and Malek el-Nomrossey. "The Family Planning Effort in Egypt: A Descriptive Sketch." In *Egypt: Population Problems and Prospects*, edited by Abdel R. Omran, 219–257. Chapel Hill, NC: Carolina Population Center, 1973.

Paidar, Parvin. *Women and the Political Process in Twentieth-Century Iran*. Cambridge, UK: Cambridge University Press, 1995.

Pateman, Carol. *The Sexual Contract*. Stanford, CA: Stanford University Press, 1988.

Peirce, Leslie. *Morality Tales: Law and Gender in the Court of Aintab*. Berkeley: University of California Press, 2003.

Phillipp, Thomas. "Feminism and Nationalist Politics in Egypt." In *Women in the Muslim World*, edited by Lois Beck and Nikki Keddie, 277–294. Cambridge, MA: Harvard University Press, 1978.

Podeh, Elie, and Onn Winckler, eds. *Rethinking Nasserism*. Gainesville: University Press of Florida, 2004.

Pollard, Lisa. *Nurturing the Nation: The Family Politics of Modernizing, Colonizing and Liberating Egypt*. Berkeley: University of California Press, 2005.

———. "Manly Men or Colonized Effeminates? Gender in Egypt's Colonial and Post-Colonial Political Experience." Paper presented at the conference "Gendering the Middle East," Middle East and Middle Eastern American Center, City University of New York, Dec. 12, 2003.

Poovey, Mary. *Uneven Developments: The Ideological Work of Gender in Mid-Victorian England*. Chicago: University of Chicago Press, 1988.

Prashad, Vijay. *The Darker Nations: A People's History of the Third World*. New York: New Press, 2007.

Ram, Kalpana. "Rationalizing Fecund Bodies: Family Planning Policy and the Modern Indian Nation-State." In *Borders of Being: Citizenship, Fertility, and Sexuality in Asia and the Pacific*, edited by Margaret Jolly and Kalpana Ram, 82–117. Ann Arbor: University of Michigan Press, 2001.

Rejwan, Nessim. *Nasserist Ideology: Its Exponents and Critics*. New York: John Wiley, 1974.

Reynolds, Nancy. "Sharikat al-Bayt al-Misri: Domesticating Commerce in Egypt: 1931–1956." *Arab Studies Journal* 7 (Fall 1999/Spring 2000): 75–99.

Rizk, Hana. "Population Policies in Egypt." In *Report of the Proceedings: The Fifth International Conference on Planned Parenthood, 24–28 October 1955, Tokyo, Japan*. London: International Planned Parenthood, 1955.

Robinson, Kathryn. "Government Agency, Women's Agency: Feminism, Fertility and Population Control." In *Borders of Being: Citizenship, Fertility, and Sexuality in Asia and the Pacific*, edited by Margaret Jolly and Kalpana Ram, 36–57. Ann Arbor: University of Michigan Press, 2001.

Rofel, Lisa. *Other Modernities: Gendered Yearnings in China After Socialism*. Berkeley: University of California Press, 1999.

Rupp, Leila. *Worlds of Women*. Princeton, NJ: Princeton University Press, 1991.

Ryan, Mary. *Mysteries of Sex: Tracing Women and Men Through American History*. Chapel Hill: University of North Carolina Press, 2006.

Ryzova, Lucy. "Egyptianizing Modernity Through 'The New Effendiyya': Social and Cultural Constructions of the Middle Class in Egypt Under the Monarchy." In *Re-Envisioning Egypt: 1919–1952*, edited by Arthur Goldschmidt et al., 124–163. Cairo: American University in Cairo Press, 2005.

Sadat, Anwar. "Opening Address." In *Proceedings of the Afro-Asian People's Solidarity Conference, Cairo, Dec. 26, 1957 to Jan. 1, 1958*. Moscow: Foreign Languages Publishing House, 1958.

Safran, Nadav. "The Abolition of the Shari'a Courts in Egypt." *Muslim World* 48 (1958): 20–28.

Scott, Joan. *Gender and the Politics of History*. New York: Columbia University Press, 1988.

Sen, Samita. "Motherhood and Mothercraft: Gender and Nationalism in Bengal." *Gender and History* 5 (Summer 1993): 231–243.

Shafik, Viola. *Popular Egyptian Cinema: Gender, Class and Nation*. Cairo: American University in Cairo Press, 2007.

Shaham, Ron. *The Family and the Courts in Modern Egypt*. Leiden: Brill, 1997.

El Shakry, Omnia. *The Great Social Laboratory: Subjects of Knowledge in Colonial and Postcolonial Egypt*. Stanford, CA: Stanford University Press, 2007.

———. "Barren Land and Fecund Bodies: The Emergence of Population Discourse in Interwar Egypt." *International Journal of Middle East Studies* 37 (Aug. 2005): 351–372.

———. "Schooled Mothers, Structured Play: Childrearing in Turn of the Century Egypt." In *Remaking Women: Feminism and Modernity in the Middle East*, edited by Lila Abu-Lughod, 126–170. Princeton, NJ: Princeton University Press, 1998.

Shamir, Shimon, ed. *From Monarchy to Republic: A Reassessment of Revolution and Change*. Boulder, CO: Westview Press, 1995.

Shanawany, Haifa. "Stages in the Development of a Population Policy." In *Egypt: Population Problems and Prospects*, edited by Abdel R. Omran, 189–218. Chapel Hill, NC: Carolina Population Center, 1973.

Sharkey, Heather. *Living with Colonialism: Nationalism and Culture in the Anglo-Egyptian Sudan*. Berkeley: University of California Press, 2003.

Sharpless, John. "Population Science, Private Foundations, and Development Aid: The Transformation of Demographic Knowledge in the United States, 1945–65." In *International Development and the Social Sciences: Essays on the History and Politics of Knowledge*, edited by Frederick Cooper and Randall Packard, 176–202. Berkeley: University of California Press, 1997.

Singham, A.W., and Shirley Hume. *Non-Alignment in an Age of Alignments*. London: Zed Press, 1986.

Smith, Hendrick. "Come to the Cairo Fair." *New York Times*, Mar. 26, 1966, p. 10.

Sonbol, Amira. *The New Mamluks: Egyptian Society and Modern Feudalism*. Syracuse, NY: Syracuse University Press, 2000.

———. "Ta'a and Modern Legal Reform." *Islam and Christian-Muslim Relations* 9 (1998): 285–294.

———. "Adults and Minors in Ottoman *Shariʿa* Courts." In *Women, the Family and Divorce Laws in Islamic History*, edited by Amira Sonbol, 236–258. Syracuse, NY: Syracuse University Press, 1996.

———. "Law and Gender Violence in Ottoman and Modern Egypt." In *Women, the Family and Divorce Laws*, edited by Amira Sonbol, 277–290. Syracuse, NY: Syracuse University Press, 1996.

Soueif, Ahdaf. "The Language of the Veil." *The Guardian*, Dec. 8, 2001 http://www.guardian.co.uk/weekend/story/0,3605,614360,00.html.

Sullivan, Earl. *Women in Egyptian Public Life.* Cairo: American University in Cairo Press, 1986.

Sunder Rajan, Rajeswari. *The Scandal of the State: Women, Law and Citizenship in Postcolonial India.* Durham, NC: Duke University Press, 2003.

Thompson, Elizabeth. *Colonial Citizens: Republican Rights, Paternal Privilege and Gender in French Syria and Lebanon.* New York: Columbia University Press, 2000.

Tomiche, Nada. "The Position of Women in the UAR." *Journal of Contemporary History* 3 (July 1968): 129–143.

Toppozada, H. K. "Progress and Problems of Family Planning in the United Arab Republic." *Demography* 5 (1968): 590–597.

Troutt Powell, Eve. *A Different Shade of Colonialism: Egypt, Great Britain, and the Mastery of the Sudan.* Berkeley: University of California Press, 2003.

Tucker, Judith. *In the House of the Law: Gender and Islamic Law in Ottoman Syria and Palestine.* Berkeley: University of California Press, 1998.

———. *Women in 19th Century Egypt.* Cambridge, UK: Cambridge University Press, 1985.

———. "Egyptian Women in the Workforce: An Historical Survey." *MERIP* 50 (Aug. 1976): 3–9, 26.

Vatikiotis, P. J. *Nasser and His Generation.* London: Croom Helm, 1978.

Verdery, Katherine. "From Parent-State to Family Patriarchs: Gender and Nation in Contemporary Eastern Europe." *East European Politics and Societies* 8 (Spring 1994): 225–255.

Waterbury, John. *The Egypt of Nasser and Sadat: The Political Economy of Two Regimes.* Princeton, NJ: Princeton University Press, 1983.

———. *Manpower and Population Planning in the Arab Republic of Egypt, Part III.* Cairo: American University Field Staff, 1972.

———. *Manpower and Population Planning in the Arab Republic of Egypt, Part IV: Egypt's Governmental Program for Family Planning.* Cairo: American University Field Staff, 1972.

Westad, Odd Arne. *The Global Cold War: Third World Interventions and the Making of Our Times.* Cambridge, UK: Cambridge University Press, 2007.

Wheelock, Kenneth. *Nasser's New Egypt.* Westport, CT: Greenwood Press, 1975.

Winegar, Jessica. *Creative Reckonings*: *The Politics of Art and Culture in Contemporary Egypt*. Stanford, CA: Stanford University Press, 2006.

Winter, Michael. "Islam and the State: Pragmatism and Growing Commitment." In *Egypt from Monarchy to Republic*, edited by Shimon Shamir, 44–58. Boulder, CO: Westview Press, 1995.

Yihong, Jin. "Rethinking the "Iron Girls": Gender and Labour During the Chinese Cultural Revolution." *Gender and History* 18 (Nov. 2006): 613–634.

al-Zayyat, Latifa. *The Open Door*. Translated by Marilyn Booth. Cairo: American University in Cairo Press, 2000.

Zeghal, Malika. "Religion and Politics in Egypt: The Ulama of al-Azhar, Radical Islam and the State: 1952–94." *International Journal of Middle East Studies* 31 (Aug. 1999): 371–399.

INDEX

Rashid, Fatma Niʻmat, 45, 49–50
Raziq, Muhammad, 129
reform, land, 51–52, 67, 198n75
reform, social, 15, 35–39, 45, 49, 51, 135
Revolution (1919), 28–34, 193n21
Revolution (1952), 10, 25, 38, 51–53, 55, 178, 184,
    198n74
rural women, 33, 170; and agricultural labor,
    67, 202nn32–33; as objects of social
    reform, 35–38;195n37; as targets of family
    planning, 131, 135–137. *See also* subaltern
    women

Saʼid, Amina, 19–20; advocacy of abortion,
    139; advocacy of daycare provision, 78;
    background, 45, 56, 112, 190n34, 196nn53–
    54; and personal status law reform, 114;
    views on veiling, 183; views of women's
    labor, 73–74, 822, 88; writings on non-
    Egyptian women, 163, 167–168, 171
Saʻid, Karima, 163, 221n25
Sadat, Anwar, 50, 157, 177–178. *See also* Free
    Officers
Sadat, Jihan, 198n81
secularism, 1, 41, 102, 104–106, 110–111, 115,
    182–183, 209n8, 209n10
Shafiq, Duriyya, 8, 55, 206n31; background,
    45, 190n34, 196n53; imprisonment by
    Nasser regime, 19, 72, 206n33; political
    activism, 49–50, 54, 65
Shaʻrawi, Huda, 9, 29, 32–33, 39–40, 93,
    207n105
Shafiq, Amina, 113
El Shakry, Omnia, 37, 190n27, 195n38, 216n32
Shaltut, Muhammad, 116, 134
el-Sharabassy, Ahmad, 133, 135
shariʻa, 101–104, 116, 208n2, 208n4, 209nn7–8.
    See also personal status laws; secularism
Shukri, Amina, 55, 212n31,
Sirri, Nahid, 154
social reform. *See* reform, social
socialism, Arab. *See* Arab socialism
socialism, state. *See* state socialism
Society of Young Egyptian Women, 33
state elites. *See* elites, state
state feminism, 12–17; contradictions of,
    58–59, 178–179, 181; definition of, 3, 7;
    and domesticity, 71–72, 75, 81, 84–89;
    female workers as symbols of, 60–61,
    69; historical roots of, 25–26; and labor
    laws, 65–66; legacies of in contemporary
    Egypt, 182–185; as middle class

ideology, 10–11; middle class women as
    beneficiaries of, 28–29; and mobilization
    of female workers, 66–68; notion of
    rights in, 110–111, 120; and subaltern
    women, 10, 181–182; transnational
    influences on, 12, 17, 155. *See also*
    Arab socialism; education, women;
    family planning; feminism, Egyptian;
    feminists; personal status laws; state
    elites; workers, women
state socialism, contemporary perceptions
    of, 178; failures of, 177; non-Western
    models of, 3, 53–54
subaltern women, 30, 32–33, 181–182. *See also*
    rural women; working class women
Suez Canal, nationalization of, 23–24, 51, 157

Third World, as a political imaginary, 156
Thompson, Elizabeth, 30

ulama, 107, 111–112, 212n32

veil (*hijab*), 1, 9, 16, 27, 41–44, 58, 62, 69–71,
    91–98, 168–169, 182–185
Verdery, Katherine, 58–59

Wafd Party, 29–31, 34, 44, 192n13
Wafdist Women's Central Committee, 29, 32
woman question, the, 2–3, 9, 13–16,
    20–21; and Arab socialism, 25; bourgeois
    feminist views of, 33, 43; and Egyptian
    nationalism, 32, 40; genealogies of,
    26–28; persistence of, 179; postwar views
    of, 45, 48. *See also* feminism, Egyptian
Women's Committee for Popular Resistance,
    48
women's organizations: Association of
    Egyptian Working Women, 64; Bint
    al-Nil Union, 49–50, 115, 197n65;
    Egyptian Feminist Union, 32–33, 45–46,
    48–50, 105–106, 161–161, 220nn9–10;
    International Alliance for Equal
    Suffrage and Citizenship, 159–161, 221n11,
    221n18; League of Women Students
    and Graduates for the University
    and Egyptian Institutes, 48; Muslim
    Women's Association, 46; National
    Women's Party, 49; Society of Young
    Egyptian Women, 33; Wafdist Women's
    Central Committee, 29, 32; Women's
    Committee for Popular Resistance, 48
women's press, 17, 27, 39; as a source for

Stanford Studies in Middle Eastern and Islamic Societies and Cultures

---

Joel Beinin and Frédéric Vairel, editors, *Social Movements, Mobilization, and Contestation in the Middle East and North Africa*
2011

Samer Soliman, *The Autumn of Dictatorship: Fiscal Crisis and Political Change in Egypt under Mubarak*
2011

Rochelle A. Davis, *Palestinian Village Histories: Geographies of the Displaced*
2010

Haggai Ram, *Iranophobia: The Logic of an Israeli Obsession*
2009

John Chalcraft, *The Invisible Cage: Syrian Migrant Workers in Lebanon*
2008

Rhoda Kanaaneh, *Surrounded: Palestinian Soldiers in the Israeli Military*
2008

Asef Bayat, *Making Islam Democratic: Social Movements and the Post-Islamist Turn*
2007

Robert Vitalis, *America's Kingdom: Mythmaking on the Saudi Oil Frontier*
2006

Jessica Winegar, *Creative Reckonings: The Politics of Art and Culture in Contemporary Egypt*
2006

Joel Beinin and Rebecca L. Stein, editors, *The Struggle for Sovereignty: Palestine and Israel, 1993–2005*
2006